RATIONALISM AND REVOLUTION
1660–1815

RATIONALISM AND REVOLUTION 1660-1815

A Documentary History of Modern Europe Volume II

Edited by
Thomas G. Barnes
Gerald D. Feldman

University of California, Berkeley
Originally published by Little, Brown and Company

UNIVERSITY
PRESS OF
AMERICA

LANHAM • NEW YORK • LONDON

Copyright © 1979 by

Thomas G. Barnes and Gerald D. Feldman

University Press of America,™ Inc.

4720 Boston Way
Lanham, MD 20706

3 Henrietta Street
London WC2E 8LU England

All rights reserved

Printed in the United States of America

ISBN (Perfect): 0-8191-0850-2
LCN: 79-66686

Copyright © 1972 by
Little, Brown and Company (Inc.)

PREFACE

"For I do not see the whole of anything; neither do those who promise to show it to us." Michel de Montaigne's frank disclaimer of his own capacity and scathing rejection of the vaunted capacities of others to see all was written almost exactly four centuries ago, in an age of fanaticisms and all-embracing visions. It is relevant for our own age of fanaticisms and all-embracing visions. Fanaticism aside, it is a particularly apt motto for authors and editors of books for introductory courses in history. Where not downright messianic, or even prophetical, such books tend to be pontifical — if not by the authors' intentions, then at least in the student's reading of them. Some notions guided us in this compilation, and it is good to make those notions and their manifestations clear at the outset, not only that we might not be thought messianic, prophetical, or pontifical, but also that those who choose and those who use this book will know what we think it does and does not do. At the outset, we make no claim that it will enable the student to "see the whole" of modern European history, or even as much of it as is treated here.

We believe that even the most general study of history requires awareness of historians' dependence upon the sources for history. It is as well that the novice understands from the start that all historiography is based on a broad but still selected body of sources. The very selectiveness of this collection reflects the nature of the historian's job in writing history. We believe that the student cannot begin to understand either history or the historian's task without himself exercising his intellect on the sources of history. This compilation, highly selective though it is, demands that the student use his critical faculties in weighing what he reads as historical evidence; indeed, it demands that he determine from the variety of sources presented what constitutes historical evidence and how evidence can be analyzed and understood in different ways. For example, a student with the psychological interests of Erik H. Erikson, another with the politico-social bent of Roland H. Bainton, and another given to the avowedly theological focus of James Atkinson would all approach Martin Luther differently, but they would all have to meet and begin with Luther's own writings.

For that reason, if for no other, this series includes a major segment of Luther, which, though it comprises only a fraction of his considerable output, provides a common ground for all who would understand Luther and Lutheranism and a common origin for each interpretation of the man and his movement. So have we in every volume of this series aimed at providing a large enough selection from major historical figures (both thinkers and doers), commentaries by lesser men, descriptions of events, laws and government directives, manifestoes and platforms, some correspondence and belles lettres, to suggest the variety of sources for Europe's past, to allow each student to bring into play his own critical acumen, and to provide illustration of men, events, and ideas which might otherwise prove elusive.

This series is intended to be a *documentary history* of Europe. By this we mean that a student using — not merely reading — these volumes can come to some understanding of modern Europe's past by the documents alone aided by the explanation of the headnotes to the selections and the longer introductory essay to each chapter, which provides context and continuity both to the documents in that chapter and with the chapters preceding and succeeding. The series is not meant to serve as a substitute for a text, but it is intended to be as self-sufficient as is necessary to fit with any textbook or narrative history, sometimes in agreement with and sometimes in contrast to the interpretations that will be found elsewhere in what a student can be expected to read in an introductory course in modern European history at any college level. We have sought to make the selections long enough to give real substance for reflection and analysis. Perforce, this has limited the number of selections and therefore has caused us to exclude some men, events, and ideas that others would think of prime importance. We have felt no call to mirror the broad consensus as to which documents are and are not important. Although our colleagues will find a number of selections that all agree are "major," they will also find many that are rarely if ever found in books of readings and a few that have not previously appeared in English. We have sought significance, freshness, insightfulness, and incisiveness in our selections, and these concerns rather than idiosyncrasy, a penchant for novelty, or a commitment to a specific historical interpretation have determined that much of the material in this series will be new and different.

ACKNOWLEDGMENTS

The permission of authors and publishers in whom copyright is vested has been acknowledged where the selection appears. We would, however, tender special thanks to those holders of copyright who allowed us to use material either gratis or for a nominal fee, a practice that is no longer universal. A number of our colleagues assisted us with sage advice and tips for finding materials, and we are in yet greater debt to Lawrence Levine, Martin Malia, Robert Middlekauff, William Slottman, and Engel Sluiter than that already incurred by many years' close service together at Berkeley. Two students, Murray Bilby and Jeffrey Diefendorf, served us as bibliographical assistants and rendered aid beyond what we paid them. Malgorzata I. Winkler of the University of California, Berkeley, Library translated the Union of Lublin from Polish, a difficult task well done. The College Department of Little, Brown and Co. was always helpful, and we perhaps tumble into invidiousness in singling out the history editor, Charles Christensen, and the three copyeditors who wrestled with the series and its authors, Jane Aaron, Lynne Marcus Gould, and Patricia Herbst. To all, our most sincere thanks.

T. G. B.
G. D. F.

CONTENTS

Chapter 1
THE PINNACLE OF FRENCH ABSOLUTISM   1

Lessons in Statecraft   3
   Louis XIV on His Mistress, *La Gloire*   4

The Fruit of Absolutist Social Mobility   8
   Monsieur Jourdain, *Le Bourgeois Gentilhomme*   9

"Bloody Ramillies," 1706   15
   Description of Battle by M. de la Colonie   15

The Old Nobility Bites Back   19
   Saint-Simon: Louis XIV as King Bee   20

Chapter 2
ABSOLUTISM IN AUSTRIA, SPAIN, AND PRUSSIA   24

Bourbon Absolutism in Spain Under Philip V   27
   Louis XIV Instructs His Grandson Philip V of Spain, 1700   27
   Philip V's Reforms of Spanish Government in Practice,
      April 3, 1711   30

The "Pragmatic Sanction" for the Austrian Succession   31
   Emperor Charles VI Promulgates the "Pragmatic Sanction"   32
   The French Ambassador Advises Caution, 1730   34

Prince Frederick of Prussia Is Instructed in Obedience
by His Father   35
   Account by Princess Wilhelmine   35

Frederick the Great's Analysis of the Garrison State   39
   An Essay on Forms of Government   40

Chapter 3
**ABSOLUTISM AND OLIGARCHY IN THE NORTH
AND EAST**   44

The "Lion of the North" Before and After Poltava, 1709   47
   On the Eve of Poltava: Charles XII and His Generals   47

After Poltava: Charles XII to the Committee of Defense in Stockholm, July 11, 1709	49
Peter the Great Deals with Mutiny in the Infantry, 1698	50
General Patrick Gordon's Diary	50
Catherine the Great and the Restructuring of Russian Law	55
The Instructions to the Commissioners for Composing a New Code of Laws	56
Intervention of Catherine the Great in Poland, 1766	60
Declaration on Behalf of the Dissidents, from the Empress Catherine II of Russia, Presented by Repnin at the Diet of the Polish-Lithuanian Commonwealth on November 4, 1766	60

Chapter 4
CONSTITUTIONALISM AND OLIGARCHY IN THE WEST   66

John Locke Caroline	69
Of the Dissolution of Governments	69
Parliament's Charter	75
The English Bill of Rights, 1689	75
Edmund Burke to His Constituents	79
On the American Revolution and English Liberties, 1777	80
William V, Prince of Orange	84
The Last Non-Absolutist Quasi-Monarch of the Dutch Republic	85

Chapter 5
WEALTH, WAR, AND EMPIRE   89

Men, Money, Munitions, Manners, and Morals	92
Instructions from the Privy Council of England to Virginia, April 19, 1626	92
The Balance of Trade, 1668	95
Josiah Child's *New Discourse of Trade*	95
The Exclusion of Slavery from England	100
"The Case of James Sommersett, a Negro, on Habeas Corpus," 1772	101
Colonel Washington of the Virginia Militia Reports a Skirmish, 1754	105
To Governor Dinwiddie	106
To Colonel Joshua Fry	107
To Governor Dinwiddie	108
To His Brother	110

Contents xi

Chapter 6
SCIENCE: THE SEARCH FOR ORDER   111

The Virtuosi Found the Royal Society   114
    Thomas Sprat's *History of the Royal Society*   114

Newton Orders the Universe   118
    Rules of Reasoning in Philosophy   118
    General Scholium   120

William Petty on Land Tax in Ireland   124
    Value in Adversity   124

Strong Medicine for Clio's Malady   129
    Bayle's *Dictionary, Historical and Critical*   129

Chapter 7
THE ENLIGHTENMENT   134

Voltaire Admires the English "Constitution"   137
    On the Parliament   137
    On the Government   140

Instruction in the Spirit of the Age of Reason   143
    The *Encyclopédie*   143

Reason Brought to Bear on Law   148
    Caesare Beccaria's *Essay on Crimes and Punishments*   148

"Virtue! Sublime Science of Simple Minds"   152
    Rousseau's *Discourse on the Moral Effects of the Arts and Sciences*   152

Chapter 8
THE CRISIS OF ABSOLUTISM   156

The Model "Enlightened Despot": Joseph II   159
    Instructions of the Empress Maria Theresa for the Tutor
        of Her Son Joseph, Field-Marshal Count Batthyány, 1751   159
    Lament of a Mother and Co-Ruler: Maria Theresa to Joseph,
        December 24, 1775   161
    Joseph on Privilege, Inequality, and Reform   161
    Joseph's "Palace Professor," Joseph von Sonnenfels,
        on the Emancipation of the Serfs, 1782   163

Louis XV Lectures the Parlement of Paris, 1766   164
    The Sovereign Power   165

The Financial Conjurer Preaches What He Does Not Practice   168
    Jacques Necker's *Treatise on the Administration
        of the Finances of France*   168

The Last Crisis of French Absolutism   171
    Talleyrand's Analysis   172

Chapter 9
THE FRENCH REVOLUTION 176

Twenty Days That Shook the World: June 8–27, 1789 Caroline 177
    Account by Arthur Young, a Visiting Englishman 178

The Constitution of 1791 and Louis, "King of the French" 186
    The Constitution of September 14, 1791 186
    Louis XVI's Proclamation of September 28, 1791 190

Virtue Enthroned 191
    Institution of Tenth-Day Festivals 192

Terror Enthroned 194
    Establishment of the Revolutionary Tribunal 194

Chapter 10
THE NAPOLEONIC ERA 198

Napoleon Ends the Revolution, December 15, 1799 199
    Proclamation of 24 Frimaire, VIII 199

Laws of "the New Justinian" 200
    The Civil Code 200

Napoleon Speaks for Himself 204
    Exhortation, Assertion, Self-Adulation, and Despair 204

RATIONALISM
AND REVOLUTION
1660–1815

THE PINNACLE OF FRENCH ABSOLUTISM
Chapter 1

"I am the State." Though Louis XIV never actually spoke these words attributed to him, they are a succinct summation of his notion of statecraft. Moreover, they represent truth, for Louis XIV did indeed become the state. With that transformation of the man into the institution, French absolutism reached its pinnacle.

The transformation was an act of will, begun in 1661 by the resolution of Louis never again to allow any minister such powers as Richelieu and Mazarin had wielded. It was a difficult choice because it meant unremitting attention to details of state, continuous personal supervision of a complicated bureaucracy whose officers had purchased their offices and therefore enjoyed a high degree of immunity against the consequences of malfeasance or misfeasance, the routine exercise of diplomacy and the conduct of war, sole ultimate determination of all domestic and foreign policy, personal rendering of justice in his council in great cases involving important persons, and the constant manifestation of his own regal person in his court, his councils, and the country at large. It led inevitably — unless his will or his health broke, and both remained nearly unimpaired until his death in 1715 at the age of seventy-six — to the submerging of his private life and personal desires beneath the well maintained surface of his personification of the state. His solace was his power and prestige, and he won a measure of both more considerable than that of any of his contemporaries, if not enough to allay the measure of remorse that assailed him in his last years.

Louis chose two courses for the greatness and glory of himself and his people. Domestically, the course was to conclude the subjugation of the nobility, particularly the old nobility, to complete the bureaucratization of French administration, central and local, and to reduce the influence of religion and the clergy, Catholic and Protestant, to the extent that their potential for challenging secular absolutism would be ended. Externally, the course was to advance French commerce and industry at the expense of other trading nations and to expand the territory of France at the expense of its neighbors. Both courses assured confrontation; neither produced complete success, though the domestic was more successful (the external proved disastrous).

Louis excluded the old aristocracy from the ruling circle of his government, choosing his ministers primarily for their talent from the new nobility of the lower echelons of the bureaucracy. He imposed taxation on the previously tax-exempt noblemen. He established a lively trade in titles of honor that brought revenue and diluted the status of nobility. In constructing the new palace at Versailles and establishing his court there, he imposed attendance on his person upon the old nobility. This was costly to them and effectively prevented them from exercising the natural leadership in the provinces that was a barrier to centralism and a power base for resistance. The importance of the old nobility declined rapidly. The fortunes of the new rose accordingly, and the "Monsieur Jourdains" so artfully pilloried by Molière became legion.

Louis completed the bureaucratization begun in the early sixteenth century, advanced by Henry IV, Richelieu, and Mazarin, by a sophisticated division of responsibility among overlapping central councils shorn of policy-making powers and by the extension of new authority and obligations to the local *intendants*. The traditional courts of Paris and the provinces, the *parlements*, a bulwark of noble power, were reduced to merely trying cases and recording royal legislation without debating constitutional issues and amendment. Louis came as close to erecting a police state as the physical limitations of the time allowed, and the *lettres de cachet* that resulted in indefinite imprisonment without trial silenced opposition.

Throughout his rule, Louis asserted temporal supremacy over the Catholic Church in France through the contrivance of Gallicanism, though after 1693 he reached an arrangement with the papacy in return for papal support in his foreign policy. His own orthodox Catholicism became more pronounced in later years partly under the influence of his devout mistress, Madame de Maintenon, and partly for reasons of state. He suppressed the proto-Calvinist Jansenist movement. In 1685 he revoked the Edict of Nantes, thus curtailing the last vestiges of Huguenot particularism and causing thousands of his wealthiest and most industrious subjects to flee for fear of persecution.

The economic policy of Louis XIV was principally the work of Jean Baptiste Colbert, the most trusted of Louis's subordinates. Brilliant and calculating, Colbert had virtually entire direction of industry, commerce, agriculture, the colonies, maritime affairs, art, and finances during the most productive years of Louis's reign. Colbert's economic program became the classical example of mercantilism in action. Self-sufficiency was his goal in industry, monopoly in trade. Twenty-two years of unremitting labor did little to raise the level of the French economy. It did, however, provide the initial stock to finance Louis's grandiose and aggressive foreign policy.

The year 1685 marks the natural dividing line in Louis's reign and in his fortunes. Before that date, two brilliantly planned and fought wars (1667–1668 and 1672–1679) gave France the initiative in European power politics and major territories in the east. After 1685, Louis faced massive coalitions of powers that literally surrounded France and wrested from Louis the diplomatic and military advantage that was vital to the success of his policy. The result was almost continuous war from 1688 to 1714 in the Low Countries, Germany, North America, and on the high seas. Tremendous effort, fine generalship, the *élan* of the French soldiers, and courage born of desperation staved off utter defeat and put a French prince on the Spanish throne. But the price in money, men, and effort was more than Louis could afford to pay. Reaction was twofold and ominous: the foreign powers waited to challenge France again and noble opposition to the throne revived. Both combined to become the nemesis of eighteenth-century French absolutism. It was a small step from the duc de Saint-Simon's prolonged sneer over the grave of Louis-the-State to a rising vociferousness on the part of the nobility against the absolutism of his successors, who were less in stature than Louis XIV either as man or as institution.

Lessons in Statecraft

Louis XIV began systematically to compose his memoirs five years after he took control of the government in 1661. He was moved by the example of Sully and Richelieu, the great ministers of his two immediate predecessors, who had justified their dominance in absolutist statecraft by lengthy political testaments. Louis's motives are intriguing. Since he would have no Sully or Richelieu, he would have to justify his own actions — and such justification to posterity was, like everything else, too important to leave to a subordinate. In 1668, Louis addressed the first of his memoirs to his seven-year-old heir apparent, who was about to come under the tutelage of his first male tutor. This excerpt from it provides a clear picture of Louis's conception of his role as well as sage advice. How wasted was the lesson; his son died in 1711, four years before Louis's death.

4

Louis XIV on His Mistress, *La Gloire*

Many reasons, all very important, my son, have decided me, at some labour to myself, but one which I regard as forming one of my greatest concerns, to leave you these Memoirs of my reign and of my principal actions. I have never considered that kings, feeling in themselves, as they do, all paternal affection, are dispensed from the obligation common to fathers of instructing their children by example and by precept. On the contrary, it has seemed to me that in the high rank in which we are placed, you and I, a public duty is added to private, and that in the midst of all the respect which is given us, all the abundance and brilliancy with which we are surrounded — which are nothing more than the reward accorded by Heaven itself in return for the care of the peoples and States confided to our charge — this solicitude would not be very lofty if it did not extend beyond ourselves by making us communicate all our enlightenment to the one who is to reign after us. . . .

I have considered, too, what I have so often experienced myself — the throng who will press round you, each for his own ends, the trouble you will have in finding disinterested advice, and the entire confidence you will be able to feel in that of a father who has no other interest but your own, no ardent wish but for your greatness. . . .

From my early infancy the very name of *rois fainéants* or *maires du palais*[1] displeased me when mentioned in my presence. But I must point out the state of affairs: grievous disturbances throughout the kingdom before and after my majority; a foreign war in which these troubles at home had lost to France thousands and thousands of advantages; a Prince of my blood and of great name at the head of my enemies; many Cabals in the State; the Parliaments still in the possession and enjoyment of a usurped authority; at my Court very little disinterested fidelity and, on this account, my subjects, though outwardly most submissive, as much a responsibility and cause of misgiving to me as the most rebellious; a minister re-established in power despite so many factions, very skilful and very adroit, but whose views and methods were naturally very different from mine, whom, nevertheless, I could not gainsay, nor abate the least portion of his credit, without running the risk of again raising against him by some misleading appearance of disgrace those very storms which had been allayed with so much difficulty. . . .

Everywhere was disorder. My Court as a whole was still very far re-

From *A King's Lessons in Statecraft: Louis XIV*, ed. Jean Longnon, trans. Herbert Wilson (New York, 1925), pp. 39–45, 47–49, 51–53, 55, 59.

[1] The last kings of the Frankish Merovingian dynasty in the seventh century were *rois fainéants* — do-nothing kings — who turned over government to the mayor of the palace, the chief household official, from whom came the dynasty of Charlemagne. — T. G. B.

moved from the sentiments in which I trust you will find it. Men of quality and officials, accustomed to continual intrigue with a minister who showed no aversion to it, and to whom it had been necessary, arrogated to themselves an imaginary right to everything that suited them. There was no governor of a city who was not difficult to govern; no request was preferred without some complaint of the past, or some hint of discontent for the future, which I was allowed to expect and to fear. The favours demanded, and extorted, rather than awaited, by this one and that, and always considerable, no longer were binding on any one, and were only regarded as useful in order to maltreat thenceforth those to whom they wished me to refuse them.

The **finances,** which give movement and action to the great organisation of the monarchy, were entirely exhausted, so much so that we could hardly find the ways and means. . . .

The **Church,** apart from its usual troubles, after lengthy disputes on matters of the schools, a knowledge of which they allowed was unnecessary to salvation for any one, with points of disagreement augmenting day by day through the heat and obstinacy of their minds, and ceaselessly involving fresh human interests, was finally threatened with open schism by men who were all the more dangerous because they were capable of being very serviceable and greatly deserving, had they themselves been less opinionated. . . .

The least of the ills affecting the order of **Nobility** was the fact of its being shared by an infinite number of usurpers possessing no right to it, or one acquired by money without any claim from service rendered. The tyranny exercised by the nobles over their vassals and neighbours in some of my provinces could no longer be suffered or suppressed save by making severe and rigorous examples. The rage for duelling — somewhat modified by the exact observance of the latest regulations, over which I was always inflexible — was only noticeable in a now well advanced recovery from so inveterate an ill, so that there was no reason to despair of the remedy.

The **administration of Justice** itself, whose duty it is to reform others, appeared to me the most difficult to reform. An infinity of things contributed to this state of affairs: the appointments filled haphazard or by money rather than by selection and merit; scant experience and less knowledge on the part of some of the judges; the regulations referring to age and service almost everywhere eluded; chicanery firmly established through many centuries, and fertile in inventing means of evading the most salutary laws. . . .

All this collection of evils, their consequences and effects, fell principally upon the people, who, in addition, were loaded with impositions, some crushed down by poverty, others suffering want from their own laziness since the peace, and needing above all to be alleviated and occupied.

It would assuredly have been to make a bad use of conditions [2] of such perfect tranquillity, such as might only be met with very rarely in several centuries, not to turn them to the only account capable of making me appreciate them, at a time when my youth and the pleasure of being at the head of my armies would have caused me to wish to have more matters to deal with abroad. But inasmuch as my chief hope in these reforms was based on my will, their foundation at the outstart rested on making absolute my will by conduct which should impose submission and respect: by rendering scrupulous justice to all to whom I owed it; but in the bestowing of favours, giving them freely and without constraint to whomsoever I would, and when it should please me, provided that my subsequent action should let others know that while giving reasons to no one for my conduct I ruled myself none the less by reason, and that in my view the remembrance of services rendered, the favouring and promoting of merit — in a word, doing the right thing — should not only be the greatest concern but the greatest pleasure of a prince.

Two things without doubt were absolutely necessary: very hard work on my part, and a wise choice of persons capable of seconding it.

I laid a rule on myself to work regularly twice every day, and for two or three hours each time with different persons, without counting the hours which I passed privately and alone, nor the time which I was able to give on particular occasions to any special affairs that might arise. There was no moment when I did not permit people to talk to me about them, provided that they were urgent; with the exception of foreign ministers who sometimes find too favourable moments in the familiarity allowed to them, either to obtain or to discover something, and whom one should not hear without being previously prepared.

I cannot tell you what fruit I gathered immediately I had taken this resolution. I felt myself, as it were, uplifted in thought and courage; I found myself quite another man, and with joy reproached myself for having been too long unaware of it. . . .

I gave orders to the four Secretaries of State no longer to sign anything whatsoever without speaking to me; likewise to the Controller, and that he should authorise nothing as regards finance without its being registered in a book which must remain with me, and being noted down in a very abridged abstract form in which at any moment, and at a glance, I could see the state of the funds, and past and future expenditure.

The Chancellor received a like order, that is to say, to sign nothing with the seal except by my command, with the exception only of letters

[2] Internal and external conditions. — T. G. B.

of justice, so called because it would be an injustice to refuse them, a procedure required more as a matter of form than of principle. . . .

Regarding the persons whose duty it was to second my labours, I resolved at all costs to have no prime minister; and if you will believe me, my son, and all your successors after you, the name shall be banished for ever from France, for there is nothing more undignified than to see all the administration on one side, and on the other, the mere title of King.

To effect this, it was necessary to divide my confidence and the execution of my orders without giving it entirely to one single person, applying these different people to different spheres according to their diverse talents, which is perhaps the first and greatest gift that Princes can possess.

I also made a resolution on a further matter. With a view the better to unite in myself alone all the authority of a master, although there must be in all affairs a certain amount of detail to which our occupations and also our dignity do not permit us to descend as a rule, I conceived the plan, after I should have made choice of my ministers, of entering sometimes into matters with each one of them, and when they least expected it, in order that they might understand that I could do the same upon other subjects and at any moment. Besides, a knowledge of some small detail acquired only occasionally, and for amusement rather than as a regular rule, is instructive little by little and without fatigue, on a thousand things which are not without their use in general resolutions, and which we ought to know and do ourselves were it possible that a single man could know and do everything. . . .

Neither you nor I, my son, will seek out men for those kinds of employment whom distance or their own obscurity hides from our view, whatever be the capability they may possess. Of necessity, one must decide from a small number whom chance presents, that is to say, from among those who are already occupying some post, or men whose birth or inclination have placed nearest to us.

I also determined to be present sometimes at the different Administrative Councils held on my behalf, at which it was only a question of regulating matters between the various jurisdictions. And if more important occupations spare you the time, you will do well to use it sometimes in this way in order by your presence to encourage in their duty those taking part, and to become personally acquainted with the Magistrates who report and give their opinion on the cases. From this assembly the men are chosen, as a rule, for governorships of provinces, for Embassies, and for other great posts.

But as regards the most important interests of the State and secret matters wherein a small number of heads is to be desired as much as anything else, and which of themselves require more time and more application than all the rest put together, in my wish not to confide them to one minister alone I considered Le Tellier, Fouquet, and Lionne to be the three possessing the best capacity to serve them usefully. . . .

Any one will tell you how distrustful I was of my courtiers on that account,[3] and how often with the view of testing their dispositions, I drew them on to praise the very things in which I thought I had failed, in order to reproach them at once, and accustom them not to flatter me.

But however veiled their intentions may have been, I will teach you, my son, a method by which it is easy to profit from all that they may say in praise of you, and that is to examine yourself secretly, and to trust to your own heart more than to their flattery; estimate it always according to the mood of those who shall give expression to it, either for a spiteful reproach for some mistake committed against their interests, or a covert exhortation to some course foreign to your purpose; persuaded, further, that you have not done enough, even when you may think you have deserved it; and that a reputation cannot be sustained without every day acquiring a greater; and lastly, that glory is a mistress whom one is never able to neglect, and of whose first favours one cannot prove worthy if one does not ceaselessly desire fresh ones.

The Fruit of Absolutist Social Mobility

Jean Baptiste Poquelin (1622–1673) — "Molière" — was the commanding literary figure of Louis XIV's age. Actor and playwright of comedies, he has been called the French Shakespeare. He was not so profound as the English master, neither was he a tragedian. But, like Shakespeare, his use of language became the norm for succeeding generations of writers because the full dramatic power and subtlety of the French tongue reached a pinnacle with him. Molière was both a prime ornament to Louis's glory in the arts and a cutting critic of the contemporary mores that were products of Louis's absolutism. With sardonic humor, Molière dissected doctors, lawyers, misers, conformists, and, in Monsieur Jourdain of Le Bourgeois Gentilhomme, *the new nobility. The valor of arms, the grace of music and dance, and the profundity of philosophy — doubtless Cartesian — are all brought to wreck on Jourdain. And, unlike so many aspiring new nobility in real life, he didn't make it.*

---

[3] On account of flattery. — T. G. B.

Monsieur Jourdain, *Le Bourgeois Gentilhomme*

ACT ONE

The overture is played by a great assemblage of instruments and the music pupil is discovered composing the air which MR. JOURDAIN *has commissioned for his concert. As the song ends the* MUSIC MASTER *and the* DANCING MASTER *enter with their attendant musicians, singers, and dancers.*

MUSIC MASTER [*to musicians*]. Come in here and wait until he comes.
DANCING MASTER [*to dancers*]. And you can stay on this side.
MUSIC MASTER [*to his pupil*]. Well, is it finished?
MUSIC PUPIL. Yes.
MUSIC MASTER [*taking manuscript*]. Let me see. . . . Very good!
DANCING MASTER. Is it something new?
MUSIC MASTER. It is an air for a serenade I set him to compose while we were waiting for our friend to awake.
DANCING MASTER. May one see what it is?
MUSIC MASTER. You will hear it when he comes. He can't be long now.
DANCING MASTER. We are both being kept pretty busy at present.
MUSIC MASTER. Yes. We have found here the very man we both needed. This fellow Jourdain with the fantastic notions of gentility and gallantry he has got into his head means quite a nice thing for us. I only wish, both for my music and your dancing, that there were more people like him.
DANCING MASTER. I can't altogether agree. For his own sake I would like him to have a little more understanding of the things we provide for him.
MUSIC MASTER. It's true that he understands little — but he pays well, and, after all, that's the great need in our line of business just now.
DANCING MASTER. Yes — though for my own part I must confess that what I long for most is applause; it is appreciation I live for. To my way of thinking there is no fate more distressing for an artist than to have to show himself off before fools, to see his work exposed to the criticism of the vulgar and ignorant. You can say what you like but there *is* no joy like that of working for people who have a feeling for the fine points of one's art, who can appreciate the beauties of a work and repay all one's trouble by praise which is really discerning. There is no reward so delightful, no pleasure so exquisite, as having one's work known and acclaimed by those whose applause confers honour.

From Molière, *Le Bourgeois Gentilhomme*, in *The Miser and Other Plays*, trans. John Wood (Harmondsworth, 1964), pp. 3–5, 10–17. Reprinted by permission of Penguin Books Ltd and John Wood.

MUSIC MASTER. I agree. My feelings exactly. There is nothing more pleasing than the recognition you speak of, but you can't live on applause. Praise alone doesn't keep a man going. One needs something more substantial than that, and, to my mind, there's no praise to beat the sort you can put in your pocket. It's true that this fellow here has no great share of enlightenment: he usually gets hold of the wrong end of the stick and applauds all the wrong things, but his money makes up for his lack of discernment. His praise has cash value. Vulgar and ignorant he may be but he's more use to us, you know, than your fine cultured gentleman who put us in touch with him.

DANCING MASTER. There's something in what you say, but I still think you set too much value on money. Cultivated people should be superior to any consideration so sordid as a mercenary interest.

MUSIC MASTER. All the same you don't refuse to take our friend's pay.

DANCING MASTER. Of course not. But I don't find that it entirely contents me. I still wish that with all his great wealth he had a little more taste.

MUSIC MASTER. So do I, and isn't that just where we are both trying to help him — so far as we can? In any case, he is giving us a chance to make a name in the world and he will make up for the others by paying while they do the praising.

DANCING MASTER. Hush! Here he comes.

Enter MR. JOURDAIN *in dressing-gown and night-cap attended by two lackeys.*

MR. JOURDAIN. Well, gentlemen, what is it to be to-day? Are you going to show me your bit of tomfoolery?

DANCING MASTER. Tomfoolery? What bit of tomfoolery?

MR. JOURDAIN. You know — your what ye may call it — your prologue or dialogue or whatever it is — your singing and dancing.

DANCING MASTER. Oh! That's what you mean!

MUSIC MASTER. You find us quite ready.

MR. JOURDAIN. I had to keep you waiting a while because I'm getting dressed up to-day like one of the quality and my tailor had sent me a pair of silk stockings so tight I thought I should never get into them. . . .

ACT TWO

MR. JOURDAIN, MUSIC MASTER, DANCING MASTER, LACKEYS.

MR. JOURDAIN. Well that wasn't too bad. Those fellows can certainly shake a leg.

DANCING MASTER. When the dancing and music are fully coordinated it will be still more effective and you will find that the little ballet we have arranged for you is a very pretty thing indeed.

MR. JOURDAIN. Yes, but that's for later, when the lady I am doing all this for is going to do me the honour of dining here.

DANCING MASTER. Everything is arranged.

MUSIC MASTER. There is just one other thing, sir. A gentleman like you, sir, living in style, with a taste for fine things, ought to have a little musical at-home, say every Wednesday or Thursday.

MR. JOURDAIN. Is that what the quality do?

MUSIC MASTER. It is, sir.

MR. JOURDAIN. Then I'll do it too.

MR. JOURDAIN *then dances a minuet under the* DANCING MASTER'S *direction.*

DANCING MASTER. A hat, sir, if you please. [MR. JOURDAIN *takes the* LACKEY's *hat and puts it on over his night-cap. The* DANCING MASTER *takes his hand and makes him dance to the tune which he sings.*] La, la, la la la la la etc. . . . once again . . . keep time if you ple-ease . . . la-la lala — now the right leg . . . la-la . . . don't move . . . your shoulders so much . . . la la la . . . la la . . . your arms . . . are hanging too limply . . . la la la . . . up with your head, point your toes outward . . . point your toes out-ward . . . la la la . . . keep your body . . . e . . . rect.

MR. JOURDAIN. Phew! What about that?

MUSIC MASTER. Well done! Well done!

MR. JOURDAIN. And that reminds me. Just show me how to make a bow to a countess. I shall need to know that before long.

DANCING MASTER. How to make a bow to a countess?

MR. JOURDAIN. Yes. A countess called Dorimène.

DANCING MASTER. Give me your hand.

MR. JOURDAIN. No. Just do it yourself. I shall remember.

DANCING MASTER. If you wish to show great respect you must make your bow first stepping backwards and then advance towards her bowing three times, the third time going down right to the level of her knee.

MR. JOURDAIN. Let me see you do it. Good!

LACKEY. Sir, your fencing master is here.

MR. JOURDAIN. Tell him to come in and give me my lesson here. [*To the* MUSIC MASTER *and* DANCING MASTER] Don't go! I'd like you to see me perform.

Enter FENCING MASTER *with* LACKEY *carrying the foils.*

FENCING MASTER [*after presenting a foil to* MR. JOURDAIN]. Come, sir, your salute! Hold yourself straight. Take the weight of your body a little on your left thigh. Legs not so far apart. Feet more in line. Wrist in line with your hip. Point of the foil level with your shoulder. Arm not quite so far extended. Left hand level with your eye. Left shoulder squared a little more. Head up. Firm glance. Advance! Keep your body steady. Engage my point in quart and lunge. One, two. As you were. Once again, repeat! Do keep your feet firm. One, two, and recover! When you make a pass, sir, it is important that the foil should be withdrawn first — so — keeping the body well covered. One, two. Come along. Engage my foil in tierce and hold it. Advance! Keep your body steady. Advance and lunge from there! One, two, and recover. As you were. Once again. One, two. Back you go. Parry, sir, parry! [*The* FENCING MASTER *scores two or three hits crying as he does so,* Parry! Parry!]

MR. JOURDAIN. Phew!

MUSIC MASTER. You do splendidly.

FENCING MASTER. I have told you before that the whole art of sword-play lies in two things only — in giving and not receiving. And, as I showed you the other day by logical demonstration, it is impossible for you to receive a hit if you know how to turn your opponent's sword from the line of your body, for which all that is needed is the slightest turn of the wrist — inward or outward.

MR. JOURDAIN. At that rate, then, a fellow can be sure of killing his man and not being killed himself — without need of courage.

FENCING MASTER. Exactly! . . .

[*The* FENCING MASTER *falls out with the* MUSIC *and* DANCING MASTERS *over the merits of their respective skills.*]
Enter the PHILOSOPHER.

MR. JOURDAIN. Ah, Mr. Philosopher. You've arrived in the nick of time with your philosophy. Come and make peace between these fellows.

PHILOSOPHER. What is it? What is it all about, gentlemen?

MR. JOURDAIN. They've got so worked up about which of their professions is the most important that they've started slanging each other and very nearly come to blows.

PHILOSOPHER. Come, come, gentlemen! Why let yourselves be carried away like this? Have you not read Seneca *On Anger?* Believe me there is nothing so base and contemptible as a passion which reduces men to the level of animals! Surely, surely, reason should control all our actions!

DANCING MASTER. But, my good sir, he's just been black-guarding the pair of us and disparaging music, which is this gentlemen's profession, and dancing which is mine.

PHILOSOPHER. A wise man is superior to any insults which can be put upon him, and the best reply to unseemly behaviour is patience and moderation.

FENCING MASTER. They had the impudence to compare their professions with mine.
PHILOSOPHER. Well, friend, why should that move you? We should never compete in vainglory or precedence. What really distinguishes men one from another is wisdom and virtue.
DANCING MASTER. I maintain that dancing is a form of skill, a science, to which sufficient honour can never be paid.
MUSIC MASTER. And I that music has been held in foremost esteem all down the ages.
FENCING MASTER. And I still stick to my point against the pair of them that skill in arms is the finest and most necessary of all the sciences.
PHILOSOPHER. In that case where does philosophy come in? I consider you are all three presumptuous to speak with such assurance before me and impudently give the title of sciences to a set of mere accomplishments which don't even deserve the name of arts and can only be adequately described under their wretched trades of gladiator, ballad singer, and mountebank! . . .

[*The* PHILOSOPHER *and the three* MASTERS *come to blows, and rush on fighting. The* PHILOSOPHER *returns, straightening his neck-band.*]

PHILOSOPHER. Let us come to our lesson.
MR. JOURDAIN. Oh, Mr. Philosopher, I'm sorry they've hurt you.
PHILOSOPHER. It is nothing. A philosopher learns how to take things as they come and I will get my own back on them with a satire in the manner of Juvenal. I'll fairly tear them to pieces. Let us think no more of it. What would you like to learn?
MR. JOURDAIN. Whatever I can, for I want, above all things, to become a scholar. I blame my father and mother that they never made me go in for learning when I was young.
PHILOSOPHER. A very proper sentiment! *Nam sine doctrina vita est quasi mortis imago.* You know Latin I suppose?
MR. JOURDAIN. Yes, but just go on as if I didn't. Tell me what it means.
PHILOSOPHER. It means that without knowledge, life is no more than the shadow of death.
MR. JOURDAIN. Ay. Your Latin has hit the nail on the head there.
PHILOSOPHER. Have you not mastered the first principles, the rudiments of the Sciences?
MR. JOURDAIN. Oh yes, I can read and write.
PHILOSOPHER. Well, where would you like to begin? Shall I teach you logic?
MR. JOURDAIN. Yes, but what is it?
PHILOSOPHER. Logic instructs us in the three processes of reasoning.
MR. JOURDAIN. And what are they, these three processes of reasoning?

PHILOSOPHER. The first, the second, and the third. The first is the comprehension of affinities, the second discrimination by means of categories, the third deduction by means of syllogisms. *Barbara, celarent, Darii, Ferio, Baralipton.*

MR. JOURDAIN. No. They sound horrible words. Logic doesn't appeal to me. Let me learn something nicer.

PHILOSOPHER. Would you like to study moral philosophy?

MR. JOURDAIN. Moral philosophy?

PHILOSOPHER. Yes.

MR. JOURDAIN. And what's moral philosophy about?

PHILOSOPHER. It is concerned with the good life and teaches men how to moderate their passions.

MR. JOURDAIN. No, we'll leave that out. I'm as hot-tempered as they make 'em and whatever moral philosophy may say I'll be as angry as I want whenever I feel like it.

PHILOSOPHER. Well, do you wish to study physics — the natural sciences?

MR. JOURDAIN. The natural sciences? What have they to say for themselves?

PHILOSOPHER. Natural science explains the principles of natural phenomena, and the properties of matter; it is concerned with the nature of the elements, metals, minerals, precious stones, plants, and animals, and teaches us the causes of meteors, rainbows, will-o'-the-wisp, comets, lightning, thunder and thunderbolts, rain, snow, hail, tempests, and whirlwinds.

MR. JOURDAIN. This is too much of a hullabaloo for me, too much of a rigmarole altogether.

PHILOSOPHER. Then what am I to teach you?

MR. JOURDAIN. Teach me to spell.

PHILOSOPHER. Willingly.

MR. JOURDAIN. And then you can teach me the almanac so that I shall know if there's a moon or not.

PHILOSOPHER. Very well. Now, to meet your wishes and at the same time treat the matter philosophically one must begin, according to the proper order of these things, with the precise recognition of the nature of the letters of the alphabet and the different ways of pronouncing them, and, in this connexion, I must explain that the letters are divided into vowels, so called because they express the various sounds, and consonants, so named because they are pronounced "con," or with, the vowels and serve only to differentiate the various articulations of the voice. There are five vowels, A, E, I, O, U.

"Bloody Ramillies," 1706

On May 23, 1706, an army of the Grand Alliance — England, the Austrian Empire, the Dutch Republic, Prussia, and other German states — under the English general Marlborough, routed a French and Bavarian army at Ramillies in Belgium. A signal victory, it was not a turning point in the War of the Spanish Succession (1701–1714), for there were no turning points, merely the bloody battles of Blenheim (1704), Ramillies and Turin (1706), Oudenarde (1708), and the bloodiest of them all, Malplaquet (1709).

In the following selection, a French dragoon officer, M. de la Colonie, with the Bavarian forces, recounts the fight at Ramillies. It was typical of the age, consisting of positioned warfare of massed infantry, where the choice of ground determined the outcome, cannon barrages, and the lightning charge of horse, in which victory went to the side that did not break and run. There was nothing civilized about eighteenth-century warfare: in a few hours on that May afternoon, 20,000 casualties fell at Ramillies.

Description of Battle by M. de la Colonie

France was very lucky in thus being able to stay the enemy's advance both on the Rhine and the Moselle, and the King marked his satisfaction by the present of a hundred thousand crowns, which he made to Maréchal de Villeroi. This General certainly rendered all the plans of the Allies abortive; their only success was a little one in Alsace, to wit, the capture of Haguenau, an almost defenceless town.

The last campaign had been so favourable to France that she became convinced the wheel of Fortune was turning in her favour, and that she should therefore take the opportunity to strike terror in the hearts of her enemies.

To bring this about a battle in Flanders would be necessary; she had in reserve, should a reverse occur, a number of fortified towns which would be a means of defence for the frontier by checking the enemy's advance and giving us time to replace our losses, and in case of success Holland and the German frontier lay open to us. By invading Holland, France could mine the resources of the enemy, for they drew therefrom their chief supplies of money and all kinds of munitions of war.

From *The Chronicles of an Old Campaigner: M. de la Colonie, 1692–1717*, ed. and trans. Walter C. Horsley (London, 1904), pp. 303–08, 311–13. Reprinted by permission of John Murray, Publishers.

Thus we began the campaign of 1706 in Flanders. Great preparations were made, and to realise our project we mobilised about the beginning of May one of the finest armies ever seen, which took up a position overlooking the Plain of Ramillies, its left resting on the wood of Waterloo, with the right in the plain itself. The enemy recalled detachments they had in the Cleves and Limburg districts and the garrisons of several of their towns to reinforce their army in every possible way to resist us, or to attack us themselves if they saw a favourable opportunity of so doing.

With these intentions the enemy appeared in the Plain of Ramillies, but owing to its vast extent, instead of posting themselves exactly opposite us, they took up a position at the end of the plain, the left of their army resting on a marsh near a village named Tavier, whilst in front of their right they had a series of very deep ravines, which rendered them unassailable at this point. The ground bordering on these ravines, although dry to all appearance, was none the less impracticable, and in this position they awaited our attack.

France was burning for the fight, her plan of campaign was decided upon, and it would never have done to have missed the first available opportunity; that which now presented itself was believed to be a favourable one, so our generals set to work to reconnoitre the plain.

The marsh which protected the enemy's left served to cover our right flank as we advanced — but the ravines on, and in front of, their right were not perceived by us, or the fact that they would prevent our attacking them there.

It was believed that neither side would have any advantage over the other in the combat; acting upon this opinion, it was decided to take the initiative and attack the enemy at once.

It was on May 23rd, the Day of Pentecost, that this action took place, as fatal to France and Spain alike as was the Battle of Hochstett (Blenheim), and although the number who perished on the field was not excessive, the losses it brought in its train later on were almost as considerable.

It appeared as if ill-fortune pursued the House of Bavaria with a greater persistence than in the case of any of the other Powers.

It had been arranged that if Bavaria was lost the Elector should obtain as compensation the Burgundian Circle or the Spanish Low Countries, and now the Battle of Ramillies snatched this Crown from him as Hochstett had robbed him of Bavaria.

So vast was the plain at Ramillies that we were able to march our army on as broad a front as we desired, and the result was a magnificent spectacle. The army began its march at six o'clock in the morning, formed into two large columns, the front of each consisting of a battalion; the artillery formed a third, which marched between the two infantry columns. The cavalry squadrons in battle formation occupied an equal extent of ground, and there being nothing to impede the view, the whole force was seen in such a fine array that it would be impossible to view a grander sight. The army had but just entered on the campaign, weather and fatigue had hardly yet had time to dim its brilliancy, and it was inspired with a courage born of confidence. The late Marquis de Goudrin, with whom I had the honour to ride during the march, remarked to me that France had surpassed herself in the quality of these troops; he believed that the enemy had no chance whatever of breaking them in the coming conflict; if defeated now, we could never again hope to withstand them. . . .

There was yet another point to which no attention had been paid, but which had an important bearing on the result, and that was the village of Tavier, which lay beyond the marsh, nearly equidistant from the enemy and ourselves. Although in order to occupy it, it was necessary for either side to cross the marsh, it was yet essential to both to seize it before the beginning of the action. The cavalry were formed on the extreme flanks of both armies on the edge of the marsh, which was but a pistol-shot in breadth and only practicable for infantry; hence, whichever infantry occupied the village, they could line its edge, open a destructive fire, and destroy the cavalry without any risk whatever. The enemy, who were the first to appreciate this fact, sent fourteen battalions across the marsh to seize it, and then our generals realized the result this would have on the course of the battle, and resolved to drive them out before the action began.

This village was the scene of the opening of the engagement, and the fighting there was almost as murderous as the rest of the battle put together. The following dragoon regiments were told off [1] for this: the King's, d'Aubigni, de Notât, and two others whose names I have forgotten; all were ordered to dismount, and were joined by the infantry regiment Greder-Suisse, the whole making five regiments of dragoons and three battalions, and finally our Bavarian brigade was added. In the order given to each it was omitted to show the details of the troops forming the detachment, or to appoint a rendezvous on our side of the marsh, so as to prevent one or another attempting anything before the rest were assembled. The units were at some distance from each other in the first instance, and being uninformed as to whom they were to work with, each took their own line to reach the village, ignorant even as to whether there was a likelihood of its being defended. Our brigade formed part of the right wing of the first infantry line, not far from the centre, and consequently some distance from the marsh when we began our advance on the village. As soon as the respective armies began to cannonade and

[1] Chosen. — T. G. B.

bombard each other, I had ordered flourishes to be played upon our hautboys, to entertain us the while, but the booming of the guns that went on all round so startled our musicians that they disappeared like a flash before anyone noticed it, and transported the melodious sounds of their instruments to some quarter where the harmonies were not quite so discordant. However, we set out, and passed along the right of our line to reach the marsh without knowing if any other troops had preceded us, or if others were to follow us; we thought, in fact, that we only were told off for the expedition, and preserved in our march all the order possible to maintain among troops anxious to win renown before the eyes of an army. The enemy's cannon, however, did some damage to our brigade, because in passing the length of the line we found ourselves exposed to several batteries, which had already opened fire upon our battalions. . . .

The enemy and their fourteen battalions perceiving us thus manœuvring on the little rise, and being ignorant of our real strength, first halted, and then proceeded to retire into the village under the impression that we were going to assault their position, and from thence kept up a continual fire upon us. But as we were nearly out of range, and under the partial protection of the rising ground, this hardly troubled us, so I forbade my men to return the fire, as my intention was only to keep them amused, and so render their further efforts abortive. We had not been here very long before we saw the general action begin, and from the place where I was situated the line of both armies were presented to my view almost in their entirety, so that hardly any of their movements escaped my notice. Following on the cannonading and bombarding, which was maintained during the completion of the final dispositions, I saw the cavalry of the enemy's left wing march to attack the Maison du Roi [2] followed by their infantry in slow time, and I was able to distinguish to perfection the great number of squadrons they had detailed for this assault. The enemy advanced in four dense lines like solid walls, while we had but three lines, the third of which was composed of several squadrons of dragoons with plenty of gaps between them. As I have already said, we had not reconnoitred the ravines which separated our left from their right; they were found impracticable, and, consequently, no important action took place thereabouts. The Allies, who knew the ground well, had concentrated the bulk of their forces to attack our right, which consisted of the Maison du Roi, in whom we had placed, perhaps, too much faith. That they were the pick of the French army cannot be denied, but they were crushed by force of numbers. The enemy's infantry, which connected with their cavalry and extended as far as the centre of their line of battle, had been reinforced in a similar manner, so that their

---

[2] Louis XIV's household guard. — T. G. B.

right flank was much denuded of troops, and remained almost immobile. Besides this, the precaution had been taken to post a corps in reserve some distance in rear to ensure the destruction of our right flank, and in this array the enemy confidently made sure of victory before even the action had actually begun.

I now saw the enemy's cavalry advance upon our people, at first at rather a slow pace, and then, when they thought they had gained the proper distance, they broke into a trot to gain impetus for their charge. At the same moment the Maison du Roi decided to meet them, for at such a moment those who await the shock find themselves at a disadvantage. But what a contrast was shown in the *mêlée* that resulted! The enemy, profiting by their superiority in numbers, surged through the gaps between our squadrons and fell upon their rear, whilst their four lines attacked in front. Naturally, our right was soon crushed. I noticed numbers of riderless horses make their escape, and in a short time the rout became general. The enemy took our lines in flank, rode them down, and completely routed them; each thought only of its retreat. Hardly any but the Maison du Roi were roughly handled on the battlefield, but brigade after brigade broke during its retreat; the enemy made numerous prisoners, and by their pursuit drove them so precipitately and in such different directions, that for more than two months after the action it was quite impossible to mobilise the army on a campaigning footing.

The Old Nobility Bites Back

Louis de Rouvroy, duc de Saint-Simon (1675–1755), came from an old noble family, distinguished in the service of a succession of French kings. In his youth he served in the war of the 1690's. In common with his peers, he was smothered in the "paternal" embrace of Louis XIV at Versailles. He fended off the crushing boredom of the court's inane round by assiduously collecting as much compromising gossip of secrets and intrigue as he could acquire. Louis disliked him and never trusted him with even the relatively innocuous duties left to the old nobility. Saint-Simon had a vision of the old nobility's becoming a "great council" of France, a counterpoise to the absolutist monarch on behalf of privilege. Louis's death brought him office in the Regency for Louis XV. His Mémoires are always arch, sometimes inaccurate, and were motivated more by malice than by policy. They give incomparable insight into Versailles, and, if allowance is made for their venom, into Louis XIV himself.

Saint-Simon: Louis XIV as King Bee

I shall pass over the stormy period of Louis XIV's minority. At twenty-three years of age [1] he entered the great world as King, under the most favourable auspices. His ministers were the most skilful in all Europe; his generals the best; his Court was filled with illustrious and clever men, formed during the troubles which had followed the death of Louis XIII.

Louis XIV was made for a brilliant Court. In the midst of other men, his figure, his courage, his grace, his beauty, his grand mien, even the tone of his voice and the majestic and natural charm of all his person, distinguished him till his death as the King Bee, and showed that if he had only been born a simple private gentleman, he would equally have excelled in fêtes, pleasures, and gallantry, and would have had the greatest success in love. The intrigues and adventures which early in life he had been engaged in — when the Comtesse de Soissons lodged at the Tuileries, as superintendent of the Queen's household, and was the centre figure of the Court group — had exercised an unfortunate influence upon him: he received those impressions with which he could never after successfully struggle. From this time, intellect, education, nobility of sentiment, and high principle, in others, became objects of suspicion to him, and soon of hatred. The more he advanced in years the more this sentiment was confirmed in him. He wished to reign by himself. His jealousy on this point unceasingly became weakness. He reigned, indeed, in little things; the great he could never reach: even in the former, too, he was often governed. The superior ability of his early ministers and his early generals soon wearied him. He liked nobody to be in any way superior to him. Thus he chose his ministers not for their knowledge but for their ignorance; not for their capacity but for their want of it. He liked to form them, as he said; liked to teach them even the most trifling things. It was the same with his generals. He took credit to himself for instructing them; wished it to be thought that from his cabinet he commanded and directed all his armies. Naturally fond of trifles, he unceasingly occupied himself with the most petty details of his troops, his household, his mansions; would even instruct his cooks, who received, like novices, lessons they had known by heart for years. This vanity, this unmeasured and unreasonable love of admiration, was his ruin. His ministers, his generals, his mistresses, his courtiers, soon perceived his weakness. They praised him with emulation and spoiled him. Praises, or, to say truth, flattery, pleased him to such an extent, that the coarsest was well received, the vilest even better relished. It was the sole means by which you could approach him. Those whom he liked owed his affection for them, to their

From *The Memoirs of the Duke of Saint-Simon*, vol. 2, trans. Bayle St. John, 8th ed. (London, 1913), pp. 357–59, 363–65.
[1] In 1661. — T. G. B.

untiring flatteries. This is what gave his ministers so much authority, and the opportunities they had for adulating him, of attributing everything to him, and of pretending to learn everything from him. Suppleness, meanness, an admiring, dependent, cringing manner — above all, an air of nothingness — were the sole means of pleasing him.

This poison spread. It spread, too, to an incredible extent, in a prince who, although of intellect beneath mediocrity, was not utterly without sense, and who had had some experience. Without voice or musical knowledge, he used to sing, in private, the passages of the opera prologues that were fullest of his praises! He was drowned in vanity; and so deeply, that at his public suppers — all the Court present, musicians also — he would hum these self-same praises between his teeth, when the music they were set to was played!

And yet, it must be admitted, he might have done better. Though his intellect, as I have said, was beneath mediocrity, it was capable of being formed. He loved glory, was fond of order and regularity; was by disposition prudent, moderate, discreet, master of his movements and his tongue. Will it be believed? He was also by disposition good and just! God had sufficiently gifted him to enable him to be a good King; perhaps even *a tolerably great King!* All the evil came to him from elsewhere. His early education was so neglected that nobody dared approach his apartment. He has often been heard to speak of those times with bitterness, and even to relate that, one evening he was found in the basin of the Palais Royale garden fountain, into which he had fallen! He was scarcely taught how to read or write, and remained so ignorant, that the most familiar historical and other facts were utterly unknown to him! He fell, accordingly, and sometimes even in public, into the grossest absurdities.

It was his vanity, his desire for glory, that led him, soon after the death of the King of Spain, to make that event the pretext for war; in spite of the renunciations so recently made, so carefully stipulated, in the marriage contract. He marched into Flanders; his conquests there were rapid; the passage of the Rhine was admirable; the triple alliance of England, Sweden, and Holland only animated him. In the midst of winter he took Franche-Comté, by restoring which at the peace of Aix-la-Chapelle, he preserved his conquests in Flanders. All was flourishing then in the state. Riches everywhere. Colbert had placed the finances, the navy, commerce, manufactures, letters even, upon the highest point; and this age, like that of Augustus, produced in abundance illustrious men of all kinds — even those illustrious only in pleasures. . . .

He early showed a disinclination for Paris. The troubles that had taken place there during the minority made him regard the place as dangerous; he wished, too, to render himself venerable by hiding himself from the eyes of the multitude; all these considerations fixed him at St. Germains soon after the death of the Queen, his mother. It was to that place he began to attract the world by fêtes and gallantries, and by making it felt that he wished to be often seen.

His love for Madame de la Vallière, which was at first kept secret, occasioned frequent excursions to Versailles, then a little card castle, which had been built by Louis XIII — annoyed, and his suite still more so, at being frequently obliged to sleep in a wretched inn there, after he had been out hunting in the forest of Saint Leger. That monarch rarely slept at Versailles more than one night, and then from necessity; the King, his son, slept there, so that he might be more in private with his mistress; pleasures unknown to the hero and just man, worthy son of Saint Louis, who built the little château.

These excursions of Louis XIV by degree gave birth to those immense buildings he erected at Versailles; and their convenience for a numerous court, so different from the apartments at St. Germains, led him to take up his abode there entirely shortly after the death of the Queen. He built an infinite number of apartments, which were asked for by those who wished to pay their court to him; whereas at St. Germains nearly everybody was obliged to lodge in the town, and the few who found accommodation at the château were strangely inconvenienced.

The frequent fêtes, the private promenades at Versailles, the journeys, were means on which the King seized in order to distinguish or mortify the courtiers, and thus render them more assiduous in pleasing him. He felt that of real favours he had not enough to bestow; in order to keep up the spirit of devotion, he therefore unceasingly invented all sorts of ideal ones, little preferences and petty distinctions, which answered his purpose as well.

He was exceedingly jealous of the attention paid him. Not only did he notice the presence of the most distinguished courtiers, but those of inferior degree also. He looked to the right and to the left, not only upon rising but upon going to bed, at his meals, in passing through his apartments, or his gardens of Versailles, where alone the courtiers were allowed to follow him; he saw and noticed everybody; not one escaped him, not even those who hoped to remain unnoticed. He marked well all absentees from the court, found out the reason of their absence, and never lost an opportunity of acting towards them as the occasion might seem to justify. With some of the courtiers (the most distinguished), it was a demerit not to make the court their ordinary abode; with others 'twas a fault to come but rarely; for those who never or scarcely ever came it was certain disgrace. When their names were in any way mentioned, "I do not know them," the King would reply haughtily. Those who presented themselves but seldom were thus characterised: "They are people I never see"; these decrees were irrevocable. He could not bear people who liked Paris.

Louis XIV took great pains to be well informed of all that passed everywhere; in the public places, in the private houses, in society and familiar intercourse. His spies and tell-tales were infinite. He had them of all species; many who were ignorant that their information reached him; others who knew it; others who wrote to him direct, sending their letters through channels he indicated; and all these letters were seen by him alone, and always before everything else; others who sometimes spoke to him secretly in his cabinet, entering by the back stairs. These unknown means ruined an infinite number of people of all classes, who never could discover the cause; often ruined them very unjustly; for the King, once prejudiced, never altered his opinion, or so rarely, that nothing was more rare. He had, too, another fault, very dangerous for others and often for himself, since it deprived him of good subjects. He had an excellent memory; in this way, that if he saw a man who, twenty years before, perhaps, had in some manner offended him, he did not forget the man, though he might forget the offence. This was enough, however, to exclude the person from all favour. The representations of a minister, of a general, of his confessor even, could not move the King. He would not yield.

The most cruel means by which the King was informed of what was passing — for many years before anybody knew it — was that of opening letters. The promptitude and dexterity with which they were opened passes understanding. He saw extracts from all the letters in which there were passages that the chiefs of the post-office, and then the minister who governed it, thought ought to go before him; entire letters, too, were sent to him, when their contents seemed to justify the sending. Thus the chiefs of the post, nay, the principal clerks were in a position to suppose what they pleased and against whom they pleased. A word of contempt against the King or the government, a joke, a detached phrase, was enough. It is incredible how many people, justly or unjustly, were more or less ruined, always without resource, without trial, and without knowing why. The secret was impenetrable; for nothing ever cost the King less than profound silence and dissimulation.

The last talent he pushed almost to falsehood, but never to deceit, pluming himself upon keeping his word — therefore he scarcely ever gave it. The secrets of others he kept as religiously as his own. He was even flattered by certain confessions and certain confidences; and there was no mistress, minister, or favourite, who could have wormed them out, even though the secret regarded themselves. . . .

ABSOLUTISM IN AUSTRIA, SPAIN, AND PRUSSIA
Chapter 2

Louis XIV's France became the model for absolutism everywhere in Europe in the early eighteenth century. The model, however, was adapted to local institutions and circumstances. Along with the Bourbon monarchy in France, three other continental dynasties were destined to play dominant roles in European power politics during the eighteenth century: the new Bourbon monarchy of Spain, a revitalized Hapsburg monarchy of Austria, and the oldest dynasty but newest power of them all, the Hohenzollern monarchy of Prussia. The new-fashioned absolutism was the key to their capacity to play those roles. By the blueprint of Louis's absolutism, Spain, Austria, and Prussia were far behind in administrative centralization. Austria — not the Holy Roman Empire but the Hapsburg dynasty's own territories — was an agglomeration of states in Eastern Europe comprising three major political entities (Austria, Hungary, Bohemia-Moravia), three major languages (German, Magyar, Slavic), at least as many cultures, and numerous fractionalized minorities. Only the person of the Hapsburg ruler united them, though "united" is too strong a word, for these territories would have been ungovernable if they had not been geographically contiguous. In Spain, the fifteenth-century union of Castile and Aragon was a dynastic, not structural, union and Olivares' manful attempt to impose centralized administrative structures had resulted in the revolt and temporary independence of the important province of Catalonia in 1640. The last Spanish Hapsburg kings of the second half of the seventeenth century were incompetents and let Olivares' work decay. Centralization was furthest advanced in Prussia. It had to be, for the Hohenzollern domain comprised a chain of territories scattered across northern Germany, from the Dutch border to the Polish border, with the center in Brandenburg. Only the strong hand of a ruler continuously evident in an efficient bureaucracy and army could give it any form and cohesion. Frederick William, the Great Elector (1640–1688), founded the Prussian civil service, drawn from the subjects of all his territories and welded into a thoroughly faithful tool of the dynasty, and the Prussian army, the presence of which in every domain represented the monarch's power. The meteoric rise of Prussia in the mid-eighteenth century under the greatest of its monarchs was firmly founded on those two institutions, fashioned a century before and brought to perfection in succeeding years.

With respect to the other principal foundation of absolutism, the subjugation of the nobility, Prussia also led Austria and Spain, though all lagged behind France. The Great Elector deprived the provincial estates of most of their power, but he had to make concessions to do it. He gave the Prussian nobility (the Junkers) greater power over their peasants, he converted their lands from feudal-service tenure to full ownership, he recognized their monopoly of rural property, and he assured them of exemption from taxes and customs duties. In Austria, the power of the provincial estates declined only toward the end of the seventeenth century when the absolutism of Leopold I (1657–1705) began to take effect. The creation of a new nobility and a rudimentary structure of central administrative councils superimposed on the provincial administration were Leopold's major devices to advance absolutism. In Spain, even under the Bourbon reorganization of the eighteenth century, the power of the old nobility remained awesome.

The new style of absolutism in Spain was instituted by Philip V (1700–1746), grandson of Louis XIV and the first Bourbon ruler. His accession touched off the War of the Spanish Succession, and from 1701 to 1714 his position was tenuous and his attention was concentrated on defending his throne. Despite the war, he turned to renovation at once. Careful, though general, instructions from Louis pointed the direction, and Philip made his power felt in increased centralization as soon as opportunity allowed. He was not a truly competent ruler, but the abilities of his queen, Elizabeth Farnese, went far toward supplying his defects. Both he and his successor, Ferdinand VI (1746–1759), avoided confrontation with the Spanish nobility, but they did accomplish a high degree of bureaucratic centralization, the further subordination of the church, and tax and economic reforms that brought a measure of prosperity and governmental solvency in peacetime.

Leopold I of Austria was an early convert to Louis's system. He created the initial impetus that carried absolutism on through a short-lived successor and three decades of rule by Charles VI (1711–1740). Charles was involved so continuously in war and diplomacy, the latter to assure the succession to his daughter Maria Theresa, that he brought the Austrian state close to bankruptcy. Leopold's ambitious foreign policy brought success against the Turks, added territory, and played a part in creating a sense of unity in his realm. Leopold also managed to break the resistance of the Hungarian nobility by repression and concession. However, he failed to halt the decline in taxes from his chief source of revenue, the lands of the serfs, because the nobility was the chief beneficiary of land-conversion schemes that removed peasant property from the tax rolls. A thoroughly Colbertian economic policy did not go far toward reviving a lagging economy. Nonetheless, Leopold built centralized institutions, especially the army, and enhanced the prestige as well as the power of the monarch at least to the extent that when his granddaughter ascended the throne in 1740 only to be imperiled by Prussia's lightning attack into her dominions, she was able to mobilize and to defend her state.

The most successful and most competent of all eighteenth-century absolutists was the Prussian king who attacked Maria Theresa's Austria: Frederick II, "the Great" (1740–1786). Historians have been fascinated by the high drama of the sensitive, gifted youth: his music was taken from him and his flute was broken by a domineering father, who detested the effete prince who would succeed him; his closet confidant was his vivacious sister Wilhelmine; his only friend was his beloved companion Katte, whose beheading the eighteen-year-old Frederick was forced to watch while he himself was under shadow of death. And historians have been no less fascinated by the vivid contrast between the youthful and the older Frederick — ruthless, insensitive, as domineering as his father, crude, snuff-stained, respectfully but unaffectionately dubbed "Old Fritz" by his subjects. His greatness depended on neither extreme of his personality. Frederick was intelligent and calculating, imbued with the same sense of dynastic destiny that had moved his father and, earlier, the Great Elector. He was also a man with a task and a high sense of duty. His ends were characteristic of the age: territorial aggrandizement and the prestige of great-power status. The means he chose to attain them was the completion of the garrison state bequeathed him by his father. The resulting absolutist state was of greater strength and reputation in proportion to its size than Louis XIV's France.

Frederick II bears comparison to Louis XIV in other ways. During his long reign he also was involved in almost continuous war. Like Louis, his reign naturally divides midway, between success in diplomacy and war and failure to achieve more by either — a stalemate of maintenance of gains at best. The generalization suggested by the experience of both Frederick and Louis is that absolutism produced an effective war machine in a centralized state largely safe from internal disorder but did not have the technical capacity to produce a healthy economy to sustain the war machine over the long, grueling haul of absolutist power politics.

Bourbon Absolutism in Spain Under Philip V

The accession to the throne of Spain of Philip duc d'Anjou, Louis XIV's grandson, in 1700 as the named successor of the last Hapsburg king, childless Charles II, raised the specter of an enormous dynastic power, a combined France and Spain, should Philip or his heir succeed also to the French throne. This was the basic issue of the War of the Spanish Succession (1713–1714). The treaties ending the war confirmed Philip V on the Spanish throne, but excluded him and his line from the French throne.

Philip went to Spain briefed by his grandfather especially in the manner of handling his reputedly very religious and very proud new subjects. Philip was indolent and dull; it was as well that the instructions were clear. Philip followed them to the letter and enjoyed considerable success.

A royal decree of April 3, 1711, reformed the entire administrative structure of Aragon, a pattern to be followed later in Castile. The reforms constituted very sophisticated centralism.

Louis XIV Instructs His Grandson Philip V of Spain, 1700

1. Never omit any of your duties, especially towards God.
2. Preserve yourself in the purity of your bringing up.
3. Cause God to be honoured in all places where you have power; procure His glory; give the example. It is one of the greatest forms of good that Kings can do.
4. On every occasion declare yourself on the side of virtue and against vice.
5. Have no attachment ever to any one.
6. Love your wife, lead a good life with her, and ask God to give you one suitable to you. I do not think you should take an Austrian woman.
7. Love the Spaniards and all your subjects attached to your Crowns and to your person; do not give preference to those who flatter you most; esteem those who for a good cause venture to displease you; these are your real friends.
8. Make your subjects happy; and, with a view to this, only engage in

From *A King's Lessons in Statecraft: Louis XIV*, ed. Jean Longnon, trans. Herbert Wilson (New York, 1925), pp. 173–76.

war when you are obliged, and after you have well considered and weighed the reasons with your Council.

9. Endeavour to keep your finances in good order; watch over the Indies and your fleets; keep your commerce in mind; live in close union with France, since there is nothing so advantageous to our two Powers as this union which nothing can withstand.

10. If you are compelled to go to war, place yourself at the head of your armies.

11. Take thought to re-establish your troops everywhere, and begin with those in Flanders.

12. Never leave your affairs for your pleasure; but make for yourself a rule of some kind which will give you occasions of liberty and distraction.

13. Of these there is hardly a more innocent one than the chase and the pleasure of some country house, provided that you do not incur too much expense thereon.

14. Pay great attention to your affairs; when people discuss them with you listen to them at length at the beginning, without deciding anything.

15. When you have attained to more knowledge, remember that it is for you to decide; but whatever be your experience, always hearken to all the advice and all the arguments of your Council before coming to this decision.

16. Do all in your power to get to know well the most important people, in order that you may make suitable use of them.

17. See that your Viceroys and Governors shall always be Spaniards.

18. Treat every one well; never say anything vexing to any one, but do honour to people of quality and merit.

19. Give evidence of your gratitude to the late King and to all who sided with choosing you as his successor.

20. Have great confidence in Cardinal Portocarrero, and show him your pleasure in the course he has pursued.

21. I think you should do something considerable for the Ambassador [1] who had the tact to ask for you and to be the first to greet you in the quality of a subject.

22. Do not forget Betmar, who has merit and is capable of being of service to you.

23. Have entire trust in the Duc d'Harcourt; [2] he is a clever and an honest man, and will only give you advice in accordance with your interests.

24. Keep all Frenchmen in good order.

25. Treat your domestic servants well, but do not allow them too much familiarity, and trust them still less; use them so long as they are well-

---

[1] The Marquis of Castel-dos-Rios. Philip V made him a Grandee of Spain. — T. G. B.
[2] The French ambassador in Madrid. — T. G. B.

Louis XIV of France to Philip V of Spain

behaved; dismiss them on the least fault they commit and never uphold them against the Spaniards.

26. Have no dealings with the Queen Dowager³ beyond what you can help; arrange for her to leave Madrid and not to go out of Spain; wherever she is keep an eye on her conduct, and prevent her mixing herself up in any affairs; regard with suspicion those who have too much to do with her.

27. Love your relations always; keep in mind the grief they have had in leaving you; keep up a close intercourse with them in great things and small; ask us for anything you need, or wish to have, which you do not find where you are; we will do the same with you.

28. Never forget that you are French, and what may happen to you when you have made secure the Spanish succession with children; visit your kingdoms; go to Naples and Sicily; make a stay in Milan, and come to Flanders; this will be an opportunity of seeing us again; meanwhile visit Catalonia, Aragon, and the other places; see what is to be done for Ceuta.

29. Throw some money to the people when you are in Spain, and especially when entering Madrid.

30. Do not appear astonished at the extraordinary figures you will meet; never make fun of them; each country has its peculiar manners and you will soon become accustomed to what at first will seem most surprising to you.

31. Avoid as far as you can granting favours to those who give money to obtain them; dispense suitably and liberally, and be chary of accepting presents except they be trifling; if sometimes you cannot help accepting them, give a more valuable one to the donor after allowing a few days to pass.

32. Keep a privy purse in which to put your own money, of which you alone have the key.

33. I will end with one of the most important pieces of advice that I can give you: never allow yourself to be ruled; be the master; have no favourites or prime minister; listen to, and consult your Council, but do you decide yourself. God, who made you King, will give you the lights which are necessary to you, so long as you have a right intention.

---

³ Marie Anne, second wife and widow of Charles II of Spain and a strong partisan of Austria's claim to the Spanish throne. — T. G. B.

Philip V's Reforms of Spanish Government in Practice, April 3, 1711

I have decided that for the moment and as a temporary measure, there should be in this realm of Aragon a commandant general, to whose care should fall its military, political, economic and administrative government, wherefore I have been pleased to elect and nominate you, the Principe Tserclaës de Tilly. At the same time I have decided that there be an audiencia, with two chambers, one for civil matters, with four ministers; and the other for criminal matters; together with a fiscal, who would assist in both chambers; and the necessary subordinates. And that there also be a regent to rule this audiencia, which I wish to be composed of persons chosen by me without restriction of province, country or origin; and in consequence of this I nominate as regent of this audiencia Don Francisco de Aperregui, the most senior oidor of the council of Navarre; for the civil chamber, Don Manuel de Fuentes y Peralta, Don Joseph de Castro y Azaujo, Don Gil Custudio de Lissa y Guebara, and Don Jaime Ric y Veyan; and for the criminal chamber, Don Agustín de Montiano, Don Lorenzo de Medina, Don Diego de Barbastro, Don Ignacio de Segovia, and Don Joseph Agustín Camargo; and as fiscal, Don Joseph Rodrigo y Villalpando. In the criminal chamber, pleas are to be judged and determined according to the custom and laws of Castile . . . and in the civil chamber, civil pleas are to be judged according to the municipal laws of this realm of Aragon, since it is my will that the said municipal laws be observed for all cases between private individuals. [And in those cases] where I intervene against one of my subjects . . . judgment is to be . . . according to the laws of Castile. The commandant general of the realm is to preside over the said audiencia. Appeals in the third instance, of both civil and criminal cases, are to be allowed to the council of Castile. [Salaries] are to be paid in the way they were before 1705.

For the levy, administration and collection of all that belongs to the royal revenue, there is to be an administrator, for which I have nominated Don Melchor Macanaz. A chamber is to be established with the name of the junta, or tribunal, of the Royal Exchequer [*Junta, o Tribunal del Real Erario*. Eight persons were to compose this tribunal]: two from the clergy, of whom one should be a bishop, abbot or *comendador*, and the other a canon of one of the churches of the realm; two from the upper nobility; two from the gentry estate [*estado de Hijosdalgo*], and two citizens of Saragossa or another of the cities in the realm. [The bishop of Huesca was named as one of the ecclesiastical members.]

From Henry Kamen, *The War of Succession in Spain, 1700–1715*, pp. 343–45. © 1969 by Henry Kamen. Reprinted by permission of Henry Kamen, Indiana University Press, and George Weidenfeld & Nicolson Ltd.

I have also resolved that this kingdom be divided into districts or *partidos,* and that in each there should be a military governor, whom I shall nominate, subordinate in all matters to the commandant general; and that the problems and measures arising in matters of government be communicated to me through the commandant general and the governors of the districts, each of whom has to care for the political and economic government of his district; and that appeals in these matters should be allowed to the council of war.

[The salaries of the commandant general and the governors were to come from the Tesorería Mayor de la Guerra, but each district in Aragon was to pay a special half-yearly tax towards this, which would be entered in the said Tesorería.]

Touching the municipal government of the cities, towns and places of this realm, the election and nomination of justices, judges and their subordinates is my responsibility, depending on the number of persons available; the same applies to the nomination of the *corregidor* or *alcalde* and his subordinates, who, in the exercise of their office and in the administration of justice, are to observe the same rules and laws as are stated and regulated for the two chambers of the audiencia.

In what touches the Church, I have no intention of prejudicing it, nor on the other hand of diminishing my *regalías* in any way. I therefore resolve that all ecclesiastical matters, and any rights of the crown [*regalías*], which were formerly administered by the justiciar of Aragon and his court, shall hereafter be administered by the regent and ministers of the audiencia, or by persons whom I may in future deputise for this.

The "Pragmatic Sanction" for the Austrian Succession

Charles VI, faced with the likelihood that he would have no male issue, promulgated the "Pragmatic Sanction" in 1713 to assure the succession to the Austrian throne of his daughter Maria Theresa, to the exclusion of all other possible successors, and to prevent division of the Hapsburg dominions. It required long, hard diplomacy to secure the guarantees of the other powers that they would respect the edict, which was far from clear in Roman Law, as the French ambassador to Charles VI pointed out in a dispatch home in 1730. Bavaria was the notable holdout. Though Prussia agreed to the Sanction, Frederick II declared it invalid and used this as the pretext to attack Austria on Maria Theresa's accession in 1740.

Emperor Charles VI Promulgates the "Pragmatic Sanction"

H.I.M.[1] called all the Privy Councillors who were in Vienna to a meeting in the usual place at 10 A.M. on the 19th of April 1713. At the prescribed time the Emperor went into the Council Chamber and placed himself under the canopy at the usual table; then he had his Councillors and Ministers of State summoned and they entered in order of rank and each went to his own place; namely, Prince Eugene of Savoy, etc. . . .

When all the said Councillors and Ministers of State were thus assembled, H.I.M. declared that his motive for calling them was to inform them that certain arrangements, rules and pacts dealing with the succession had been drawn up, between his father the late Emperor,[2] his late brother Joseph, then King of the Romans, and himself, at that time King-designate of Spain; and these had been confirmed by all parties on oath in the presence of different Councillors and Ministers of the Emperor; but as few of the said Councillors and Ministers were now alive, H.I.M. had considered it necessary not only to make this declaration to those present but also to inform them of the said laws and pacts and have the documents read to them.

Immediately after this H.I.M. ordered his Court-Chancellor Count von Seilern to read the said documents.

And the said Count read in a loud and audible voice the opening of the original instrument which the Emperor, as King of Spain, signed and sealed when he accepted the Spanish throne. Then he read from beginning to end all the acts of succession signed and sealed by the Emperor Leopold and the King of the Romans, respectively, together with the notary's certificate attached. Then he read the rest of the Spanish instrument, containing the agreement and engagement which the present Emperor had then made, with the notary's certificate similarly attached, which acts are dated Vienna, 12 Sept. 1703.

When this had been done, H.I.M. said further to the above-mentioned Councillors and Ministers, that the acts which had just been read made it clear that there existed an arrangement and a mutual pact concerning the succession, and that this was drawn up for all perpetuity and confirmed upon oath as between the Josephine and Caroline branches of the family. Consequently, apart from the hereditary kingdoms and provinces of Spain which were ceded to him by the Emperor Leopold and the Emperor Joseph of glorious memory, the death of the said Emperor his brother without male heirs had placed H.I.M. in possession of all the

From *Select Documents of European History*, vol. 3, 1715–1920, ed. H. Butterfield (London, 1931), pp. 1–4. Reprinted by permission of Methuen & Co. Ltd.
[1] His Imperial Majesty. — T. G. B.
[2] Leopold I. — T. G. B.

Charles VI of Austria and the Pragmatic Sanction

other kingdoms and hereditary possessions. These were to be kept in their entirety, without any kind of division, being possessed according to the law of primogeniture by the male heirs of a lawful marriage so long as any were alive; but were to pass in the same way to his daughters by lawful marriage, if there were a default of masculine posterity on his part (from which may God preserve him). In all this the order and law of primogeniture were always to be maintained.

Further, failing any legitimate descendants, either male or female, to H.I.M., the said right of succession to all the said hereditary kingdoms and possessions, without division, would pass in the above-mentioned way — always keeping the order of primogeniture — to the daughters of the Emperor Joseph and to their legitimate descendants; and similarly the said Archduchesses would enjoy all the other privileges and prerogatives, according to the said law and ordering of the succession.

This being the case, after the Caroline branch now reigning, and after the Josephine branch consisting of the daughters left behind by the Emperor Joseph, the said rights of succession with everything depending thereto shall belong, and shall remain, and shall be in every way reserved to the sisters of H.I.M. and all the other lines of the Archducal House, according to the law of primogeniture and in the order which that law determines.

The law and these regulations and pacts concerning the succession were established for all perpetuity and confirmed by the oath of the Emperors, the father and brother of H.I.M., as well as by his said Imperial Majesty himself, and as they had no other object but the glory of God and the keeping together of all the hereditary possessions without partition, H.I.M. firmly adhered to them and counted upon the said Councillors and Ministers doing the same; he exhorted them and ordered them to observe everything in these pacts and regulations with as much care and attention as he, and also to see that others observe them and maintain them; and for this reason H.I.M. excused the said Councillors and Ministers from their vow of secrecy in this case. After which H.I.M. and they the Councillors and Ministers retired.

I certify that everything took place as I have stated it above; and in witness of this I have signed the present act and put my seal to it.

George Frederick von Schickh
Vienna   19 April 1713

The French Ambassador Advises Caution, 1730

The proposal is a very indefinite one. We should not be wise if we gave a guarantee without knowing what we were undertaking. The whole subject is really full of doubts and difficulties. All the states which are in the possession of the Emperor have their own different statutes and usages [in regard to the order of the succession]. It is doubtful whether the kingdoms of Bohemia and Hungary have lost their right of election, and even if they can have lost it, one might ask whether the Emperor can dispose of it to the profit of his daughters. This would be prejudicing the rights of people of Hungarian descent, who go back to the daughter of Ladislaus VI, King of Hungary and Bohemia. She carried her rights over these two kingdoms to her husband Ferdinand I. Anne of Austria, one of the daughters of this marriage, became the wife of Albert, Duke of Bavaria. She alone has a direct and unbroken line of descendants, and they are the princes of the House of Bavaria. And this is where His Electoral Highness [of Bavaria] undoubtedly draws part of his family claims to the Austrian succession in Germany. There is just the same obscurity when we come to the case of the three Austrias. One would have to see the original letters of investiture and then examine all the pacts which the House of Austria has made. The Emperor would find himself in an embarrassing position if he were asked to communicate all the necessary documents in order to show how far the dispositions which he has made are valid. This would lead to the disclosure of many abuses and usurpations which have been allowed to pass but which have not become any the more legitimate for that. Then there is another question as to whether the fief of Milan is masculine or not. If the Empire were to make a decision on this point I am not sure that it would adjudge the fief to be feminine. The right of settling who has the reversion [in the case of the failure of direct heirs] is another question and it is the most important question of all. Can the princes of the House of Austria actually change the order of succession, while they are pretending merely to be working out its implications, as the Emperor cleverly makes out in his Pragmatic Sanction? It appears from some of the documents that if the daughters of the Austrian House have entirely renounced their rights in favour of the masculine line in Germany, they have however reserved those rights in the event of the male line becoming extinct, and the very existence of these reservations must imply that they had the right of reversion. One could say a great deal about the renunciations made by the daughters of the Emperor Joseph. One might ask whether the many precautions that have been taken to make these renunciations water-tight are not really so many

From *Select Documents of European History*, vol. 3, 1715–1920, ed. H. Butterfield (London, 1931), pp. 4–6. Reprinted by permission of Methuen & Co. Ltd.

arguments against the validity of these very renunciations. Finally the Emperor himself admits in his Pragmatic Sanction that he is introducing a new law, and this admission raises a point that can be used as an important argument against him.

Prince Frederick of Prussia Is Instructed in Obedience by His Father

The intense dislike that Frederick William I conceived for his frivolous son stemmed from his intensely militaristic notion of kingship and his hatred of culture, which he thought was the pursuit of the weak, and of his son's genuine sensibility and profound stubbornness. Prince Frederick, the future Frederick the Great, in this, as in everything else he undertook, worked hard to deserve his father's animosity. The prince's adolescent resolve to run away from his brutish father was taken in 1730 in league with two young officer-companions, Katte and Keith. Frederick and Katte were caught, Keith escaped. The prince and Katte were condemned by court-martial for desertion. Katte was executed before Frederick's eyes, and if Frederick had not broken and taken an oath of filial obedience he probably would have been executed also. Thus the "drillmaster of Prussia" made his son a soldier and a king.

The account of Princess Wilhelmine, Prince Frederick's sister, is accurate and as low-key as such a harrowing tale can be. Her sympathies were mixed; then, too, so were Prince Frederick's.

Account by Princess Wilhelmine

An unknown person brought her [1] a letter which enclosed one from my brother to me. She brought it to me at once. I could not receive it without feelings of the deepest emotion. The letter was written in pencil, and its contents read as follows (I have copied every word from the original, which I keep as a most precious relic.):

Dear Beloved Sister:
I am to be declared an arch-heretic by the court-martial before which I am

From *Memoirs of Wilhelmine, Margravine of Bairuth*, ed. and trans. Princess Christian of Schleswig-Holstein (New York, 1888), pp. 160–65.
[1] Wilhelmine's maid. — T. G. B.

shortly to appear. It will not require any great difficulty to do this. You can, therefore, imagine what a creature they are going to make me out. I do not in the least care about the ban which they will pronounce over me, if only my dear sister will not bear me false witness. How thankful I am that neither bolts nor bars can prevent my assuring you of my sincere friendship! Yes, dearest sister, there are still people in this almost depraved century who are devoted enough to procure me the means of expressing my devotion to you. If I only know that you are happy, dear sister, then my prison will become an abode of contentment and satisfaction. "*Chi ha tempo, ha vita,*" [2] let this comfort us. I wish, with all my heart, that we needed no interpreter to go to and fro between us. May those happy hours return once more, during which your Principe and my Principessa (we called my guitar and his flute by these names) brought forth such sweet harmonies. To speak plainly, may I soon again be able to tell you, by word of mouth, that nothing in this world can ever lessen my affection for you. Good-by.

The Prisoner [3]

This letter touched me deeply, and I cried over it.

"How deeply I pity my poor brother!" I said to Mademoiselle von Sonnsfeld; "he is still able to joke in the midst of his sore trouble. Goodness only knows what misery is in store for him. I must answer him. You will not forbid my having this comfort? The same person who brought me his letter so safely will find means of letting my answer reach him."

Mademoiselle von Sonnsfeld did not wish at once to damp my joy, but by degrees she made me understand the great danger I exposed myself to if I carried out my intention of writing.

The court-martial assembled on the 1st of November. As my governess was aware of the agitated state I was in, she hid this news from me, the more so as she knew that my brother's fate was to be decided by it.

Although I did not at that time know of what took place, I will here continue my account of these tragic events, so as not to break the thread of my narrative.

The court-martial was held at Potsdam. It was composed of two major-generals, two colonels, two lieutenant-colonels, two majors, two captains, and two lieutenants. The whole army were obliged to draw lots as to who was to constitute it, as every one declined to have anything to do with it.

The lots fell on Major-generals Dönhoff and Linger, and Colonels Derchow and Panewitz. I do not remember the names of the colonels and captains, but the lieutenants were Einsiedel and one other from the king's regiment. They had all to take their oath on the Bible. Dönhoff and Linger voted for pardon being granted; but Einsiedel, Derchow, and the others, all Grumkow's creatures, and favorites of the king, condemned my brother and Katt to the scaffold. A monstrous and unheard-of sen-

---

[2] "Who has time has life." — T. G. B.
[3] Prince Frederick. — T. G. B.

tence in a civilized land! Seckendorf now stepped in as mediator, and begged for mercy for both criminals, particularly my brother. It was granted him only with much trouble, for my father's rage had increased. For Katt he could obtain nothing — not even a reprieve. His sentence was therefore pronounced. He heard it without moving a muscle, and with the most heroic firmness. He merely answered, "I submit to the king's will, and to that of Providence. I can die without fear, for I have nothing to reproach myself with, and I suffer for a good cause." He then prepared himself for the awful trial before him. Next day he was told that the king wished his execution to take place away from Berlin. This rather startled him, but he soon regained his composure.

As soon as he was left alone he called the officer of the guard, and gave him the snuffbox containing the portraits of my brother and me, saying, "Keep this, and think sometimes of me. Do not, however, show the box to any one, as it might do harm to the high personages who are represented on it." Katt then wrote three letters — one to his grandfather, one to his father, and one to his brother-in-law. When the clergyman came to him, he said, "I have greatly sinned before God. My great ambition was the cause of many faults, of which I repent sincerely. The crown prince's favor made me blind to all else. I now know how vain are all earthly things. I repent truly of all my sins, and pray death to lead me to everlasting peace." The day was spent in conversing in this manner. Towards evening Major Schenk came with tears in his eyes and told Katt that everything was ready for his departure, adding, "The king has commanded me to be present at your execution, and to accompany you to the place where it is to be carried out. I have twice over begged to be excused from this mission, but the king insisted, so I could but obey. Would to God that his heart had been softened, and that I might have been the bearer of your pardon!"

"You are very kind," Katt replied, "but I do not wish to escape from my fate. I give my life for a master whom I love most dearly, and by doing so give him the greatest proof of my devotion. Happiness without end awaits me." With these words he stepped cheerfully and smilingly into the carriage.

Before starting he took leave of many officers and soldiers of the gendarmerie who had assembled to witness his departure. It was nine o'clock in the morning when he reached Küstrin. The scaffold had been erected in front of my brother's windows, from which the bars had been removed. It was on a level with the window, and only a few paces from it.

As soon as they had reached the interior of the fortress Schenk said to Katt, "Keep up your courage, for a fearful trial is before you."

"Say rather that it is the greatest comfort that could have been given me," he replied.

My unfortunate brother had, the day before, witnessed all these preparations without knowing their purpose. He expected his own death-warrant. Early in the morning the governor of the fortress, General Lepel, and the president, Münichow, entered my brother's prison and endeavored to prepare him as best they could for the terrible news they had to communicate to him. They brought him a plain brown suit of clothes, the counterpart to that which Katt wore (my brother would not take it off afterwards, till it had to be literally torn off him). As soon as the crown prince heard what was in store for him he was seized with frantic despair, which grew only greater and greater as he was forced to approach the window. He tried to throw himself out of it. Then he exclaimed, "For God's sake postpone the execution! I will write to the king that I will solemnly renounce the crown if only I can save Katt's life."

As my brother saw him mount the scaffold he called out to him, "I am miserable, dear Katt. I am the cause of your misfortune; oh, that I were in your place!" Katt, then kneeling down, replied, "Had I a thousand lives, my beloved prince, I would lay them all down for you." One of the attendants then stepped forward to blindfold him, but he waved him back. He then said, in a firm voice, "My God, into Thy hands I commend my spirit." He had scarcely uttered these words when his head fell. In falling he had still stretched out his hand towards the window at which my brother was standing. The poor prince had fainted away. He was laid on his bed, where he remained insensible for several hours. Fever then attacked him, and his condition was not to be described. Katt's body had been left lying in such a position that my brother could not escape seeing it. As no one knew what to do with the crown prince, and the doctors feared for his life, they sent for a clergyman. But the cruel emotions my brother had been through were not so easily got over, and he became calmer only when quite exhausted. Great bodily weakness, accompanied by floods of tears, at last succeeded the violent fits of despair, and he sank into melancholy, which lasted some time. Even now we never dare mention this terrible scene to him. Katt's body remained lying on the scaffold till sundown. It was then buried in a corner of the fortress near the bastions. I am here going to insert a letter Katt wrote to his grandfather, and also a verse which was found written on the window of his prison.

> Sir, and Honored Grandfather,
> I cannot express to you with what pain and anxiety I write these lines. I, who have been the sole object of your constant solicitude; I, to whom you looked for the advancement of your family; I, whom you educated in principles that should have made me fit to serve God and my neighbors; I, who never parted from you without having been honored by some of your kind advice; I, who was the joy, pride, and support of your old age; I, miserable creature, am the cause of all your grief and pain. Instead of sending you good news, I must tell you of my being sentenced to death — a sentence which has just been communicated to me. Do not take my sad fate too much to heart. We must bow to

the will of Providence. If we are tried by reverses, the strength will be given us to endure them. Nothing is impossible to God: He can help when He sees fit. I put all my trust in the Almighty, that He may yet soften the king's heart, and incline him to show me mercy. The king was at all times gracious towards me. If God wills it otherwise, then I shall not cease to praise Him, for He orders all for our best. I shall patiently submit to any alternative your influence and other people's may obtain from the king. Meanwhile I entreat your forgiveness for all my misdeeds, and hope that God, who forgives the greatest of sinners, will also have mercy on me. Will you not also follow His example, and grant your pardon to him who signs himself, sir, and much esteemed grandfather,

Your devoted and respected grandson,

2d November, 1730
Katt

The following are the lines he wrote on his window. There is more cleverness in them than poetry:

Wouldst thou the fruit of a clear conscience reap?
Take time, and patience keep.
Wouldst of the writer ask? Then Katt replies,
"Cheerful and hopeful in his cell he lies."

Underneath them was written: "To those who wish to read these lines be it known that he who wrote them was imprisoned on the 16th of August, 1730, by order of the king. He still hopes to be liberated, though the manner in which he is watched makes him fear something terrible."

Frederick the Great's Analysis of the Garrison State

Frederick's collected essays and memoirs constitute a multivolume corpus of literature, written in the only tongue he owned to be civilized, French. The volumes testify to Frederick's continuing intellectualism. Their bulk is sometimes more impressive than their profundity. This is true of considerable parts of his "Essay on Forms of Government," but some paragraphs of it are arresting, for they describe the state-in-arms that he inherited, advanced, preserved, and bequeathed to his successor and, indeed, for better and for worse, to the world from that day to the final grotesque immolation in Hitler's bunker in Berlin in May, 1945. The Prussian garrison state was not ancient Sparta, neither was it the prototype of Nazi Germany. It did, though, place a tragic emphasis on arms and the values of war.

An Essay on Forms of Government

If we look back into the most remote antiquity, we shall find that the people whose history has descended to us led pastoral lives, and did not form social bodies. What the book of Genesis relates of the history of the Patriarchs is sufficient proof. Previous to this small Jewish nation, the Egyptians must in like manner have been dispersed over those countries which the Nile did not submerge; and many ages no doubt passed away before the vanquished river would permit the people to assemble in small towns. From the Grecian history we learn the names of founders of states, and of those legislators who first assembled the Greeks in bodies. This nation was long in a savage state, as well as all the nations of the globe. Had the annals of the Etruscans, and those of the Samnite, Sabine and other tribes, come down to us, we should assuredly have learnt that they lived in distinct families, before they were assembled and united.

The Gauls were forming into societies at the time they were conquered by Julius Caesar; but it appears Great Britain had not attained this point of perfection, when the conqueror first passed into that island with his Roman legions. In the age of this great man, the Germans could only be compared to what the Iroquois and Algonquins, or some equally savage people, are at present. They existed by hunting and fishing, and on their milk and herds. A German thought himself debased by cultivating the earth; this was a labour performed by the slaves he had taken in war. The Hercynian forest, at that time, almost wholly covered the vast extent of country which at present composes the German empire. The nation could not be populous, for want of sufficient food; and this no doubt was the true cause of the prodigious emigrations of the northern people, who hastened southward in search of lands ready cleared, under a less rigorous climate. . . .

That general instinct, in men, which leads them to procure for themselves the greatest possible happiness, occasioned the creation of various forms of government. Some imagined that, by confiding themselves to the guidance of a few sages, they should find this great happiness; hence the aristocratic form. Others preferred an oligarchy. Athens, and most of the Grecian republics, chose a democratical government. Persia, and the east, bowed beneath despotism. The Romans, for a time, had kings; but, weary of the tyranny of the Tarquins, they changed the monarchy into an aristocracy. Presently tired of the severity of the Patricians, who oppressed them by usury, the people left the city, and did not return to Rome till the senate had first approved the tribunes, elected by Plebeians for their defence against the power of the great. The people afterward rendered their

From Frederick II, *Political, Philosophical, & Satyrical Miscellanies*, Posthumous Works, vol. 5, trans. T. Holcroft (London, 1789), pp. 5–9, 15–16, 18–21.

authority almost supreme. Those who seized violently on government, and who, following the guidance of the passions and of caprice, reversed the laws and overturned those fundamental principles which had been established for the preservation of society, were denominated tyrants.

But, however sage the legislators, and those who first assembled the people in bodies were, however good their intentions might be, not one of these governments is found to have maintained its perfect integrity. And why? Because men are imperfect, consequently so are their works: because the citizens, employed by the prince, were blinded by individual interest, which always overthrows the general good: and, in fine, because there is no stability on earth. . . .

I once more repeat, the sovereign represents the state; he and his people form but one body, which can only be happy as far as united by concord. The prince is to the nation he governs what the head is to the man; it is his duty to see, think, and act for the whole community, that he may procure it every advantage of which it is capable. If it be intended that a monarchical should excel a republican government, sentence is pronounced on the sovereign. He must be active, possess integrity, and collect his whole powers, that he may be able to run the career he has commenced. Here follow my ideas concerning his duties.

He ought to procure exact and circumstantial information of the strength and weakness of his country, as well relative to pecuniary resources as to population, finance, trade, laws, and the genius of the nation whom he is appointed to govern. If the laws are good they will be clear in their definitions; otherwise, chicanery will seek to elude their spirit to its advantage, and arbitrarily and irregularly determine on the fortunes of individuals. Law-suits ought to be as short as possible, to prevent the ruin of the appellants, who consume in useless expences what is justly and duly their right. This branch of government cannot be too carefully watched, that every possible barrier may be opposed to the avidity of judges and counsellors. Every person is kept within the limits of their duty, by occasional visits into the provinces. Whoever imagines himself to be injured will venture to make his complaints to the commission; and those who are found to be prevaricators ought to be severely punished. It is perhaps superfluous to add that the penalty ought never to exceed the crime; that violence never ought to supersede law; and that it were better the sovereign should be too merciful than too severe.

As every person who does not proceed on principle is inconsistent in his conduct, it is still more necessary that the magistrate who watches over the public good should act from a determinate system of politics, war, finance, commerce, and law. Thus, for example, a people of mild manners ought not to have severe laws, but such as are adapted to their character. The basis of such systems ought always to be correspondent to the greatest good society can receive. Their principles ought to be conformable to the situation of the country, to its ancient customs, if they are good, and to the genius of the nation.

. . . Men are wicked. Care must especially be taken not to suffer surprise, because whatever surprises intimidates and terrifies, which never happens when preparations are made, however vexatious the event may be which there is reason to expect. European politics are so fallacious that the most sage may become dupes, if they are not always alert, and on their guard.

The military system ought, in like manner, to rest on good principles, which from experience are known to be certain. The genius of the nation ought to be understood; of what it is capable, and how far its safety may be risked by leading it against the enemy. The warlike customs of the Greeks and Romans are interdicted, in these ages. The discovery of gunpowder has entirely changed the mode of making war. A superiority of fire at present decides the day. Discipline, rule, and tactics have all been changed, in order that they may conform to this new custom; and the recent and enormous abuse of numerous trains of artillery, which incumber armies, obliges others, in like manner, to adopt this method; as well to maintain themselves in their posts as to attack the foe in those which they shall occupy, should reasons of importance so require. So many new refinements have, therefore, so much changed the art of war that it would, at present, be unpardonable temerity in a general who, in imitation of Turenne, Condé, or Luxembourg, should risk a battle according to the dispositions made by those great commanders, in the age in which they lived. Victory then was carried by valour and strength: it is at present decided by artillery; and the art of the general consists in his near approach to the army of the enemy, without suffering his own troops to be destroyed previous to the attack. To gain this advantage, it is necessary he should silence the fire of the enemy, by the superiority of that with which it is opposed.

The art of castrametation, or of deriving all possible advantage from the situation of the ground, will however remain eternally unchanged in the military system. Should new discoveries continue to be made, the generals who then shall live must of force comply with these novelties, and change whatever may need correction in tactics.

There are states which, from their situation and constitution, must be maritime powers: such are England, Holland, France, Spain and Denmark. They are surrounded by the sea, and the distant colonies which they possess oblige them to keep a marine, to maintain communication and trade between the mother country and these detached members. There are other states, such as Austria, Poland, Prussia, and even Russia, some of which may well do without shipping; and others that would commit an unpardonable fault, in politics, were they to divide their forces by employing a part of their troops at sea, of the services of which they indispensably stand in need by land.

The number of troops which a state maintains ought to be in proportion to the troops maintained by its enemies. Their force should be equal, or the weakest is in danger of being oppressed. It perhaps may be objected that a king ought to depend on the aid of his allies. The reasoning would be good were allies what they ought to be; but their zeal is only lukewarm; and he who shall depend upon another as upon himself will most certainly be deceived. If frontiers permit them to be defended by fortresses, there must be no neglect in building, nor any expense spared to bring them to perfection. Of this France has given an example, and she has found the advantage of it on different occasions.

But neither politics nor the army can prosper if the finances are not kept in the greatest order, and if the prince himself be not a prudent economist. Money is like the wand of the necromancer, for by its aid miracles are performed. Grand political views, the maintenance of the military, and the best conceived plans for the ease of the people, will all remain in a lethargic state, if not animated by money. The economy of the sovereign is the more useful to the public good, because if he have not sufficient funds in reserve, either to supply the expenses of war, without loading his people with extraordinary taxes, or to succour citizens in times of public calamity, all these burthens will fall on the subjects, who will be without the resource, in such unhappy times, of which they will then stand in the most need.

No government can exist without taxation, which is equally necessary to the republic and to the monarchy. The sovereign who labours in the public cause must be paid by the public; the judge the same, that he may have no need to prevaricate. The soldier must be supported that he may commit no violence, for want of having whereon to subsist. . . .

ABSOLUTISM AND OLIGARCHY IN THE NORTH AND EAST
Chapter 3

By the early eighteenth century the larger states of the European heartland were monotonously absolutist. On the peripheries of Europe, however, the pattern of statecraft was more diverse. Though it was monarchical everywhere in the larger states to the west, the north, and the east, Britain and Poland could not be called absolutist by any stretch of the imagination, Sweden became absolutist for a generation and then reverted to oligarchy, Denmark entered a relatively benign absolutism in 1660 that lasted until 1848, and Russia grafted Western European absolutism onto its native stem of despotism and conditioned both by a degree of oligarchism to produce a hybrid regime that lasted until 1917.

The reasons for such diversity on the periphery of Europe are many, but two are worthy of particular attention: the degree of vitality of traditional institutions and the accident of strong monarchs. Britain is a very special case; its proto-absolutism was shattered by a revolution founded in the "traditional institution" of Parliament. In Scandinavia strong representative institutions and elective kingship made the emergence of absolutism difficult. Both Danish and Swedish absolutism were born in military defeat in the second half of the seventeenth century, in wars that pointed up national feebleness stemming from noble divisiveness. In both states, exceptional personalities — Frederick III in Denmark and Charles XI in Sweden — seized the opportunity of the moment, challenged the nobility both in the estates and in the provinces, and effected something approaching absolutist monarchy. Absolutism advanced and survived in Denmark over the eighteenth century primarily because the Danish kings withdrew into relative isolation and avoided the pressures that would have been placed on the state by involvement in European power politics. In Sweden, the work of Charles XI (1660–1697) was undone in two decades by the disastrous bid for international power of Charles XII (1697–1718). "The Lion of the North," Charles XII was a somewhat uncritical admirer of Louis

XIV's absolutism. His short reign also divided naturally in the middle like Louis's. From his accession in 1697 at the age of fifteen to his defeat and flight at Poltava in 1709, he held off invasion by powerful enemies and then turned to the offensive against Denmark, Poland, Saxony, and Russia; after his loss to a Russian army at Poltava, he passed five years in exile and four more brutally destructive years attempting to restore his lost hegemony. With his death in action in 1718, the Swedish nobility reasserted itself and established an oligarchy almost on the English model that lasted until 1772.

In Russia the only traditional institutions by the late seventeenth century were the tsar and the Russian Orthodox Church. For a century the Russian nobility had been tamed to the harness of state service, either in the civil bureaucracy or in the army, and there was no real institutional base for the defense of noble privilege. The church was for all practical purposes a tool of the tsar. Thus, the emergence of a powerful tsar meant that absolutism on the Western European model could be established almost by fiat. That tsar was Peter the Great, who ruled jointly with his half-brother from 1682 to 1696, and alone from 1696 to 1725. Crude and ferocious in his ruthlessness — any challenge to his power provoked instant, brutal reprisal — he was also a visionary. The vision was bifocal but Western in its orientation. Internally, Peter sought to establish a modern Western absolutist monarchy with a Western technology to sustain it. He was skillful in his eclecticism, and he was no slavish imitator of Western devices. Although his bureaucratic reorganization was modeled on Sweden's, his court on Versailles, his local administration on various Western models, and his army partly on the Prussian example, all were blended with Russian practices. In completing the subservience of the church, by the system of the Procurator and the Holy Synod, and of the nobility, by the Table of Ranks, Peter created entirely anew. Significantly, for his technology he did not choose the products of absolutism but those of oligarchy. England and the Dutch Republic, in both of which he had sojourned, provided him with the models for his shipyards, mines, foundries, cloth factories, canals, ports, and even tobacco retailing. Externally, Peter sought to make Russia a European power. His new capital, St. Petersburg, was a window on the West, as close to the West as he could get and still be on Russian soil. Russia's aggressive urge under Peter stemmed from drives to become a Baltic power on the one hand and a Black Sea power on the other. Sweden was the victim of the former drive, the Turks of the latter. Both drives brought Russia into propinquity with the West, and, after 1725, Russian fortunes and those of the West were inextricably joined.

Peter built well enough so that his reforms and modernization survived six bizarre creatures — three women, one of them a transvestite, two male children, and one man — who reigned but hardly ruled from 1725 to 1762. A tsar worthy of Peter the Great finally arose from a palace revolution by a German princess, who with the aid of her lover overthrew her tsar-husband after six months on the throne and with his murder consolidated power in her own hands. Catherine II, also called "the Great" (1762–1796), faced the task of bringing the nobility back into line. Four decades without a strong monarch had enabled the nobility to use their monopoly of office in the bureaucracy and army as a power base for the reassertion of their privileges. They had made and murdered tsars during that quasi-interregnum, and their increasing oppression of the peasantry provoked rebellions that constantly threatened the survival of the state. Catherine did an abrupt about-face from Peter's policy and moved toward the nobility, increasing rather than restricting their privileges. Not only did she allow them increased power over their peasants, but she ended state service, exempted the nobility from personal taxes, and created noble assemblies in the provinces to which she devolved most provincial governmental functions. In short, she advanced oligarchy rather than repressed it. In the process she sought and managed to tie the nobility as firmly to the institution of the tsar as had her predecessors by a quite opposite policy. In one sense, Catherine established mixed monarchy in Russia two centuries after it had disappeared nearly everywhere else in Europe. Nonetheless, the initiative still rested with the tsar, and this combination of powers and interests enabled both the tsar and the Russian aristocracy to survive beyond their time.

Catherine enjoyed some reputation as an enlightened despot, ostensibly because of her patronage of the French philosophes of the Enlightenment. Her attempt to reform the Russian legal structure is generally cited as the principal manifestation of her lukewarm enlightenment. The legal reform can also be seen as a further step in the Westernization-modernization of Russia, continuing the trend begun by Peter. Catherine's economic policy was also advanced, although hardly more so than that of other absolutist states; but her fiscal policy, which produced inflation and incurred heavy foreign indebtedness, was deleterious. In her foreign policy she also returned to Peter's emphasis, ending the anti-Prussian policy of her immediate predecessors. She moved onto the offensive once more against the Turks. And she directed the full thrust of her conquest toward Poland.

Poland as a viable state disappeared in three steps. It was divided among Russia, Prussia, and Austria in 1772, between Russia and Prussia in 1793, and again among Prussia, Russia, and Austria in 1795, with the largest territorial share going to Russia. Catherine intervened in Polish affairs from the early years of her reign by the device of "protecting" minorities within Poland. Poland's failure to resist such intervention grew from its feebleness: structural, institutional, and social. It was a noble-dominated loose federation of fifty or so little oligarchies without any effective central authority. An eleventh-hour attempt to reform government and society in 1792, by a thoroughly alarmed Polish nobility chastened by the first partition and intellectually stimulated by the doctrines of the Enlightenment, came too late and in fact provoked the second partition. The Polish nobility awoke too late to the realization that responsibility is the price of privilege — especially when absolutist powers existed across the borders ready to pounce.

The "Lion of the North" Before and After Poltava, 1709

Charles XII's decision to invade Russia in 1707 was taken with bravado and insufficient men and materiel, stretched out over too-long lines of supply, and without sound planning. Charles was twenty-five; he had begun fighting at eighteen and had never stopped. He bears comparison with Napoleon, but only to a point, because the latter was a master of logistics. Charles's decision to invade Russia, however, was as disastrous as Napoleon's (and Hitler's). The climax came at the small Russian fortress of Poltava. Relying on non-Swedish infantry, without sufficient artillery and without the equipment required for siege — particularly without a genius such as the French siege-master Marshal Vauban, as Charles's siege-master, Gyllenkrok, readily admitted — Charles lost his entire army of 14,000 in June, 1709, and was forced to flee to Turkey for a long exile. His declaration to the Committee of Defense in Stockholm was written near the Black Sea.

On the Eve of Poltava: Charles XII and His Generals

GYLLENKROK. Does your Majesty intend to besiege Poltava?
CHARLES. Yes, and you must make the siege, and tell us on what day we will take the fortress. That is what Vauban used to do in France, and you are our little Vauban.

From *Select Documents of European History*, vol. 2, 1492–1715, ed. W. F. Reddaway (London, 1930), pp. 195–96. Reprinted by permission of Methuen & Co. Ltd.

GYLLENKROK. God help us, with such a Vauban as I! But, however great a man he may have been, I think that he would have been embarrassed if he had not had all he thought necessary for a siege.

CHARLES. We have enough necessary military material to take such a wretched little fort as Poltava.

GYLLENKROK. The fort is itself not strong, but the garrison of 4,000 men, besides Cossacks, makes it strong.

CHARLES. If they see that we attack it in earnest, they will give up at the first cannon-shot fired at them.

GYLLENKROK. That seems to me improbable. I rather believe that the Russians will defend themselves to the last. I see that your Majesty's infantry will be ruined.

CHARLES. We shall not need to use our infantry, but will use Mazeppa's Zaporavians.[1]

GYLLENKROK. I beg your Majesty, for God's sake, to reflect whether it is possible for such works to be carried on by a people that never have put their hands to such things; by men with whom no one can talk without an interpreter, and who will immediately run away if the work is difficult and they see their comrades fall.

CHARLES. I assure you that the Zaporavians will do everything that we wish, and that they will not run away, for we are ready to pay them well for their work.

GYLLENKROK. But even if the Zaporavians allow themselves to be used for the work, your Majesty has no cannon which can make a breach in the palisades.

CHARLES. If you can shoot one down you can shoot a hundred down.

GYLLENKROK. I am also of that opinion, but I fear that when a hundred are shot down we shall have no more ammunition.

CHARLES. You must not paint the thing so black. You are accustomed to sieges abroad, and consider such an undertaking impossible if you have not everything. But we must do with our little means what others do with great.

GYLLENKROK. I should be inexcusable if I made unnecessary difficulties, but I know that nothing is to be done with our cannon, and that therefore at last it will be the duty of the infantry to take the fortress, in doing which they will be entirely destroyed.

CHARLES. I assure you no storm will be necessary.

GYLLENKROK. But I do not understand how the town can be taken, unless perhaps some extraordinary piece of good luck favours us.

CHARLES (*laughing*). Yes; we must do exactly what is extraordinary; by that we will get fame and glory.

GYLLENKROK. Yes. God knows that this is an extraordinary undertaking, but I fear that it will also have an extraordinary end.

[1] Cossacks. — T. G. B.

CHARLES. Make now all the preparations necessary, then you will see how soon all will be finished.

CHARLES (*to* PIPER). Even if the good God should send down an angel from heaven to tell me to give up Poltava I would still remain standing here.

REHNSKJÖLD (*to* GYLLENKROK). The King wishes to have a little amusement till the Poles come.

GYLLENKROK (*to* REHNSKJÖLD). It is a costly pastime, which demands such a number of human lives. The king could find some better employment.

REHNSKJÖLD (*to* GYLLENKROK). If his Majesty's will is so, we must be content with it.

GYLLENKROK (*to* CHARLES). I know that the world judges every undertaking according to the result, and everybody will believe that it was I that advised your Majesty to make this siege. If it should miscarry, I humbly beg you not to put the blame of it on me.

CHARLES (*to* GYLLENKROK). No, you are not to blame for it. We take the responsibility on ourselves, but you can be sure that the affair will have a speedy and lucky end.

After Poltava: Charles XII to the Committee of Defense in Stockholm, July 11, 1709

It is a long time since we had news from Sweden, or could find a chance to write from here. In the meantime our position was good, and all went well, so that we could expect soon to regain such a superiority over the enemy as to work our will with him. But on the 28th of last month, by an unlucky chance, the Swedish troops were beaten in a battle, not at all by reason of the enemy's fighting-skill or numbers, for at first he was everywhere driven back, but his position was so strong as to cause loss of the Swedes, who, despite all the enemy's advantages, were so keen to fight that they attacked and pursued him everywhere; whence it came about that most of the foot were lost and even the horse suffered a great disaster. The loss is full great, but we are thinking out plans for preventing the enemy from gaining the superiority or even the smallest profit. [Gives orders for comprehensive recruiting, and for the strictest custody of Russian prisoners with a view to exchange.]

From *Select Documents of European History*, vol. 2, 1492–1715, ed. W. F. Reddaway (London, 1930), p. 197. Reprinted by permission of Methuen & Co. Ltd.

Peter the Great Deals with Mutiny in the Infantry, 1698

The Strelitz was a fierce and poorly disciplined infantry, founded by Ivan the Terrible as palace guards; it bore the brunt of Russian warfare throughout the seventeenth century. Its members were mutinous in peacetime, controllable if at all only by their great noble (boyar) officers, and after 1682 the tsar had gradually moved them to the western frontier. Their last revolt is described below by Patrick Gordon, the Scottish general in the service of the tsar as a "technological acquisition" from the West, who crushed them. Some 2,000 of them were tortured and executed; the Strelitz as a force ceased to exist. Peter was not unusually ruthless in this case. He was more moderate than some of his predecessors and some of his successors to Stalin's death in 1953.

General Patrick Gordon's Diary

JUNE 8 [1698]. A report spread that the four Strelitz regiments at Toropetz were disposed to insurrection and disobedience. An equerry was, therefore, sent to get information of their doings.

JUNE 9. An order was issued to detach four officers and forty men of the Butirki regiment, to be sent against the Strelitz regiments; the same numbers were detached from the other regiments in Moscow. One hundred and forty Strelitz deserters were ordered to be arrested, and sent to the cities of the Ukraine.

JUNE 10. Accounts were received of the four Strelitz regiments that had been stationed in the camp at Welikije Luki, and were then in Toropetz, that they were discontented at the dismissal of the rest of the army, and the orders given to them to go to various towns, and were inclined to disturbance.

JUNE 11. Two captains returned from Toropetz, and reported that the Strelitzes, after repeated secret consultations, had resolved not to march to the stations appointed for them, but to go straight to Moscow, and that they had required their officers to lead them thither. On their refusing, they had deposed them, and had chosen four men from every regiment to lead them; they were firmly resolved on coming to Moscow. This news caused no little consternation among the high authorities. In a council hastily called together, it was resolved to send against them an army corps composed both of infantry and cavalry; and I was to go before with the infantry, till the cavalry were collected. I was, therefore, sent for and

From *Passages from the Diary of General Patrick Gordon* (Aberdeen, 1859), pp. 188–93.

informed of the matter. After it had been fixed that five hundred men of my regiment, and a like number of each of the three regiments stationed in Moscow, should go, I selected the officers and men that should be used. . . .

JUNE 17. On Friday, at six o'clock, I marched with the infantry, and came to Tschernewa, ten versts.[1] Here I found a nobleman's servant, who said that he had spent the previous night with the Strelitzes, and that they were marching with all speed to reach the convent of Woskressensk that night. This news made me hasten on to get there before them. After advancing five versts farther, I rested a little, and sent a report to the Boyar, requesting him, at the same time, to send me some cavalry. I then crossed the river, and, lest the mutineers should reach the convent before me, I pushed on before with what horsemen I could muster. Two versts from the convent, the scouts brought to me four Strelitzes, who said that they were sent, one man from each regiment, to take a petition to the Boyar. Reading it, I found in it nothing but a catalogue of their services, with exaggeration of their grievances, and a prayer for leave to come to Moscow to visit their homes, wives, and children, as well as to petition for their necessities. I sent them on to the Generalissimo; and having learned from these deputies that the Strelitzes were still fifteen versts off, and could not reach the convent that night, I gave orders to mark off a camp near the convent, as the most convenient place. I arrived at the place fixed upon about sunset, and immediately received information from my scouts that the Strelitzes had reached the river, and were crossing at a shallow place. Hearing this, I hastened thither with what horsemen I had with me. I spoke to them in a calm tone, and advised them to return across the river, and encamp on the other side. Not heeding this, they turned into a line, and remained stationed on a meadow beside the river, outside the village. I returned as quickly as possible to bring up our infantry. I made the first two regiments march through the village, and take post in the best position, while the other two were stationed on the fields by the Moscow road. I then rode down to the Strelitzes, and had a conversation with them; but I found them very refractory in all that we required of them. However, I persuaded them to send two other deputies to the Generalissimo, which they did. After a mutual promise that no movement should take place that night, they returned to their camp, leaving a strong guard in the lane. . . . After which I went to the Generalissimo, and consulted with him what was to be done. After mature deliberation, it was resolved that I should repair to their camp and intimate to them: (1) That they should turn back and repair to the places assigned them; (2) That they should give up one hundred and forty deserters who had run away from Welikije Luki to Moscow, as well

---

[1] A verst is about two-thirds of a mile. — T. G. B.

as the ringleaders of the present insurrection, and disobedience to the commands of his Majesty; (3) That in the appointed places his Majesty should give them the usual pay, and either bread or money, according to the local prices; (4) That the present fault should be forgiven them; and (5) That even the others, who were more guilty, should not suffer severe punishment.

Taking the six deputies with me, I went to their camp, where I communicated the orders to assemble and hear the gracious concessions of his Majesty. When about two hundred had come together, I let the deputies communicate the orders given, and then employed all the rhetoric I was master of to induce them to return to obedience, and give in a petition, confessing their guilt in having transgressed his Majesty's orders. But they answered that they were all determined to die or else go to Moscow, though it were only for eight or three days; after that they would go wherever his Majesty should order. When I told them that they would not be permitted to go to Moscow, and that they must not think of it, they replied that they would rather die than not get to Moscow. With that began two old fellows among them to aggravate their privations, and half a dozen confirmed what they said, and kept up the disturbance. I advised that each regiment should hold a consultation apart, and that they should consider well what they did, and what they were refusing. But they rejected all advice, and declared that they were all of one mind. I then intimated that I would withdraw from the camp and wait an answer outside, adding the threat, that if they did not embrace the gracious offers of his Majesty now, they needed not expect such conditions again, when once we should be obliged to use compulsion to bring them to obedience. But to all this they paid no heed. I then rode out of their camp, and waited at some distance for a quarter of an hour; after which I sent to ask their final answer. Finding no alteration of their mind, I took my departure with an indication of sorrow. After inspecting the best approaches to the rebels, and holding a consultation with the Generalissimo and others, it was resolved to draw up the army, and plant the cannon, and use force. I brought up the infantry and twenty-five cannon to a fit position, surrounded their camp on the other side with cavalry, and then sent an officer to summon and exhort them once more to submit. As they again declined, I sent yet another to demand a categorical decision. But they rejected all proposals of compromise, and boasted that they were as ready to defend themselves by force as we were to attack. Seeing that all hope of their submission was vain, I made a round of the cannon be fired. But as we fired over their heads, this only emboldened them more, so that they began to wave their colours and throw up their caps, and prepare for resistance. At the next discharge of the cannon, however, seeing their comrades fall on all sides, they began to waver. Out of despair, or to protect themselves from the cannon, they made a sally by a lane, which, however, we had occupied with a strong body. To make yet surer, I brought up several detachments to the spot, so as to command the hollow way along which they were issuing. Seeing this, they returned to their camp, and some of them betook themselves to the barns and outhouses of the adjoining village. At the third discharge of the guns, many of them rushed out of the camp towards the infantry and cavalry. After the fourth round of fire, very few of them remained in their waggon rampart; and I moved down with two battalions to their camp, and posted guards round it. During this affair, which lasted about an hour, a few of our men were wounded. The rebels had twenty-two killed on the spot, and about forty wounded, mostly mortally. We had all the prisoners brought to the convent, and shut up in vaulted houses and other places. A list of their horses was then made, and orders given not to touch their property; only the ammunition and the regimental waggons were brought to head quarters, and an account of them taken. The next thing was to send an officer to Moscow with an account of the business. The whole afternoon we were occupied collecting the arms scattered about on the camp and fields.

JUNE 19. Information having been got as to a few of the ringleaders, from some who thought to gain favour for themselves, several influential individuals were called up and examined. One of the regiments was then mustered. The greater part of the influential men and others being examined, it was frankly confessed that some had been the ringleaders and guilty rebels. Those that were found good we put on the one side, and the bad on the other. In the afternoon, another regiment was proceeded with in the same way. . . .

JUNE 21. We mustered another regiment of the Strelitzes, and examined various individuals, putting them to the torture; whereon they confessed the wicked designs they had meant to carry out when they got to Moscow. Word was despatched to Moscow twice or thrice of all that was going on.

JUNE 22. Twenty-four individuals were found guilty, on their own confession, of the most shocking crimes, and of having designed, when they got to Moscow, to massacre certain Boyars, and to extort an increase of pay, and a new regulation of their services. On these we pronounced sentence of death, to consist in beheading. They were confined apart, and directed to confess, receive the eucharist, and prepare for death.

JUNE 23. Those condemned yesterday were beheaded. The fourth regiment was mustered in the same way.

JUNE 24. I wrote to his Majesty, giving a short account of the previous events.

JUNE 25. On this and following days, we were engaged from morning to night in hearing cases; many were put to the torture, of whom a few confessed.

JUNE 27. An order arrived to send the less guilty Strelitzes to the various convents, and there keep them closely imprisoned.

JUNE 28. Some Strelitzes that had confessed themselves guilty were hanged.

JUNE 29. His Majesty's birthday was celebrated, first by divine service, and then by a feast, at which his health was drunk, with discharge of cannon. A great many Strelitzes were sent under strong guard to various convents.

JUNE 30. Many rebels of the regiment of Colonel Hundertmark were interrogated and put to the torture; but none would confess himself guiltier than the others. They were therefore informed that they must cast lots, as the tenth man must die, which they did. About two hundred persons were knouted in the afternoon.

JULY 1. Forty-five men of Hundertmark's regiment, on whom the lot had fallen, were brought out. They were told that if they would only name the ringleaders of the rising, the rest should go free. After a pause, they began to mutter and to name one or two, who, being tortured, without much ado pled guilty; three or four more were then named, who were also tortured, and confessed after a few strokes. They were then set apart and bid prepare for death; and the others, on whom the lot had fallen, were set free.

JULY 2. To-day, seventy men were hanged by fives and three on one gallows. Numbers more were sent away to confinement. . . .

JULY 4. In the morning, the four Strelitzes condemned last Saturday were brought out and beheaded. With few exceptions, all those executed submitted to their fate with great indifference, without saying a word, only crossing themselves; some took leave of the lookers-on. One hundred and thirty had been executed, about seventy had been killed in the engagement or died of their wounds, eighteen hundred and forty-five been sent to various convents and prisons, and twenty-five remained in this convent.

JULY 6. This day, after devotion, I, with many more, were confirmed by the Archbishop of Anura [Ancyra], called Petrus Paulus de St. Joseph, of the Carmelite order; I takeing the name of Leopoldus, and my son Theodorus that of Joseph.

JULY 19. I was called to Preobraschensk. The gracious letter of his Majesty was read, in which our services were commended. The same was read to the soldiers, who were promised a ruble a piece, besides that they were all to be treated at his Majesty's table. We also were sumptuously treated, especially in drink.

SEPTEMBER 17. Many Strelitzes were brought up and put to the torture, his Majesty being desirous to institute a stricter examination than ours.

SEPTEMBER 19. I was unwell and kept the house. A sharp enquiry was made into the Strelitz business.

SEPTEMBER 20. More Strelitzes put to the question.[2] A number were directed to prepare for death.

SEPTEMBER 23. In the afternoon, I went to Preobraschensk, but in vain: every body about the court was engaged in arresting more of the adherents of the Princess Sophia, and putting the Zarina [3] in the convent.

SEPTEMBER 30. A number of Strelitzes were executed.

OCTOBER 3. I was at Preobraschensk, and saw the crocodile, swordfish, and other curiosities, which his Majesty had brought from England and Holland.

NOVEMBER 14. Orders were issued not to give support to any of the wives or children of the executed Strelitzes.

Catherine the Great and the Restructuring of Russian Law

Catherine's instructions to a special assembly for a new code of laws, in 1767, won her the title "the Great" in the circles of the Enlightenment (the philosophes were very free with the ascription "the Great"). Contemporaries viewed the assembly, composed of 564 deputies, as a proto-parliamentary body that might well be continued after it settled the new code, but the code was never drafted, and after several sessions, the assembly ceased to meet. The whole affair inspired later historians to see Catherine's enlightened despotism merely as a front. This view is based on the assumption that the Instructions of 1767, obviously reflecting the Enlightenment ideas of Beccaria and Montesquieu, was an act of enlightened despotism. In fact, the Instructions drew heavily on Roman Law, both in structure and in provisions, and the motivation behind them is obviously the same as that which made the reception of the Roman Law in earlier centuries in the West the handmaiden of absolutism: a desire to centralize the administration of law by a comprehensive written code subject to the least possible particularism in implementation.

---

[2] Tortured. — T. G. B.
[3] The Dowager Tsarina Proskovia, widow of Peter's half-brother and joint-tsar, Ivan, whose death in 1696 left Peter sole tsar. — T. G. B.

The Instructions to the Commissioners for Composing a New Code of Laws

O Lord my God, hearken unto me, and instruct me; that I may administer Judgment unto thy People; as thy sacred Laws direct to judge with Righteousness!

1. The Christian Law teaches us to do mutual Good to one another, as much as possibly we can.

2. Laying this down as a fundamental Rule prescribed by that Religion, which has taken, or ought to take Root in the Hearts of the whole People; we cannot but suppose, that every honest Man in the Community is, or will be, desirous of seeing his native Country at the very Summit of Happiness, Glory, Safety, and Tranquillity.

3. And that every Individual Citizen in particular must wish to see himself protected by Laws, which should not distress him in his Circumstances, but, on the Contrary, should defend him from all Attempts of others, that are repugnant to this fundamental Rule.

4. In order therefore to proceed to a speedy Execution of what *We* expect from such a general Wish, *We,* fixing the Foundation upon the above first-mentioned Rule, ought to begin with an Inquiry into the natural Situation of this Empire.

5. For those Laws have the greatest Conformity with Nature, whose particular Regulations are best adapted to the Situation and Circumstances of the People, for whom they are instituted.

This natural Situation is described in the three following Chapters.

CHAPTER I

6. Russia is an European State.

7. This is clearly demonstrated by the following Observations: The Alterations which *Peter the Great* undertook in Russia succeeded with the greater Ease, because the Manners, which prevailed at that Time, and had been introduced amongst us by a Mixture of different Nations, and the Conquest of foreign Territories, were quite unsuitable to the Climate. *Peter the First,* by introducing the Manners and Customs of Europe among the European People in his Dominions, found at that Time such Means as even he himself was not sanguine enough to expect.

CHAPTER II

8. The Possessions of the Russian Empire extend upon the terrestrial Globe to 32 Degrees of Latitude, and to 165 of Longitude.

From *Documents of Catherine the Great,* ed. W. F. Reddaway (Cambridge University Press, 1931; reissued by Russell & Russell, 1971), pp. 215–219, 222–223.

9. The Sovereign is absolute; for there is no other Authority but that which centers in his single Person, that can act with a Vigour proportionate to the Extent of such a vast Dominion.

10. The Extent of the Dominion requires an absolute Power to be vested in that Person who rules over it. It is expedient so to be, that the quick Dispatch of Affairs, sent from distant Parts, might make ample Amends for the Delay occasioned by the great Distance of the Places.

11. Every other Form of Government whatsoever would not only have been prejudicial to Russia, but would even have proved its entire Ruin.

12. Another Reason is; That it is better to be subject to the Laws under one Master, than to be subservient to many.

13. What is the true End of Monarchy? Not to deprive People of their natural Liberty; but to correct their Actions, in order to attain the *supreme Good*.

14. The Form of Government, therefore, which best attains this End, and at the same Time sets less Bounds than others to natural Liberty, is that which coincides with the Views and Purposes of rational Creatures, and answers the End, upon which we ought to fix a stedfast Eye in the Regulations of civil Polity.

15. The Intention and the End of Monarchy, is the Glory of the Citizens, of the State, and of the Sovereign.

16. But, from this Glory, a Sense of Liberty arises in a People governed by a Monarch; which may produce in these States as much Energy in transacting the most important Affairs, and may contribute as much to the Happiness of the Subjects, as even Liberty itself.

CHAPTER III

17. *Of the Safety of the Institutions of Monarchy.*

18. The intermediate Powers, subordinate to, and depending upon the supreme Power, form the essential Part of monarchical Government.

19. *I* have said, that the intermediate Powers, subordinate and depending, proceed from the supreme Power; as in the very Nature of the Thing the Sovereign is the Source of all imperial and civil Power.

20. The Laws, which form the Foundation of the State, send out certain Courts of Judicature, through which, as through smaller Streams, the Power of the Government is poured out, and diffused.

21. The Laws allow these Courts of Judicature to remonstrate, that such or such an Injunction is unconstitutional, and prejudicial, obscure, and impossible to be carried into Execution; and direct, beforehand, to which Injunction one ought to pay Obedience, and in what Manner one ought to conform to it. These Laws undoubtedly constitute the firm and immoveable Basis of every State.

CHAPTER IV

22. There must be a political Body, to whom the Care and strict Execution of these Laws ought to be confided.

23. This Care, and strict Execution of the Laws, can be nowhere so properly fixed as in certain Courts of Judicature, which announce to the People the newly-made Laws, and revive those, which are forgotten, or obsolete.

24. And it is the Duty of these Courts of Judicature to examine carefully those Laws which they receive from the Sovereign, and to remonstrate, if they find any Thing in them repugnant to the fundamental Constitution of the State, &c. which has been already remarked above in the third Chapter, and twenty-first Article.

25. But if they find nothing in them of that Nature, they enter them in the Code of Laws already established in the State, and publish them to the whole Body of the People.

26. In Russia the Senate is the political Body, to which the Care and due Execution of the Laws is confided.

27. All other Courts of Judicature may, and ought to remonstrate with the same Propriety, to the Senate, and even to the Sovereign himself, as was already mentioned above.

28. Should any One inquire, wherein the Care and due Execution of the Laws consists? I answer, That the Care, and due Execution of the Laws, produces particular Instructions; in consequence of which, the before-mentioned Courts of Judicature, instituted to the End that, by their Care, the Will of the Sovereign might be obeyed in a Manner conformable to the fundamental Laws and Constitution of the State, are obliged to act, in the Discharge of their Duty, according to the Rules prescribed.

29. These Instructions will prevent the People from transgressing the Injunctions of the Sovereign with impunity; but, at the same Time, will protect them from the Insults, and ungovernable Passions of others.

30. For, on the one Hand, they justify the Penalties prepared for those who transgress the Laws; and, on the other, they confirm the Justice of that Refusal to enter Laws repugnant to the good Order of the State, amongst those which are already approved of, or to act by those Laws in the Administration of Justice, and the general Business of the whole Body of the People.

CHAPTER V

31. *Of the Situation of the People in general.*

32. It is the greatest Happiness for a Man to be so circumstanced, that,

if his Passions should prompt him to be mischievous, he should still think it more for his Interest not to give Way to them.

33. The Laws ought to be so framed, as to secure the Safety of every Citizen as much as possible.

34. The Equality of the Citizens consists in this; that they should all be subject to the same Laws.

35. This Equality requires Institutions so well adapted, as to prevent the Rich from oppressing those who are not so wealthy as themselves, and converting all the Charges and Employments intrusted to them as Magistrates only, to their own private Emolument.

36. General or political Liberty does not consist in that licentious Notion, *That a Man may do whatever he pleases.*

37. In a State or Assemblage of People that live together in a Community, where there are Laws, Liberty can only consist *in doing that which every One ought to do, and not to be constrained to do that which One ought not to do.*

38. A Man ought to form in his own Mind an exact and clear Idea of what Liberty is. *Liberty is the Right of doing whatsoever the Laws allow:* And if any one Citizen could do what the Laws forbid, there would be no more Liberty; because others would have an equal Power of doing the same.

39. The political Liberty of a Citizen is the Peace of Mind arising from the Consciousness, that every Individual enjoys his peculiar Safety; and in order that the People might attain this Liberty, the Laws ought to be so framed, that no one Citizen should stand in Fear of another; but that all of them should stand in Fear of the same Laws. . . .

CHAPTER VII

64. *Of the Laws in particular.*

65. Laws carried to the Extremity of Right, are productive of the Extremity of Evil.

66. All Laws, where the Legislation aims at the Extremity of Rigour, may be evaded. It is Moderation which rules a People, and not Excess of Severity.

67. Civil Liberty flourishes, when the Laws deduce every Punishment from the peculiar Nature of every Crime. The Application of Punishment ought not to proceed from the arbitrary Will, or mere Caprice of the Legislator, but from the Nature of the Crime; and it is not the Man, who ought to do Violence to a Man, but the proper Action of the Man himself.

68. Crimes are divisible into four Classes.

69. The first Class of Crimes is that against Religion.

70. The second, against Manners.
71. The third, against the Peace.
72. The fourth, against the Security of the Citizens.
73. The Punishments inflicted upon these ought to flow from the specific Nature of the very Crime.

Intervention of Catherine the Great in Poland, 1766

Throughout most of the eighteenth century, Poland-Lithuania was a client state of Russia. Until the reign of Catherine II, the tsar had no special interest in its partition. However, in 1764 she arranged for her former lover, Poniatowski, to be elected king of Poland, to act as a veritable agent of Catherine, raising Austrian fears of a direct Russian takeover of Poland. The following "Declaration" of Catherine on behalf of the Dissidents — the approximately one-third of the population of Poland that was Ukrainian and White Russian ("Greek" Orthodox) and German ("Protestant") — was intended less to secure their religious and political rights than to provide a pretext for Russian invasion. The First Partition, in 1772, prevented an upset of the balance of power in the east. It was the death knell of Polish independence. Throughout the nineteenth century, even in the twentieth century, Russia used the pretext of protecting the rights of minorities to intervene in the internal politics of neighboring states.

Declaration on Behalf of the Dissidents, from Empress Catherine II of Russia, Presented by Repnin at the Diet of the Polish-Lithuanian Commonwealth on November 4, 1766

The unity of religion and the glory of contributing to human happiness are not only the reasons that induce Her Imperial Majesty to reiterate, in a most pressing manner, her intervention in favor of the Greek and Protestant subjects of the Kingdom of Poland toward ending their

From Herbert H. Kaplan, *The First Partition of Poland* (New York, 1962), pp. 191–95. Reprinted by permission of Columbia University Press.

oppression, under which they groan, and toward returning them to the condition of equal citizens and as free members in the State.

The undersigned, in order to clarify all which was expressed, submits this point which is attested by the laws of the Polish nation: that the Greeks and the Protestants, in the most prosperous times of the Commonwealth, always received the prerogative they demand today and that they received them peacefully without any restriction as other inhabitants of the Nation obtained them.

This prerogative was assured by all that constitutes the bond of nations, namely by solemn agreements which established law between them and their compatriots. This law, however, can be claimed at all times to be fulfilled and cannot be violated or abolished by civil constitutions of only one part of the State.

One cannot avoid acknowledging as an invariable principle that a constant refusal to do justice to the claims of the Greeks and the Protestants would necessarily lead them to extricate themselves from all obligations toward a community whose advantages they did not share; that a prolonged refusal would make of them a community of completely free people and give them the right to choose judges among their neighbors who would judge between them and their equals; and, if unable to avoid persecution, no law, either human or divine, could condemn them if they were to ally themselves to these neighbors.

In times past, the Commonwealth had been in danger of this, but had happily succeeded in preventing it by the sanction which treaties formed with foreign powers gave to the domestic policy of Poland.

Now, the maintenance of the tranquillity of the Commonwealth belongs not only to the inhabitants of the land but also to the neighbors, who, treating with the Commonwealth, contracted with her members.

It is thus that Russia, in virtue of the Treaty of 1686, and the other powers in concert with her, in consequence of the Treaty of Oliva, engage in watching over the security of each part of the Commonwealth to prevent discord between them, to procure exact justice, and the enjoyment for each and all that which constitutes reciprocal and common rights.

Therefore, it is for the reason of executing the provisions of the treaties, that the Empress desires to regain for the Greek and Protestant subjects all their rights and the security of their preservation. [The Empress] cannot place any limits on the protection she grants to the Greeks and Protestants without compromising the glory and the dignity of her Crown and the confidence of her friends.

Without any expectation of obtaining a reward but merely for the purpose of emphasizing the necessity of the Commonwealth's agreeing to the principle in which she is interested, Her Imperial Majesty finds it impossible to renounce her desire to help the Commonwealth.

Being a good neighbor and sincere friend, Her Imperial Majesty has always been and will continue to be happy for every success of the Commonwealth. It was greatly satisfying to her when she was able to help the confederated Commonwealth to regain its internal peace, to preserve its liberty, and to elect a *Piast*.

Everyone could see then the friendliness, generosity, and readiness with which Her Imperial Majesty offered the aid for which she had been asked. She was always interested in the affairs concerning her neighbor the Commonwealth in order to ensure happiness to all its citizens. She was asked to help freely elect a ruler from amongst the nation. She gave her assistance with readiness.

Although she was successful in this matter, she would consider her work imperfect if one part of the citizens was excluded from its fortunate results. She would be of the opinion that her aim was not fully accomplished as long as any difference remained in the country between the Dissidents and other citizens.

Therefore Her Imperial Majesty considers it a matter of her honor to show that the confidence, which the whole Commonwealth puts in her friendship is fully justified and not to limit the assistance which she may offer for the happiness of one part of the nation.

Her Imperial Majesty renews her application to the present *Diet* to put a halt to this source of unending discord and thus restore tranquillity to the Commonwealth.

She recommends this affair to the King and the entire Nation to treat it with the regard and attention it merits for its importance to the general welfare. Her Imperial Majesty looks upon it in two ways, namely, a spiritual as well as a temporal interest.

Concerning the first [the Commonwealth], without having annulled the rights of the Greeks and the Protestants, has, however, illegally multiplied the abuses to such a point that freedom of religion has been reduced to nothing or nearly so.

The undersigned demands in the name of Her Imperial Majesty, his Sovereign, that these abuses be redressed and that in the future, neither these nor any new abuses be introduced. This can be attained when the present Diet resolves the following:

1. Churches lawfully belonging to the Dissidents which were unlawfully taken from them are to be given back. No obstacle is to be made to the renovation or reconstruction of such as were damaged by time or fire. No opposition is to be made to baptisms, marriages, services for the dead, preaching of God's word in the churches or to the sick. The ecclesiastics, both for the Greeks and Protestants, are to have permission to accomplish the above-mentioned acts, and . . . all that belongs to the administration of the Sacraments and the divine services of every respective religion without any opposition. Together, these constitute entire liberty of the Divine Service.

2. For the establishment of this lasting and general religious freedom in the entire State, the present Diet will resolve that in all cities, towns, and villages in which the Greeks or Protestants have neither churches nor chapels it will be permitted to members of those religions who wish to settle there, to have churches, cemeteries, priests and pastors, and [complete freedom in the] administration of the Sacraments to the people of their religions.

3. Freedom of religion is a divine right which concerns everyone. Therefore, it is the obligation of every well-governed State to permit this advantage to all its inhabitants and not to subordinate one religion. It is evident, according to this principle, that the tribute exacted by the Catholic clergy from the Dissidents for burials, marriages, and baptisms is illegal. The variations as to its proportions in different provinces would suffice to show it has no legal title. Abuses of so pernicious a nature cannot be made lawful by any particular constitution if those interested have not established it by their free votes. It appears, therefore, most just to reform this abuse. Yet if all the Estates agree that some distinction should preserve the dominant religion in a free State, it would be necessary to establish a measure of payment which would be considered honorary rather than a tribute.

4. The Greek Seminary in Mohilev will not be disturbed in any fashion, and will, in freedom and tranquillity, give education to youths of the Greek persuasion without any hindrance from anyone.

5. The Bishop and Bishoprics of Belorussia with all their dependencies will be, for all time, preserved for the Greek religion as well as the churches belonging to the Greek and Protestant communities.

6. No priest or pastor of the Greeks or Protestants is to be cited under any pretext before an ecclesiastical court. They belong exclusively to the secular jurisdiction.

7. Marriages between persons of different religions are to be permitted, and children are to follow the religion of either parent, depending on the child's sex.

In a word, the Greeks and the Protestants are to enjoy the exercise of their religion and the protection that equity and reason owe to every inhabitant: This is no more than a strict right.

Justice demands the reestablishment of the Greeks and Protestants to their temporal prerogatives which Her Imperial Majesty, impelled by the friendship she feels as a neighboring power as well as by obligations of her Crown, insists can alone secure the happiness and good order of the Kingdom of Poland.

The equality of nobility is the foundation of Polish liberty and the most positive guarantee of her Constitution. All laws which have intended, from time to time, to divest the Greek and the Protestant *szlachta* from their prerogatives, were the unfortunate source of troubles and disunion. One part of the State, thinking to reap great advantages by elevating themselves at the expense of another part of the Nation, destroyed the real and only tie which cemented a national union.

In time of peace and general harmony, in which everything conspires to the establishment of a complete and lasting happiness, when the laws regain their former force by the zeal and unanimity of patriots, and promise to render the Commonwealth more flourishing than ever, all the Estates ought to comprehend that no durable prosperity and happiness can be anticipated if they are not perfectly united. To maintain one part of the Nation in the exclusive possession of the charges and dignities against the ancient laws of the Commonwealth which grants to every religion an equal right in the government of the land, would be to sacrifice the national greatness to a particular interest.

This principle of the public law of Poland which, in times of trouble and discord, was almost demolished by a succession of civil Constitutions made by one part of the State, is precisely that on which Her Imperial Majesty founds her request for negotiation with those subjects of the Commonwealth who differ only by their religion in order to determine their share in the administration of the State and connection with the Crown. Until a perfect understanding on this point is established, and the solicitations of the divers Estates in the Commonwealth are satisfied, Her Imperial Majesty will feel her obligations to be unfulfilled. The aid which she accorded to the whole Nation for the public welfare cannot be refused to a part of the Nation so considerable as the Greek and Protestant communities. The heart of Her Imperial Majesty could not be satisfied if she had only procured an apparent tranquillity for the Commonwealth; if she had preserved her from the violence which had menaced her laws, her liberties, and her institutions only to abandon one part of the Nation to the persecutions of the other; if she had contributed to put into execution certain laws only to augment and perpetuate the power of abuses. Her Imperial Majesty could not be satisfied even if one part of the Nation had received her assistance, gladly and with benefit, while another part, even more considerable, with equal claim to her solicitude, also having invoked her support and contributed to render it efficacious, still continued to groan under persecution.

Religion, obligation, amicable and good neighborly relations, the engagement of treaties, the honor attached to their execution, the desire to answer the hopes of the whole Nation, enjoin Her Imperial Majesty the absolute necessity of continuing these efforts in order to bring about the reestablishment of the Greeks and Protestants in the enjoyment of the rights, both spiritual and secular, which are their due as members of a free Nation.

Her Imperial Majesty is persuaded that the good offices of a friendly and neighboring power will suffice to render general the feelings which the most sensible and patriotic of the Nation now entertain. Those who still oppose these sentiments ought to be looked upon only as enemies to themselves and to the country. No private consideration will deter Her Imperial Majesty from the end she has in view. She considers it her obligation to employ against [her opponents] every means likely to effect the restoration of the general tranquillity, and she believes she could not employ herself more worthily.

[Signed by Prince Repnin]

CONSTITUTIONALISM AND OLIGARCHY IN THE WEST
Chapter 4

"He that will, with any clearness, speak of the dissolution of government, ought in the first place to distinguish between the dissolution of the society and the dissolution of the government." Locke's distinction between government and society lies at the base of modern constitutionalism and the concept of democracy, not just in Britain and its American derivative but throughout the entire democratic world. In the preponderantly absolutist Europe of 1690 this distinction was starkly novel. Absolutism, in theory and in practice, presumed that society and government were the same, that the enemy of one was the enemy of the other, that the dissolution of government was the destruction of society, that the monarch was both the head of the body politic and the head of the body social. Locke's distinction severed the body politic and the body social: Not only did society precede government, but, although the destruction of society always meant the destruction of government, the destruction of government did not necessarily result in the destruction of society. Indeed, the continuation of a bad government might well destroy society, and society then must dissolve the government in order to survive. Machiavelli had postulated the preservation of the state — in effect, the government — as the transcendent morality in politics. Locke substituted the preservation of society. He made the state secondary, its government ancillary, to society, the center of political concern.

Though Locke did not appeal to history or legal precedent for justification of his theory (he appealed to fundamental natural law revealed by reason), his *Two Treatises on Government* reflected historical fact and became the principal rationalization of historical events to future generations of Englishmen. The *Two Treatises* were written between 1679 and 1683 as an unpublished contribution to the controversy raging in Parliament and the country over whether the Catholic duke of York should be excluded from succeeding his brother Charles II as king. When published in 1690, the *Two Treatises* appeared to justify the "Glorious Revolution" of 1688, which had forced the "abdication" of that same Catholic, then King James II, and called to his place William III of Holland and his wife, Mary, daughter of James II. As a justification, the work has continued to affect the historical interpretation of the events of 1688. As a reflection of historical fact, the *Two Treatises* recognized the existence of an oligarchy that enjoyed the greatest part of the property of England and had as its primary vested interest the protection of that property. The *Two Treatises* simply declared that, as men of property had risen against Charles I to defend their property against his incursions, so men of property must resist the incursions of his successor, James II. The predecessors of these men of property had originally explicitly contracted to form government to protect their property. The government now threatening their property had broken the contract; it must be changed. In 1688, it was.

The events leading to 1688 and the "Glorious Revolution" itself were more complicated than that, of course. But Locke's emphasis on oligarchy and property was sound historically. The oligarchy was the political nation, composed of landowners and great merchants, who alone, as Locke described them, enjoyed the property and the leisure afforded by it sufficient to enable them to participate in political life. Yet these men had a fiduciary responsibility to ensure that government protected the right to life, liberty, and property of all people in the society. Their action in 1688, therefore, was in defense not merely of their own property but of all property, all life, all liberty. They acted on behalf of all, and thus their action prevented the destruction of society either from above by the king or from below by the masses.

The establishment of William and Mary on the throne "abdicated" by James II was the triumph of the oligarchy. That triumph was institutionalized in Parliament. Part of the institutionalization was legislative. The Bill of Rights is the most extraordinary legislative act ever passed in Parliament, and though neither subsequent constitutional theory nor contemporary law recognized it as being any more or less immutable than any other Act of Parliament, the Bill of Rights displaced the Magna Carta as the keystone, if not the fundamental law, of the British constitution. Most of the institutionalization of 1688 was practice not theory: the preeminence of Parliament, its indispensability in the routine of government, and its continuing reflection of the interests of all in the debates and acts of the oligarchic few.

By the end of the eighteenth century the claim of the oligarchic few that they acted for all was becoming strained. The first half of the century had witnessed the evolution of responsible government, that is, the necessary reliance of the king on a minister who could gain and maintain control of Parliament. Implicit in this reliance was the identification of the monarch with the oligarchy's interests. With the accession of George III in 1760, the relationship was changed for almost twenty years by the monarch's demand that the oligarchy identify its interests with him. The shift was subtle but significant, and it effectively divided the oligarchy in Parliament. Outside Parliament, the religious revival of John Wesley and the vocal pressure of John Wilkes on behalf of the lower middle class of London for influence in Parliament spurred a demand for reform of government, both executive and parliamentary. Across the Atlantic, the demand of the American colonies either that their "virtual representation" in Parliament be made a reality or that they be left to govern themselves (they really desired the latter), issued in American independence. The villain was less George III than the oligarchy in Parliament. One Member of Parliament, Edmund Burke, in the 1770's and 1780's lent an exceptional mind and voice to the causes of reducing monarchical influence in Parliament, parliamentary reform, and the American colonies. Burke's advocacy of these causes was the climax and the swan song of the indisputable dominance of the landed and merchant oligarchy in Parliament and society. British oligarchy was given a new, short lease on life by the horror inspired by the French Revolution, but a short lease was all it was.

The golden age of the Dutch oligarchy ended with the republic's call to William III of Orange in 1672 to defend the country against invasion by Louis XIV. The republic remained virtually at war for forty years. Regental oligarchy had to submerge its assertiveness or the republic would have disappeared. Peace did not bring either the prosperity or the ease from external threat that their effort in war had led the Dutch to expect, and regental vitality and responsibility did not survive the wars with Louis XIV. Factionalism, corruption, self-satisfaction, luxury, increasing insensitivity to the needs of the state and the populace as a whole, and social exclusiveness marked the oligarchy of the eighteenth century. Another stadtholder-less period, from 1702 to 1747, bankrupted the political and moral credit of the oligarchy.

The last stadtholder, William V (1751–1795), unimaginative and backward-looking though hardworking and ambitious, from 1782 to 1787 faced incipient revolution from nonregental middle-class townsmen, sometimes led by extremist agitators. The regental oligarchs were ground between these "Patriots" and the stadtholder; as an independent political force the regental oligarchy did not survive the "Patriot" opposition. The "Patriot" revolt was put down only by the intervention of Prussian troops. In 1795 the "Patriots" exiled in France returned with the French Revolutionary army to overthrow William V and to establish the Batavian Republic. The last republican phase of the Dutch Republic created a representative government that did not survive the French Revolution. Ironically, the Batavian Republic ensured the reaction that restored a prince of Orange, not as stadtholder of the republic but as king of the Netherlands.

John Locke

The following is from the final chapter of the Second Treatise on Civil Government *by John Locke (1632–1704). It is the summation of his political philosophy. Confidant, assistant, and secretary to Anthony Ashley Cooper, second earl of Shaftesbury, leader of the parliamentary opposition to the succession of James II, Locke lived in exile in Holland from 1684 to 1689. Returning with the accession of William and Mary, he held minor office and published his highly influential tractates on politics, human understanding, money, religion, and education in the the early 1690's. His political theory, advanced primarily in the* Two Treatises, *was the starting point for the political theory of the French philosophes of the Enlightenment, provided the framework and much of the rhetoric for the American Declaration of Independence in 1776, and has dominated British political theory to this day.*

Section 221 is worth close attention; it was used by the American colonists to justify their resistance to parliamentary "taxation without representation" and other acts in the years preceding 1775. Sections 224 to 226 demonstrate why one past revolution was respectable although future revolutions could not be, providing the base for the remaining sections, which postulate "legislative" government as the means to stability. In his theory Locke shifted responsibility and power from the king to "the legislative," a shift that the "Glorious Revolution" of 1688 created in fact.

Of the Dissolution of Governments

211. He that will, with any clearness, speak of the dissolution of government, ought in the first place to distinguish between the dissolution of the society and the dissolution of the government. That which makes the community, and brings men out of the loose state of Nature into one

From John Locke, *Second Treatise on Civil Government*, ch. 19, in *Two Treatises on Civil Government* (London, 1884), pp. 301–03, 306–12, 318–20.

politic society, is the agreement which every one has with the rest to incorporate and act as one body, and so be one distinct commonwealth. The usual, and almost only way whereby this union is dissolved, is the inroad of foreign force making a conquest upon them. For in that case (not being able to maintain and support themselves as one entire and independent body) the union belonging to that body, which consisted therein, must necessarily cease, and so every one return to the state he was in before, with a liberty to shift for himself and provide for his own safety, as he thinks fit, in some other society. Whenever the society is dissolved, it is certain the government of that society cannot remain. Thus conquerors' swords often cut up governments by the roots, and mangle societies to pieces, separating the subdued or scattered multitude from the protection of and dependence on that society which ought to have preserved them from violence. The world is too well instructed in, and too forward to allow of this way of dissolving of governments, to need any more to be said of it; and there wants not much argument to prove that where the society is dissolved, the government cannot remain; that being as impossible as for the frame of a house to subsist when the materials of it are scattered and displaced by a whirlwind, or jumbled into a confused heap by an earthquake.

212. Besides this overturning from without, governments are dissolved from within:

First. When the legislative is altered, civil society being a state of peace amongst those who are of it, from whom the state of war is excluded by the umpirage which they have provided in their legislative for the ending all differences that may arise amongst any of them; it is in their legislative that the members of a commonwealth are united and combined together into one coherent living body. This is the soul that gives form, life, and unity to the commonwealth; from hence the several members have their mutual influence, sympathy, and connection; and therefore when the legislative is broken, or dissolved, dissolution and death follows. For the essence and union of the society consisting in having one will, the legislative, when once established by the majority, has the declaring and, as it were, keeping of that will. The constitution of the legislative is the first and fundamental act of society, whereby provision is made for the continuation of their union under the direction of persons and bonds of laws, made by persons authorized thereunto, by the consent and appointment of the people, without which no one man, or number of men, amongst them can have authority of making laws that shall be binding to the rest. When any one, or more, shall take upon them to make laws whom the people have not appointed so to do, they make laws without authority, which the people are not therefore bound to obey; by which means they come again to be out of subjection, and may constitute to themselves a new legislative, as they think best, being in full liberty to resist the force of those who, without authority, would impose anything upon them. Every one is at the disposure of his own will, when those who had, by the delegation of the society, the declaring of the public will, are excluded from it, and others usurp the place, who have no such authority or delegation.

213. This being usually brought about by such in the commonwealth, who misuse the power they have, it is hard to consider it aright, and know at whose door to lay it, without knowing the form of government in which it happens. Let us suppose, then, the legislative placed in the concurrence of three distinct persons: — First, a single hereditary person having the constant, supreme, executive power, and with it the power of convoking and dissolving the other two within certain periods of time. Secondly, an assembly of hereditary nobility. Thirdly, an assembly of representatives chosen, *pro tempore,* by the people. Such a form of government supposed, it is evident —

214. First, that when such a single person or prince sets up his own arbitrary will in place of the laws which are the will of the society declared by the legislative, then the legislative is changed. . . .

215. Secondly, when the prince hinders the legislative from assembling in its due time, or from acting freely, pursuant to those ends for which it was constituted, the legislative is altered. . . .

216. Thirdly, when, by the arbitrary power of the prince, the electors or ways of election are altered without the consent and contrary to the common interest of the people, there also the legislative is altered. For if others than those whom the society hath authorized thereunto do choose, or in another way than what the society hath prescribed, those chosen are not the legislative appointed by the people.

217. Fourthly, the delivery also of the people into the subjection of a foreign power, either by the prince or by the legislative, is certainly a change of the legislative, and so a dissolution of the government. For the end why people entered into society being to be preserved one entire, free, independent society, to be governed by its own laws, this is lost whenever they are given up into the power of another.

218. Why, in such a constitution as this, the dissolution of the government in these cases is to be imputed to the prince is evident, because he, having the force, treasure, and offices of the State to employ, and often persuading himself or being flattered by others, that, as supreme magistrate, he is incapable of control; he alone is in a condition to make great advances towards such changes under pretence of lawful authority, and has it in his hands to terrify or suppress opposers as factious, seditious, and enemies to the government. . . .

221. There is, therefore, secondly, another way whereby governments are dissolved, and that is, when the legislative, or the prince, either of them act contrary to their trust.

First: the legislative acts against the trust reposed in them when they endeavour to invade the property of the subject, and to make themselves, or any part of the community, masters or arbitrary disposers of the lives, liberties, or fortunes of the people.

222. The reasons why men enter into society is the preservation of their property; and the end while they choose and authorize a legislative is that there may be laws made, and rules set, as guards and fences to the properties of all the society, to limit the power, and moderate the dominion of every part and member of the society. For since it can never be supposed to be the will of the society that the legislative should have a power to destroy that which every one designs to secure by entering into society, and for which the people submitted themselves to legislators of their own making; whenever the legislators endeavour to take away and destroy the property of the people, or to reduce them to slavery under arbitrary power, they put themselves into a state of war with the people, who are thereupon absolved from any farther obedience, and are left to the common refuge which God hath provided for all men against force and violence. Whensoever, therefore, the legislative shall transgress this fundamental rule of society, and either by ambition, fear, folly, or corruption, endeavour to grasp themselves, or put into the hands of any other, an absolute power over the lives, liberties, and estates of the people; by this breach of trust they forfeit the power the people had put into their hands for quite contrary ends, and it devolves to the people, who have a right to resume their original liberty, and by the establishment of a new legislative (such as they shall think fit), provide for their own safety and security, which is the end for which they are in society. . . .

224. But it will be said this hypothesis lays a ferment for frequent rebellion. To which I answer:

First: no more than any other hypothesis. For when the people are made miserable, and find themselves exposed to the ill usage of arbitrary power, cry up their governors as much as you will for sons of Jupiter, let them be sacred and divine, descended or authorized from Heaven; given them out for whom or what you please, the same will happen. . . .

225. Secondly: I answer, such revolutions happen not upon every little mismanagement in public affairs. Great mistakes in the ruling part, many wrong and inconvenient laws, and all the slips of human frailty will be borne by the people without mutiny or murmur. But if a long train of abuses, prevarications, and artifices, all tending the same way, make the design visible to the people, and they cannot but feel what they lie under, and see whither they are going, it is not to be wondered that they should then rouse themselves, and endeavour to put the rule into such hands which may secure to them the end of which government was at first erected. . . .

226. Thirdly: I answer, that this power in the people of providing for

John Locke

their safety anew by a new legislative when their legislators have acted contrary to their trust by invading their property, is the best fence against rebellion, and the probablest means to hinder it. For rebellion being an opposition, not to persons, but authority, which is founded only in the constitutions and laws of the government; those, whoever they be, who, by force, break through, and, by force, justify their violation of them, are truly and properly rebels. For when men, by entering into society and civil government, have excluded force, and introduced laws for the preservation of property, peace, and unity amongst themselves, those who set up force again in opposition to the laws, do *rebellare* — that is, bring back again the state of war, and are properly rebels, which they who are in power, by the pretence they have to authority, the temptation of force they have in their hands, and the flattery of those about them being likeliest to do, the properest way to prevent the evil is to show them the danger and injustice of it who are under the greatest temptation to run into it. . . .

228. But if they who say it lays a foundation for rebellion mean that it may occasion civil wars or intestine broils to tell the people they are absolved from obedience when illegal attempts are made upon their liberties or properties, and may oppose the unlawful violence of those who were their magistrates when they invade their properties, contrary to the trust put in them, and that, therefore, this doctrine is not to be allowed, being so destructive to the peace of the world; they may as well say, upon the same ground, that honest men may not oppose robbers or pirates, because this may occasion disorder or bloodshed. If any mischief come in such cases, it is not to be charged upon him who defends his own right, but on him that invades his neighbour's. . . .

229. The end of government is the good of mankind; and which is best for mankind, that the people should be always exposed to the boundless will of tyranny, or that the rulers should be sometimes liable to be opposed when they grow exorbitant in the use of their power, and employ it for the destruction, and not the preservation, of the properties of their people? . . .

231. That subjects or foreigners attempting by force on the properties of any people may be resisted with force is agreed on all hands; but that magistrates doing the same thing may be resisted, hath of late been denied; as if those who had the greatest privileges and advantages by the law had thereby a power to break those laws by which alone they were set in a better place than their brethren; whereas their offence is thereby the greater, both as being ungrateful for the greater share they have by the law, and breaking also that trust which is put into their hands by their brethren.

232. Whosoever uses force without right — as every one does in society who does it without law — puts himself into a state of war with those

against whom he so uses it, and in that state all former ties are cancelled, all other rights cease, and every one has a right to defend himself, and to resist the aggressor. . . .

240. Here it is like the common question will be made, Who shall be judge whether the prince or legislative act contrary to their trust? This, perhaps, ill-affected and factious men may spread amongst the people, when the prince only makes use of his due prerogative. To this I reply. The people shall be judge; for who shall be judge whether his trustee or deputy acts well and according to the trust reposed in him, but he who deputes him and must, by having deputed him, have still a power to discard him when he fails in his trust? If this be reasonable in particular cases of private men, why should it be otherwise in that of the greatest moment, where the welfare of millions is concerned and also where the evil, if not prevented, is greater, and the redress very difficult, dear, and dangerous?

241. But, farther, this question, Who shall be judge? cannot mean that there is no judge at all. For where there is no judicature on earth to decide controversies amongst men, God in heaven is judge. He alone, it is true, is judge of the right. But every man is judge for himself, as in all other cases so in this, whether another hath put himself into a state of war with him, and whether he should appeal to the supreme Judge, as Jephtha did.

242. If a controversy arise betwixt a prince and some of the people in a matter where the law is silent or doubtful, and the thing be of great consequence, I should think the proper umpire in such a case should be the body of the people. For in cases where the prince hath a trust reposed in him, and is dispensed from the common, ordinary rules of the law, there, if any men find themselves aggrieved, and think the prince acts contrary to, or beyond that trust, who so proper to judge as the body of the people (who at first lodged that trust in him) how far they meant it should extend? But if the prince, or whoever they be in the administration, decline that way of determination, the appeal then lies nowhere but to Heaven. Force between either persons who have no known superior on earth, or which permits no appeal to a judge on earth, being properly a state of war, wherein the appeal lies only to Heaven; and in that state the injured party must judge for himself when he will think fit to make use of that appeal and put himself upon it.

243. To conclude. The power that every individual gave the society when he entered into it can never revert to the individuals again, as long as the society lasts, but will always remain in the community; because without this there can be no community — no commonwealth, which is contrary to the original agreement; so also when the society hath placed the legislative in any assembly of men, to continue in them and their successors, with direction and authority for providing such successors,

The Bill of Rights

the legislative can never revert to the people whilst that government lasts; because, having provided a legislative with power to continue for ever, they have given up their political power to the legislative, and cannot resume it. But if they have set limits to the duration of their legislative, and made this supreme power in any person or assembly only temporary; or else, when, by the miscarriages of those in authority, it is forfeited; upon the forfeiture of their rulers, or at the determination of the time set, it reverts to the society, and the people have a right to act as supreme, and continue the legislative in themselves or place it in a new form, or new hands, as they think good.

Parliament's Charter

The Bill of Rights was the parliamentary enactment into law of a Declaration of Rights that accompanied the offer of the crown to William III and Mary II following the "Glorious Revolution" of 1688. It was not a condition of the offer but was freely accepted by the new monarchs. It recited the misdeeds of James II somewhat luridly, gave credence to the notion that he had abdicated and, therefore, had not been deposed, and extended statutory authority for the enjoyment of a number of individual rights. Its overall effect, however, was to strengthen Parliament. It remains in effect today.

The English Bill of Rights, 1689

AN ACT FOR DECLARING THE RIGHTS AND LIBERTIES OF THE SUBJECT AND SETTLING THE SUCCESSION OF THE CROWN. Whereas the lords spiritual and temporal, and commons, assembled at Westminster lawfully, fully, and freely representing all the estates of the people of this realm, did upon the thirteenth day of February, in the year of our Lord one thousand six hundred eighty eight,[1] present unto their Majesties, then called and known by the names and stile of William and Mary, prince and princess of Orange, being present in their proper persons, a certain declaration in writing, made by the said lords and commons, in the words following, *viz.*

From 1 William & Mary, sess. 2, c. 2 (1689), *Statutes of the Realm*, vol. 6 (London, 1819), pp. 142–44.

[1] 1688/9 — T. G. B.

Whereas the late King James The Second, by the assistance of divers evil counsellors, judges, and ministers employed by him, did endeavour to subvert and extirpate the protestant religion, and the laws and liberties of this kingdom.

By assuming and exercising a power of dispensing with and suspending of laws, and the execution of laws, without consent of parliament.

By committing and prosecuting divers worthy prelates, for humbly petitioning to be excused concurring to the said assumed power.

By issuing and causing to be executed a commission under the great seal for erecting a court called, *The court of commissioners for ecclesiastical causes.*

By levying money for and to the use of the crown, by pretence of prerogative, for other time, and in other manner, than the same was granted by parliament.

By raising and keeping a standing army within this kingdom in time of peace, without consent of parliament, and quartering soldiers contrary to law.

By causing several good subjects, being protestants, to be disarmed, at the same time when papists were both armed and employed, contrary to law.

By violating the freedom of election of members to serve in parliament.

By prosecutions in the court of King's bench, for matters and causes cognizable only in parliament; and by divers other arbitrary and illegal courses.

And whereas of late years, partial, corrupt, and unqualified persons have been returned and served on juries in trials and particularly divers jurors in trials for high treason, which were not freeholders.

And excessive bail hath been required of persons committed in criminal cases, to elude the benefit of the laws made for the liberty of the subjects.

And excessive fines have been imposed; and illegal and cruel punishments inflicted.

And several grants and promises made of fines and forfeitures, before any conviction or judgment against the persons, upon whom the same were to be levied.

All which are utterly and directly contrary to the known laws and statutes, and freedom of this realm.

And whereas the said late King James the Second having abdicated the government, and the throne being thereby vacant, his highness the Prince of Orange (whom it hath pleased Almighty God to make the glorious instrument of delivering this kingdom from popery and arbitrary power) did (by the advice of the lords spiritual and temporal, and divers principal persons of the commons) cause letters to be written to the lords spiritual and temporal, being protestants; and other letters to the several

The Bill of Rights

counties, cities, universities, boroughs, and cinque-ports, for the choosing of such persons to represent them, as were of right to be sent to parliament, to meet and sit at Westminster upon the two and twentieth day of January, in this year one thousand six hundred eighty eight,[2] in order to such an establishment, as that their religion, laws, and liberties might not again be in danger of being subverted: upon which letters, elections have been accordingly made.

And thereupon the said lords spiritual and temporal, and commons, pursuant to their respective letters and elections, being now assembled in a full and free representative of this nation, taking into their most serious consideration the best means for attaining the ends aforesaid; do in the first place (as their ancestors in like case have usually done) for the vindicating and asserting their ancient rights and liberties, declare

That the pretended power of suspending of laws, or the execution of laws, by regal authority, without consent of parliament, is illegal.

That the pretended power of dispensing with laws, or the execution of laws, by regal authority, as it hath been assumed and exercised of late, is illegal.

That the commission for erecting the late court of commissioners for ecclesiastical causes, and all other commissions and courts of like nature are illegal and pernicious.

That levying money for or to the use of the crown, by pretence of prerogative, without grant of parliament, for longer time, or in other manner than the same is or shall be granted, is illegal.

That it is the right of the subjects to petition the King, and all committments and prosecutions for such petitioning are illegal.

That the raising or keeping a standing army within the kingdom in time of peace, unless it be with consent of parliament, is against law.

That the subjects which are protestants, may have arms for their defence suitable to their conditions, and as allowed by law.

That election of members of parliament ought to be free.

That the freedom of speech, and debates or proceedings in parliament, ought not to be impeached or questioned in any court or place out of parliament.

That excessive bail ought not to be required, nor excessive fines imposed; nor cruel and unusual punishments inflicted.

That jurors ought to be duly impanelled and returned, and jurors which pass upon men in trials for high treason ought to be freeholders.

That all grants and promises of fines and forfeitures of particular persons before conviction, are illegal and void.

And that for redress of all grievances, and for the amending, strengthening and preserving of the laws, parliaments ought to be held frequently.

[2] 1688/9 — T. G. B.

And they do claim, demand, and insist upon all and singular the premisses, as their undoubted rights and liberties; and that no declarations, judgments, doings or proceedings, to the prejudice of the people in any of the said premisses, ought in any wise to be drawn hereafter into consequence or example. To which demand of their rights they are particularly encouraged by the declaration of his highness the prince of Orange, as being the only means for obtaining a full redress and remedy therein. Having therefore an entire confidence, That his said highness the Prince of Orange will perfect the deliverance so far advanced by him, and will still preserve them from the violation of their rights, which they have here asserted, and from all other attempts upon their religion, rights, and liberties. The said lords spiritual and temporal, and commons, assembled at Westminster, do resolve, That William and Mary prince and princess of Orange be, and be declared, King and Queen of England, France and Ireland, and the dominions thereunto belonging, to hold the crown and royal dignity of the said kingdoms and dominions to them the said prince and princess during their lives, and the life of the survivor of them; and that the sole and full exercise of the regal power be only in, and executed by the said prince of Orange, in the names of the said prince and princess, during their joint lives; and after their deceases, the said crown and royal dignity of the said kingdoms and dominions to be to the heirs of the body of the said princess; and for default of such issue to the princess Anne of Denmark and the heirs of her body; and for default of such issue to the heirs of the body of the said prince of Orange. And the lords spiritual and temporal, and commons, do pray the said prince and princess to accept the same accordingly. And that the oaths hereafter mentioned be taken by all persons of whom the oaths of allegiance and supremacy might be required by law, instead of them; and that the said oaths of allegiance and supremacy may be abrogated.

I A.B. do sincerely promise and swear, That I will be faithful, and bear true allegiance, to their Majesties King William and Queen Mary:

So help me God.

I A.B. do swear, That I do from my heart abhor, detest, and abjure as impious and heretical, that damnable doctrine and position, That princes excommunicated or deprived by the pope, or any authority of the see of Rome, may be deposed or murdered by their subjects, or any other whatsoever. And I do declare, That no foreign prince, person, prelate, state, or potentate hath, or ought to have any jurisdiction, power, superiority, pre-eminence, or authority, ecclesiastical or spiritual, within this realm:

So help me God.

Upon which their said Majesties did accept the crown and royal dignity of the kingdoms of England, France, and Ireland, and the dominions thereunto belonging, according to the resolution and desire of the said lords and commons contained in the said declaration. And thereupon their Majesties were pleased, That the said lords spiritual and temporal, and commons, being the two houses of parliament, should continue to sit, and with their Majesties royal concurrence make effectual provision for the settlement of the religion, laws and liberties of this kingdom, so that the same for the future might not be in danger again of being subverted; to which the said lords spiritual and temporal, and commons, did agree and proceed to act accordingly. Now in pursuance of the premises, the said lords spiritual and temporal, and commons, in parliament assembled, for the ratifying, confirming and establishing the said declaration, and the articles, clauses, matters, and things therein contained, by the force of a law made in due form by authority of parliament, do pray that it may be declared and enacted, That all and singular the right and liberties asserted and claimed in the said declaration, are the true, ancient, and indubitable rights and liberties of the people of this kingdom, and so shall be esteemed, allowed, adjudged, deemed, and taken to be, and that all and every the particulars aforesaid shall be firmly and strictly holden and observed, as they are expressed in the said declaration; and all officers and ministers whatsoever shall serve their Majesties and their successors according to the same in all times to come. . . .

Edmund Burke to His Constituents

Edmund Burke (1729–1797) long sought conciliation of the American colonies and spoke forcefully for it in Parliament on several occasions. He still hoped for reconciliation, though the war was already two years old and the Declaration of Independence almost a year old, when he wrote to the sheriffs of Bristol in April, 1777. Burke had represented that commercial city, with close ties to the colonies and second in size only to London, since 1774. He was the intellectual light of the faction of Whigs who grouped behind Lord Rockingham, favoring reform and leading the opposition to Lord North, the most pliable and long-tenured of George III's handpicked prime ministers leading the "king's interest" in Parliament. North's suspension of habeas corpus in 1777 was directed at silencing these vocal critics in Britain. It prompted the following letter.

Burke's argument owes much to Locke. It has the same basis in pragmatism that undergirded Locke's theory and the same emphasis on civil liberties. The fear that those liberties were diminishing in Britain as the result of the war with the colonies seemed to raise the specter of the tyranny of the 1680's. Now, though, it was more the parliamentary oligarchy — Locke's "legislative" — than the king that posed the threat.

On the American Revolution and English Liberties, 1777

The act of which I speak [1] is among the fruits of the American war — a war in my humble opinion productive of many mischiefs, of a kind which distinguish it from all others. Not only our policy is deranged, and our empire distracted, but our laws and our legislative spirit appear to have been totally perverted by it. We have made war on our colonies, not by arms only, but by laws. As hostility and law are not very concordant ideas, every step we have taken in this business has been made by trampling on some maxim of justice or some capital principle of wise government. What precedents were established, and what principles overturned (I will not say of English privilege, but of general justice), in the Boston Port, the Massachusetts Charter, the Military Bill, and all that long array of hostile acts of Parliament by which the war with America has been begun and supported! Had the principles of any of these acts been first exerted on English ground, they would probably have expired as soon as they touched it. But by being removed from our persons, they have rooted in our laws, and the latest posterity will taste the fruits of them.

Nor is it the worst effect of this unnatural contention, that our *laws* are corrupted. Whilst *manners* remain entire, they will correct the vices of law, and soften it at length to their own temper. But we have to lament that in most of the late proceedings we see very few traces of that generosity, humanity, and dignity of mind, which formerly characterized this nation. War suspends the rules of moral obligation, and what is long suspended is in danger of being totally abrogated. Civil wars strike deepest of all into the manners of the people. They vitiate their politics; they corrupt their morals; they pervert even the natural taste and relish of equity and justice. By teaching us to consider our fellow-citizens in an hostile light, the whole body of our nation becomes gradually less dear to us. The very names of affection and kindred, which were the bond of charity whilst we agreed, become new incentives to hatred and rage when

From *The Works of the Right Honorable Edmund Burke*, vol. 2, 3d ed. (Boston, 1869), pp. 202–03, 209–11, 222–23, 229–30, 243–45.

[1] The suspension of habeas corpus. — T. G. B.

the communion of our country is dissolved. We may flatter ourselves that we shall not fall into this misfortune. But we have no charter of exemption, that I know of, from the ordinary frailties of our nature. . . .

I think I know America — if I do not, my ignorance is incurable, for I have spared no pains to understand it — and I do most solemnly assure those of my constituents who put any sort of confidence in my industry and integrity, that everything that has been done there has arisen from a total misconception of the object: that our means of originally holding America, that our means of reconciling with it after quarrel, of recovering it after separation, of keeping it after victory, did depend, and must depend, in their several stages and periods, upon a total renunciation of that unconditional submission which has taken such possession of the minds of violent men. The whole of those maxims upon which we have made and continued this war must be abandoned. Nothing, indeed, (for I would not deceive you,) can place us in our former situation. That hope must be laid aside. But there is a difference between bad and the worst of all. Terms relative to the cause of the war ought to be offered by the authority of Parliament. An arrangement at home promising some security for them ought to be made. By doing this, without the least impairing of our strength, we add to the credit of our moderation, which, in itself, is always strength more or less.

I know many have been taught to think that moderation in a case like this is a sort of treason — and that all arguments for it are sufficiently answered by railing at rebels and rebellion, and by charging all the present or future miseries which we may suffer on the resistance of our brethren. But I would wish them, in this grave matter, and if peace is not wholly removed from their hearts, to consider seriously, first, that to criminate and recriminate never yet was the road to reconciliation, in any difference amongst men. In the next place, it would be right to reflect that the American English (whom they may abuse, if they think it honorable to revile the absent) can, as things now stand, neither be provoked at our railing or bettered by our instruction. All communication is cut off between us. But this we know with certainty, that, though we cannot reclaim them, we may reform ourselves. If measures of peace are necessary, they must begin somewhere; and a conciliatory temper must precede and prepare every plan of reconciliation. Nor do I conceive that we suffer anything by thus regulating our own minds. We are not disarmed by being disencumbered of our passions. Declaiming on rebellion never added a bayonet or a charge of powder to your military force; but I am afraid that it has been the means of taking up many muskets against you. . . .

I have always wished, that as the dispute had its apparent origin from things done in Parliament, and as the acts passed there had provoked the war, that the foundations of peace should be laid in Parliament also. I have been astonished to find that those whose zeal for the dignity of our body was so hot as to light up the flames of civil war should even publicly declare that these delicate points ought to be wholly left to the crown. Poorly as I may be thought affected to the authority of Parliament, I shall never admit that our constitutional rights can ever become a matter of ministerial negotiation.

I am charged with being an American. If warm affection towards those over whom I claim any share of authority be a crime, I am guilty of this charge. But I do assure you, (and they who know me publicly and privately will bear witness to me,) that, if ever one man lived more zealous than another for the supremacy of Parliament and the rights of this imperial crown, it was myself. Many others, indeed, might be more knowing in the extent of the foundation of these rights. I do not pretend to be an antiquary, a lawyer, or qualified for the chair of professor in metaphysics. I never ventured to put your solid interests upon speculative grounds. My having constantly declined to do so has been attributed to my incapacity for such disquisitions; and I am inclined to believe it is partly the cause. I never shall be ashamed to confess, that, where I am ignorant, I am **diffident**. I am, indeed, not very solicitous to clear myself of this imputed incapacity; because men even less conversant than I am in this kind of subtleties, and placed in stations to which I ought not to aspire, have, by the mere force of civil discretion, often conducted the affairs of great nations with distinguished felicity and glory.

When I first came into a public trust, I found your Parliament in possession of an unlimited legislative power over the colonies. I could not open the statute-book without seeing the actual exercise of it, more or less, in all cases whatsoever. This possession passed with me for a title. It does so in all human affairs. No man examines into the defects of his title to his paternal estate or to his established government. Indeed, common sense taught me that a legislative authority not actually limited by the express terms of its foundation, or by its own subsequent acts, cannot have its powers parcelled out by argumentative distinctions, so as to enable us to say that here they can and there they cannot bind. . . .

==Civil freedom,== Gentlemen, is not, as many have endeavored to persuade you, a thing that lies hid in the depth of abstruse science. It ==is a blessing and a benefit, not an abstract speculation;== and all the just reasoning that can be upon it is of so coarse a texture as perfectly to suit the ordinary capacities of those who are to enjoy, and of those who are to defend it. Far from any resemblance to those propositions in geometry and metaphysics which admit no medium, but must be true or false in all their latitude, social and civil freedom, like all other things in common life, are variously mixed and modified, enjoyed in very different degrees, and shaped into an infinite diversity of forms, according to the temper and circumstances of every community. The *extreme* of liberty (which is its abstract perfection, but its real fault) contains nowhere, nor ought to obtain anywhere; because extremes, as we all know, in every point which relates either to our duties or satisfactions in life, are destructive both to virtue and enjoyment. Liberty, too, must be limited in order to be possessed. The degree of restraint it is impossible in any case to settle precisely. But it ought to be the constant aim of every wise public counsel to find out by cautious experiments, and rational, cool endeavors, with how little, not how much, of this restraint the community can subsist: for liberty is a good to be improved, and not an evil to be lessened. It is not only a private blessing of the first order, but the vital spring and energy of the state itself, which has just so much life and vigor as there is liberty in it. But whether liberty be advantageous or not, (for I know it is a fashion to decry the very principle,) none will dispute that peace is a blessing; and peace must, in the course of human affairs, be frequently bought by some indulgence and toleration at least to liberty: for, as the Sabbath (though of divine institution) was made for man, not man for the Sabbath, government, which can claim no higher origin or authority, in its exercise at least, ought to conform to the exigencies of the time, and the temper and character of the people with whom it is concerned, and not always to attempt violently to bend the people to their theories of subjection. The bulk of mankind, on their part, are not excessively curious concerning any theories whilst they are really happy; and one sure symptom of an ill-conducted state is the propensity of the people to resort to them. . . .

Liberty is in danger of being made unpopular to Englishmen. Contending for an imaginary power, we begin to acquire the spirit of domination, and to lose the relish of honest equality. The principles of our forefathers become suspected to us, because we see them animating the present opposition of our children. The faults which grow out of the luxuriance of freedom appear much more shocking to us than the base vices which are generated from the rankness of servitude. Accordingly, the least resistance to power appears more inexcusable in our eyes than the greatest abuses of authority. All dread of a standing military force is looked upon as a superstitious panic. All shame of calling in foreigners and savages in a civil contest is worn off. We grow indifferent to the consequences inevitable to ourselves from the plan of ruling half the empire by a mercenary sword. We are taught to believe that a desire of domineering over our countrymen is love to our country, that those who hate civil war abet rebellion, and that the amiable and conciliatory virtues of lenity, moderation, and tenderness to the privileges of those who depend on this kingdom are a sort of treason to the state.

It is impossible that we should remain long in a situation which breeds such notions and dispositions without some great alteration in the national character. Those ingenuous and feeling minds who are so fortified against all other things, and so unarmed to whatever approaches in the shape of disgrace, finding these principles, which they considered as sure means of honor, to be grown into disrepute, will retire disheartened and disgusted. Those of a more robust make, the bold, able, ambitious men, who pay some of their court to power through the people, and substitute the voice of transient opinion in the place of true glory, will give into the general mode; and those superior understandings which ought to correct vulgar prejudice will confirm and aggravate its errors. Many things have been long operating towards a gradual change in our principles; but this American war has done more in a very few years than all the other causes could have effected in a century. It is therefore not on its own separate account, but because of its attendant circumstances, that I consider its continuance, or its ending in any way but that of an honorable and liberal accommodation, as the greatest evils which can befall us. . . . Let us not be amongst the first who renounce the maxims of our forefathers. . . .

William V, Prince of Orange

Dutch wealth and strength were universally envied in the seventeenth century and were still to be reckoned with in the eighteenth. However, political stability appeared to elude the hardy republic throughout its existence. The tension between the powerful and assertive oligarchies of the Dutch cities and the hereditary stadtholder of the House of Orange was always considerable and resulted in two long periods in the seventeenth and eighteenth centuries in which there was no stadtholder. The United Netherlands was a republic by virtue of the oligarchical independence of the regent class. The republic was always subject to the pressure toward monarchy of the Orange stadtholder. The regents ultimately needed the symbol and the authority of the stadtholder office in order for the republic to survive. The stadtholder never had sufficient executive power to become independent of the regent oligarchies — in short, he never had sufficient power to establish an effective monarchy, let alone an absolutist monarchy.

The report of the Prussian minister, Renfner, to King Frederick William II of Prussia, dated February 23, 1792, concerning the prince of Orange, his Prussian wife, their two sons, and the routine of the stadtholder's life is revelatory of the prince and his weaknesses and the large measure of influence exercised over him by his Prussian wife. These personal shortcomings and disadvantages compounded the weak-

ness of the office symbolically evidenced in the absence of monarchical pomp in his court. William V in 1792 was virtually a client of Prussia and Britain, for a few years earlier he had been saved from probable overthrow only by those powers. They were in no position to help him in 1795 when the remnants of the "Patriot" faction in the republic rose in support of a French Revolutionary army, composed in part of exiled "Patriots," to drive William into exile. Ironically, after the Revolutionary and Napoleonic episodes, Prince William, whose character is analyzed by Renfner, was established as king of the Netherlands, and his house is one of the few European royal houses that still possesses its throne.

The Last Non-Absolutist Quasi-Monarch of the Dutch Republic

The public voice is unjust toward him and he is worth more than his reputation. Born with a spirit, with a right sense and a sound judgment, endowed with a memory of prodigious grasp, better instructed in the complicated constitution of his country than the majority of those who have studied it professionally, susceptible of a certain application, liking good and seeking to do it, what might not have grown from so excellent a ground if it had been cultivated with care? But fate willed that all conspired to mar the upbringing of William V: the premature death of his father, a doting mother, an ambitious guardian, a sickly childhood, governors and teachers that had knowledge neither of the world nor of reality. Thence [came] his prejudices, his distrust of himself, his suspicious character, his extreme weakness, his insouciance, his disorder in work.

The Stadtholder of the United Provinces is undoubtedly the busiest prince in Europe. All matters that happen in the Republic and which concern it, within or without it, are reported to him. He is obliged to know all, to read all, to enter into all the details of the different branches of the administration, to follow from near or far all the deliberations of the States,[1] to intervene in the endless discussions that arise among the provinces, in the towns, and also among the regents. All that concerns the army and the navy is his province. He appoints the majority of the employees of the Republic. He is alone charged with the burden of official entertainments; everywhere he is obliged to pay for them personally. To be equal to such onerous cares there must be a strict division

From Henry de Peyster, *Les Troubles de Hollande, 1780–1795* (Paris, 1905), pp. 318–20, 321–22. Trans. Thomas G. Barnes.

[1] That is, the States-General of the Dutch Republic and the States of the individual provinces, especially Holland — the representative bodies that together constituted the sovereign power. — T. G. B.

of the day, a rigorous economy of time, and there never was one more prodigal of time than the Prince of Orange. His daily audiences, already so tedious in themselves, are prolonged without necessity from two o'clock until five, six, or seven o'clock in the evening. He loses whole mornings to drill a wretched troop of guards or to mount a parade; often the work that he does ought to be done by his clerks or his aides-de-camp, and he neglects his princely duties. In this there is neither order nor method. All the papers that come to him are piled pell-mell in his office and the handling of them left to chance without consulting whether they are pressing or not. Sometimes and by whim he surrounds himself with two or three secretaries, some more inept than others, and he sets himself to dispatch everything that comes to hand. Other times, when he exerts himself in an important matter, of a paper that ought to be carried in his name to the States, he takes the pen himself and one is amazed to see coming forth very well done compositions that are successful at the first stroke. Present him with the most intricate matter; he untangles it with precision at first sight, but soon his ideas vacillate, he confuses them, mixes them up, sets himself to consider them and usually ends by choosing the worst. In the time of troubles,[2] when he was so badly served, how many mistakes hasn't he been led to? And nevertheless there is not a single one of them of which he may not have predicted the unfortunate outcome. "You are going to make me do a foolish thing," he always said, "but since you want it, I shall sign." This lack of strength is his greatest misfortune and renders him incorrigible, even though he himself knows his faults, which he would be the first to deplore. . . .

It is not easy to conduct business with the Prince of Orange. No one is more obliging, indeed, on first meeting than he. Propose to him what you will, he will never fail to answer you, "that he will try to please you," but this phrase is banal and proves nothing, and the object requested remains there. One would gain nothing in returning impetuously to the charge. . . . By means of his being impatient, he would end by a show of temper. The only way to arrive at the goal with him is to bring him back to it imperceptibly in the conversation, to represent the thing to him as a benefit of which he will be the author. . . .

In the matter of some most essential negotiation . . . , try to agree with Lord van de Spiegel and you have won the cause. Only, that the interest of England should not be involved, for on this article he [William V] is deaf to all remonstrances and, pursuant to the bias innate in his house [of Orange] and which seems bound to perpetuate itself from generation to generation, he sees safety only in the Court of London, and he knows no other fear than that it will be displeased with him. . . .

[2] The "time of troubles" was the proto-revolutionary period, 1786–1787, when the Patriots threatened civil war and were put down only by a show of force by Prussian troops dispatched with British sanction. — T. G. B.

As long as the Princess of Orange [3] will choose to content herself with the degree of influence that she exercises today, it depends upon her to maintain it. One can trust to her insight and wisdom, that she will not seek to extend the sphere of her activity. She would risk altering her domestic happiness and exciting, perhaps, the defiance of a nation that loves its Stadtholder and would not care to see him entirely dependent on his spouse. William V, with all his faults, is not least dear to the people because of his goodness and his affability. The Princess shares in this attachment, but she conditions it by the consciousness of her dignity, and this is well whatever the critics may say. If the Hollanders had not been contained by the respect she commands, they would go as far as familiarity. . . .

The Crown Prince [4] excels over his younger brother in the matter of talent and aptitude, gentleness and popularity; he learns quickly what he wants to study, he works easily, he is interested in everything and applies himself from this moment to everything that concerns his country. Prince Frederick, with an understanding less easy, with less natural aptitude, compensates for this disadvantage by assiduity and perseverance, and his conversation, by being a bit slower is only that much more sure. His first impression is [of one] cold and reserved, but he attaches himself so much more strongly to those to whom he takes a liking, and one can say that his heart always goes hand-in-hand with his reason. However, despite all these solid qualities, he would be perhaps less suited to the Stadtholdership than his elder brother. He would bring to it a greater strength and a more reflective judgment, but by all appearances, less activeness and less suppleness in handling people. Ever since the Crown Prince has been on his own, one has noticed two faults that merit attention: an extreme severity toward the military and a hidden penchant for miserliness. . . .

In Holland the only day that imposes upon foreign representatives the obligation of a kind of ceremonial towards the representatives of the sovereign [power] is New Year's Day. One visits in person the President for the week [and] those of the council-board of the Province of Holland and the Grand Pensionary,[5] and one carries cards to the most distinguished members of the government.

The duties that one is called upon to render to the Court of Orange are not tiring either. From November 1 to Easter there is a public court every two weeks, to which are admitted all who have obtained the honor of presentation [to the Court], even including Jews. The company, being

---

[3] The princess, William V's wife, was Wilhemina, sister of King Frederick William II (1786–1797) of Prussia and niece of Frederick the Great. — T. G. B.
[4] Wliam (1772–1184), from 1814 King William I of the Netherlands. — T. G. B.
[5] The Grand Pensionary was the leader of the States of Holland; from 1788 to 1795, the office was held by Pieter-Laurens van de Spiegel, mentioned above. — T. G. B.

a scramble in this matter, is perforce numerous, and in fact on solemn occasions the crowd is sometimes 1,200 to 1,400 persons. The Princess gets off with making the tour of the halls, after which she turns to amusement. Everyone is permitted to do as much; refreshments are served and the reception finishes at ten o'clock [A.M.]. The great galas are March 8 and August 7, the birthdays of the Prince and the Princess of Orange. Visits are made to the Prince in the morning, and usage dictates that His Highness receive the foreign representatives in a body at about two o'clock. There is a reception in the evening; otherwise, neither celebration nor dinner. . . .

The presentation of strangers is still the simplest thing in the world. One takes them to the Prince's audience without the least ceremony and likewise to the Princess's, if it is a day when she will see people. If not, it suffices to ask the hour, and one is sure to be admitted in the course of the day, either before dinner or at supper.

WEALTH, WAR, AND EMPIRE
Chapter 5

"The state and posture of gladiators" was nothing new in the European experience during the late seventeenth and eighteenth centuries. War had been a corollary of the growth of European states from the beginning. Besides territorial aggrandizement, war had been undertaken for commercial advantage: This motivation was present in the Crusades and the later wars with the Turks, and it was paramount in the rivalry among the northern Italian city-states in the late Middle Ages and the Renaissance. From the opening of the New World by Columbus' great voyage of 1492, Spanish, Portuguese, and, shortly afterward, French traders had come to blows in and around the Americas. The English joined the fray later in the sixteenth century, and their raids along the Spanish Main, as well as their illicit slave trade to the Spanish colonies, were major causes of the dispatch of the Armada in 1588. In the seventeenth century, the Dutch battled the Portuguese in Brazil and the English in the Far East; the first two of three wars that the Dutch fought with the English from 1652 to 1678 were primarily mercantile in origin. The greatest commercial and colonial warfare in the history of the European world, however, was that between England and France, which began in 1689 in conjunction with the continental war of the League of Augsburg and ended only with Napoleon's defeat at the Battle of the Nile, in August, 1798. This worldwide, continuing confrontation was the climax of the first great period of European overseas imperialism, begun in the fifteenth century.

From the outset, European imperialism in the New World involved some colonization, that is, the settling of Europeans in the overseas territories. Colonization meant exploitation of the crude resources of the territories — from the precious metals of Spain's colonies to the furs of French Canada to the timber of New England — and increasing eagerness to find new agricultural products — sugarcane in the West Indies, tobacco in Virginia and Maryland, and the other great primary staples of the eighteenth century elsewhere — and fisheries. The state played varying roles in the colonial venture, ranging from the tight control exercised by the Spanish, Portuguese, and French governments to the mixture of joint-stock company colonies, individual proprietary colonies, and royal colonies of the English to the practically autonomous joint-stock companies of the Dutch. In all the colonies, religion, Catholic or Protestant, played a somewhat inflated part as the moral armor to shield the colonists from the terrors of the wilds. In the case of some of the English colonies, religious particularism was a major cause for the establishment of the colonies.

During the seventeenth century the interests of governments in their colonies increased. This reflected a growing awareness of the value of the colonies for trade, albeit primarily as producers of raw materials and consumers of manufactured goods from the homeland, and a developed theory of economic nationalism (a better name than the traditional "mercantilism") applicable to domestic, colonial, and foreign commerce. Economic nationalism was highly individualistic and ranged from the very tight system of Colbert in France to the freer structure of England and the quite liberal policies of the Dutch. In applicability to the colonies each system tended to be highly restrictive: The colonies existed for the homeland alone, and interlopers were to be excluded. The governing concept of economic nationalism was balance of trade, measured by the amount of precious metal a nation acquired or lost by trade. Sir Josiah Child was the principal English economic theorist on trade, and his speculation reflects traditional and universal notions of balance of trade and a critical awareness of the inadequacies of those notions.

One institution was common to all European colonies in the New World's tropics and subtropics: slavery. Originally slavery consisted of the enslavement of indigenous populations in Spanish America; by the early seventeenth century it meant the enslavement of Africans transported from Africa at the cost of terrible suffering and loss of life. The economic advantages of black slaves overcame scruples against slavery deep in the European culture. The mounting cry against slavery in the eighteenth century was moved by the ideals of the Enlightenment and, in England, by a revival of religious concern. The cry was expressed with unusual eloquence in the argument of an English lawyer that resulted in banning slavery at least on home soil.

The great Anglo-French confrontation from 1689 to 1798 determined that one of these powers would establish the largest empire in history. In the struggle, the stakes were trade and empire, the fronts were North America, India, and the Continent, the pattern was of long periods of cold war punctuated by short, sharp periods of hot war. England was the victor, on balance. The corollary consequences of this "Second Hundred Years' War" were far-reaching: It contributed to the rise of Prussia, Britain's Continental ally from 1755; it was a cause of the coming of the French Revolution by destroying the finances of France; it ensured British hostility to the Revolution and Napoleon; and, finally, it contributed immediately to the loss of Britain's major colonies, which became the United States of America.

This great, continuing confrontation was grafted onto the predominantly dynastic rivalries that divided the European states. Throughout this period, war was the logical extension of diplomacy, and diplomacy was dynastic. The pattern had been established in the sixteenth century and brought to a high point of sophistication during the Thirty Years' War (1618–1648), an essentially dynastic struggle between the Austrian Hapsburgs and other small German houses, among the German houses, and between French Bourbons and Spanish Hapsburgs. The Dutch and the Scandinavian houses were less dynamic and more peripheral to the main issues. In the second half of the seventeenth century, all war turned on Louis XIV and his France, his ambitions, his aggression, and his bid for hegemony. The eighteenth century was peculiarly the century of "wars of succession" to thrones — Spain (1701), Poland (1733), Austria (1740), Bavaria (1778) — until the wars of the French Revolution in the 1790's One of these wars of succession, the Austrian, became the parent of two more wars on the Continent, in 1744 and 1756, because of the archrivalry between Frederick II's Prussia and Maria Theresa's Austria.

In the "Second Hundred Years' War" the decisive epoch was the Seven Years' War from 1756 to 1763. Like all the Anglo-French wars beginning in 1689, this war had a North American theater of operations. Unlike the earlier wars, however, it also had a major theater of operations in India. What is striking about the war is that it began not on the Continent in 1756 but two years earlier in the woods of what is now western Pennsylvania, in a skirmish between some Virginia militiamen and some French regulars. Voltaire spoke of the "cannonshot fired in America [that] gave the signal that set Europe in a blaze"; he was guilty of only one inaccuracy — it was not a cannon but a musket — and only slight exaggeration when we consider the subsequent Prussian-Austrian rivalry. The results of the war, though, are not open to question. France lost an entire empire except for a few islands. England gained accordingly, even though its victory planted the seeds of the loss of its most valuable colonies.

Men, Money, Munitions, Manners, and Morals

Virginia was England's principal overseas colony in 1626. It was a company-colony under charter from the king, and both James I and Charles I took unusual and sometimes unwelcome interest in it. Tobacco was already the staple, too much so as these instructions indicate. The first African slaves had been imported in 1619 to work the tobacco plantations. Insufficient English settlement plagued the colony, and the Indian massacre of 1622 did not help. The concern with morals was real enough but had less to do with Puritanism than with the fear that immorality brought disorder.

Instructions from the Privy Council of England to Virginia, April 19, 1626

Instruccions from the Lords of his Majestie's most honourable Privy Councell to Sir George Yardley, knight, Governour of Virginia, and to the Councell of State there.

1. That you, Sir George Yardley, doe use your best endeavours to bee ready with such shipps and vesselles, men and provision, as you have furnished for that purpose, upon the first faire winde and weather to put to sea and to saile directly for Virginia unlesse you shall finde it requisite for the good of the plantacion and people's healths to touch at the Somer Islandes [1] by the way, whence after you have refreshed you shall proceed on to Virginia, and upon your arrival there according to your comission graunted by his most excellent Majestie under the great seale etc. take upon you the present government of that collonie.

2. That in the first place you bee carefull Almighty God may bee duely and daily served both by yourselfe and all the people under your charge which may drawe down a blessing upon all your endeavours.

3. That you faile not by the first shipp to send us a list of all the severall plantacions, the place where they are planted, the distance betweene the plantacions, the number of the people in every plantacion distinguished by their sexes, ages, professions and condicions and also by the place of every one's birth and the names of their parentes heere in England; what armes, munition, boates or shipps, dwelling houses and other

From *Acts of the Privy Council of England, March 1625 to May 1626* (London, 1934), pp. 436–39. Reprinted by permission of the Controller of Her Britannic Majesty's Stationery Office.

[1] Bermuda. — T. G. B.

buildinges, what impaled groundes, provisions of food or store of tame cattell are in every of the said plantacions.

4. That you diligently and particularly inquire by oath and all other lawfull meanes what landes, goodes, servantes, tenantes, houses, boates, shipps, debtes, etc. were in November 1623 belonging to the late company; how and to whome they have since beene disposed, by what order and authority they have beene so disposed and what you shall finde remayning to reserve to the publique use; all which you are to certifie under your hand and the seale of the collonie.

5. That all new commers bee well entertained and lodged in houses by the ould planters till they can house themselves, that they bee not suffered to sitt downe straggling but injoyned to live by those already planted or in sufficient numbers by themselves and if they bee unprovided of landes fitt to manure then to bee permitted to sett downe upon the companie's land upon the condicions expressed in the Treasurer's and Councell's letter sent immediately after the massacre in August 1622.[2]

6. That all new commers bee exempted the first yeare from going in person or contributing to the warre save onely in defence of the place where they shall inhabite and that onely when the enemye shall assaile it but all others in the collonie shalbe rated to the maintenance of the warres proporcionably to their abillities, neither shall any man bee priviledged from going to the warrs that is above 17 yeares ould and under 60, respect being had to the quallitie of the persons, that officers bee not forced to goe as private souldiers or in places inferior to their degrees unlesse in case of extreame necessitie.

7. That a marchant bee not constrained to take tobacco at 3 shillings the pound in exchange for his wares, but that it bee lawfull for him to make his owne baigaine for his goodes hee so changeth, notwithstanding any proclamacion there published to the contrary.

8. That you call for the charter parties [3] that the masters of the shipps bring along with them and strictly examine whither they have truely performed the condicions of their contractes especially to inquire whither they have not pestred their shipps with passengers and whither they have given sufficient and wholesome food and drinke during the voyage and as you finde to certifie the Lords of his Majestie's Privy Councell or the Commissioners for Virginia.

9. That you be carefull that the good shipp the *Anne* wherein you are to imbarque yourselfe and the *James* that goeth in consort with you bee not pestred with passengers and that the masters of the same shipps doe

---

[2] More than three hundred of the Virginia colony were taken by surprise and killed by the Indians on March 22, 1622, ending the "era of friendliness" that had obtained before. The immediate cause of the massacre was the shooting of a chief by two white youths who suspected that he had killed their master. — T. G. B.

[3] Shipping contracts. — T. G. B.

give the said passengers suff[i]cient and wholesome food and drinke during the voyage.

10. That in regard you may daily expect the comming of a forreigne enemy,[4] wee require you soone after your first landing that you publish by proclamacion through the collonie that no person whatsoever upon the arrival of any shipp or shipps shall dare to goe aboard without expresse warrant from you, the governor and councell, least by that meanes they bee surprized, to the great prejudice if not the overthrowe of the whole plantacion.

11. To avoyd that intollerable abuse of ingrossing[5] commodities and forestalling the markett that you require all masters of shipps not to breake bulke till theire arrivall at James cittie[6] or otherwise without speciall order from you the govenor and councell.

12. That you endeavour by severe punishment to suppresse drunkenesse and that you bee carefull that the great quantities of wine and strong drinke bee not sould into the handes of those that are likeliest to abuse it but as neere as you can it maybee equally disposed for the comfort and reliefe of the whole plantacion; and if any marchant or other for private lucre shall bring in any rotten or unwholesome wines or strong drinke such as may endanger the healths of the people that you suffer it not to bee sould there but to cause them to shipp it backe againe.

13. And whereas your tobacco falleth every day more and more to a baser price, wee require you to use your best indeavour to cause the people there to applie themselves to the raising of more staple commodities as likewise to the impaling of gardens and orchardes and inclosing of groundes for all manner of cattell whereby the store of the countrey may bee advanced in abundance.

14. That you cause the people to plant such store of corne[7] as there maye bee a whole yeare's provision before hand in the collonie least in relying upon one single harvest by drought, blasting or otherwise they fall into such wantes and famines as formerly they have endured.

15. And that you may the better avoyd the treachery of the savages and prevent such dangers as heeretofore have fallen upon the countrey, wee strictly forbidd all persons whatsoever to receive into their houses the person of any Indian or to parley commerce or trade with them without the speciall licence and warrant given to that purpose according to your commission inflicting severe punishment upon the offenders.

16. And whereas by the last letters from Virginia wee are given to understand that of those that are now nominated for councellors there some are dead and others are coming home; wee doe authorize you, the

---

[4] England was at war with Spain and on the verge of war with France. — T. G. B.
[5] Hoarding. — T. G. B.
[6] Jamestown. — T. G. B.
[7] Grain. — T. G. B.

Governor, to make choyce of such as you in your judgment shall thinke most fitt to supply their places and to administer to them an oath as you are directed by your commission that so in these dangerous times there may not bee wanting a sufficient number to governe in the affaire of that collonie as also to minister the oathe of allegiance and supremacye to all such as come thither with an intention to plant and reside there which if any shall refuse hee is to bee returned and shipped from thence home, the same oathe to bee administered to all other persons when you shall see it fitt, as marriners, marchantes etc. to prevent any danger by espyes.

17. And to conclude that in all things according to your best understanding you indeavour the extirpating of vice and the encouragement of virtue and goodnes.

The Balance of Trade, 1668

Sir Josiah Child (1630–1699) came from an old London merchant family. He amassed a fortune as a supplier to Cromwell's navy and was a large stockholder in and a member of the board of the prime English trading establishment, the East India Company. He was also a highly original economic theorist. He was a "moderate" economic nationalist, much influenced by the liberal Dutch practice, and a strong advocate of low interest rates as a spur to England's trade vitality. This is the burden of his A New Discourse of Trade, *written about 1668, from which this selection is taken. He questioned two underlying assumptions of strict mercantilist theory: that exports could be expanded without reciprocity in imports and that export of precious metal was by definition detrimental. He was uncompromising in his belief that the trade of the colonies was to be reserved to the homeland.*

Josiah Child's *New Discourse of Trade*

That the greatness of this kingdom depends upon foreign trade, is generally acknowledged, and therefore the interest of trade not unbecoming persons of the highest rank; and of this study, as well as others, it may be said, there is an infinity in it, none, though of the largest intellects and experience, being able to fathom its utmost depth.

From Josiah Child, *A New Discourse of Trade*, ch. 9, new ed. (London, 1775), pp. 141–48, 152–57, 162–64.

Among other things relating to trade, there hath been much discoursed of the *balance of trade;* the right understanding whereof may be of singular use, and serve as a compass to steer by, in the contemplation and propagation of trade for public advantage.

The balance of trade is commonly understood two ways.

1. Generally; something whereby it may be known whether this kingdom gaineth or loseth by foreign trade.

2. Particularly; something whereby we may know by what trades this kingdom gains, and by what trades it loseth.

For the first of these:

It is the most general received opinion, and that not ill-grounded, that this balance is to be taken by a strict scrutiny of what proportion the value of the commodities exported out of this kingdom bear to those imported; and if the exports exceed the imports, it is concluded the nation gets by the general course of its trade, it being supposed that the overplus is imported in bullion, and so adds to the treasure of the kingdom; gold and silver being taken for the measure and standard of riches.

2. This rule is not only commonly applied to the general course of foreign trade, but to particular trades to and from this nation to any other.

Now, although this notion have much of truth in it, and was ingeniously and worthily started by him that first published it, and much good hath accrued to the kingdom by our lawmakers (noblemen and gentlemen) resenting [1] it; yet, if the difficulty of the scrutiny, whereby to reduce it into practice, and the many accidents that may accrue, be seriously weighed, it will appear too doubtful and uncertain as to our general trade, and in reference to particular trades fallible and erroneous.

That it will not hold as to foreign trade in general, appears:

1. From the difficulty and impossibility of taking a true account, as well of the quantity as of the value of commodities exported and imported.

The general rule for this hath been the custom-house books; but that they cannot be in any measure certain, will easily be granted. For:

1. As to the quantity, if it be considered that many fine commodities, of small bulk and great value, as points, laces, ribbands, fine linen, silks, jewels, *&c.* are imported by stealth; and that also, in many out-ports and creeks of England and Wales, commodities of bulk are both imported and exported oftentimes by indirect means, that never are registered; besides also, of what is entered, there may be, though not considerable in London, yet in other parts much difference in the quantities and qualities.

2. As to the value, how shall the compute be made, seeing the rates of the customs are in no kind proportionable? our own commodities being

---

[1] That is, being sensible of, appreciating. — T. G. B.

some rated very low, as drapery, silk wares, haberdashery, and all manufactures of iron; others high, as lead and tin; and fish in English shipping nothing; and for foreign commodities imported the rates are yet more unequal: so that the value rated for the customs cannot be a due measure.

Besides, foreign commodities imported by English shipping should be valued only at their first cost and charges abroad, and those by foreign shipping with the increase of the homeward freight.

2. From the many accidents that fall out in trade, without the true knowledge whereof a right balance cannot be made; as:

1. Accidents that diminish the stock sent out; as losses at sea, bad markets, bankruptcies, also confiscations, seizures and arrests, which fall out often on several occasions.

Now, if by any of these, or such-like, the original stock comes to be impaired and lessened, the value of the commodities imported in return may be far less than the value of the commodities exported, and yet may be the full product, and so the nation no gainer, though the exports were more in value than the imports.

2. Accidents whereby the stock sent out comes to be extraordinarily advanced in sale abroad; from whence it may fall out, that the commodities imported in return may appear to be of a much greater value than the commodities exported, and yet be no more than the real produce of them, and so the nation no loser, but a gainer thereby, although the imports exceed the exports. . . .

Here let me glance at my old theme, and desire the reader to consider seriously, whether it may, not improperly, be said of all kingdoms and countries, where the interest of money runs higher than their neighbours, that a part of their estates are owned by absentees, and consequently they shall be sure to be kept poor, whether their importations or their exportations exceed. . . .

For, in case the trade of England should be carried on by absentees, then the supposition upon which this notion is grounded (*viz.* that when the exports overbalance the imports, the surplusage is returned into England in bullion) will prove a mistake, and the contrary will be true, *viz.* that the surplusage will be conveyed into foreign parts, to the places of the residence of such absentees.

2. The second thing I am to illustrate is, that this rule, barely considered, is fallible and erroneous, as to particular and distinct trades.

This will appear, if it be considered, that a true measure of any particular trade, as to the profit or loss of the nation thereby, cannot be taken by the consideration of such trade in itself singly, but as it stands in reference, and is subservient to the general trade of the kingdom; for it may so fall out, that there may be some places to which little of our English manufactures are exported, and yet the commodities we have from thence may be so necessary to the carrying on our trade in general, or some other particular trades, that without them the nation would greatly decline and decay in trade.

Now, in this case, if we should measure such a particular trade by the aforesaid notion of the balance, we should find the imports abundantly exceed the exports, and so be ready to conclude against such trade as destructive; whereas, notwithstanding, it may in truth be a very necessary beneficial trade, and to the very great advantage of the nation. . . .

Thus having demonstrated that these notions touching the balance of trade, though they are in their kind useful notions, are in some cases fallible and uncertain; if any shall ask, How shall we then come to be resolved of the matter in question?

I answer, first, The best and most certain discovery, to my apprehension, is to be made from the increase or diminution of our trade and shipping in general; for, if our trade and shipping diminish, whatever profit particular men may make, the nation undoubtedly loseth; and, on the contrary, if our trade and shipping increase, how small or low soever the profits are to private men, it is an infallible indication that the nation in general thrives: for I dare affirm, and that categorically, in all parts of the whole world, wherever trade is great, and continues so, and grows daily more great, and increaseth in shipping, and that for a succession not of a few years, but of ages, that trade must be nationally profitable. . . .

Where a great trade is driven, especially where much shipping is employed, whatever becomes of the poor merchant that drives the trade, multitudes of people will be certain gainers, as his Majesty and his officers of custom, besides shipwrights, butchers, brewers, bakers, ropemakers, porters, seamen, manufacturers, carmen, lightermen, and all other artificers and people that depend on trade and shipping, which indeed, more or less, the whole kingdom doth.

But it may be said again, If this increase of trade depend upon, and proceed from our ordinary importations, for which our ready money goes out, it will impoverish us.

I answer, In some cases it may be so, and in some cases (as I have already demonstrated) it may be otherwise, but that will best be known by the effects: for, if we are impoverished, our general trade and our shipping will necessarily and visibly grow less and less, and must rationally and unavoidably do so; for that, being impoverished, we shall lose our tools (our stock) to drive a great trade with: whereas, on the contrary, if our trade in the gross bulk of it (tho' we may decline in some) do still increase, especially our shipping, for a long tract of years, it is an infallible proof of our thriving by our trade, and that we are still getting more tools (more stock) to trade with.

Some there are would limit this discovery to the increase and diminution of our coin and bullion: but, because that is more secret and indiscernible, it cannot, I conceive, afford so clear a demonstration as the other, if any at all; for that money seems to vulgar observers most plentiful, when there is least occasion for it; and, on the contrary, more scarce, as the occasions for the employment thereof are more numerous and advantageous; according to which we should seem to have most money when we have the least trade, and yet then certainly the nation gets least. This is apparent to those that will observe, that when the East-India company have a great sale to make, then money is generally found to be scarce in London, not that it is so in reality more than at other times, but because that extraordinary occasion engageth men to employ quantities, which they provide and lay aside for that purpose. . . .

What is to be done in England, to improve the trade thereof to such a degree as to equalize or over-balance our neighbours in our national profit by our foreign trade? . . .

The method I propose for the further answering of this great question, is (following my own principle, that if trade be great, and much English shipping employed, it will be good for the nation in general, whatever it may be for private merchants) first to lay down some general rules for the enlargement of trade in England; and then some ways of reducing those general rules into use and practice. The general rules for the enlargement of trade are not many.

I. Increase hands } in trade.
II. Increase stock }
III. Make trade easy and necessary, *i.e.*, make it our interest to trade.
IV. Make it the interest of other nations to trade with us. . . .

IVth General rule, To make it the interest of other nations to trade with us.

1. Being in a good condition of strength at home, in reference to the navy, and all other kind of military preparations for defence (and offence upon just occasion given) will render us wise and honourable in the esteem of other nations, and consequently oblige them not only to admit us the freedom of trade with them, but the better terms for, and countenance in, the course of our trade.

2. To make it the interest of others to trade with us, we must be sure to furnish them at as cheap or cheaper rates than any other nation can or doth; and this I affirm can never be done without subduing usury especially, and doing those other things before-mentioned, that will conduce to the increase of our hands and stock; for our being in a condition to sell our neighbours cheaper than others, must be when it is principally an effect of many hands and much stock. . . .

3. The well contrivement and management of foreign treaties may very much contribute to the making it the interest of other nations to trade with us, at least to the convincing of foreign princes wherein and how it is their interest to trade with us.

4. Public justice and honesty will make it the interest of other nations to trade with us, that is, that when any commodities pass under a public common seal (which is in a kind the public faith of the nation) they may be exact in length, breadth, and nature, according to what they ought to be by their seals.

The like care ought to be taken for the true packing of our herrings and pilchards, formerly mentioned.

5. If we would engage other nations to trade with us, we must receive from them the fruits and commodities of their countries, as well as send them our's; but it is our interest, by example, and other means (not distasteful) above all kinds of commodities to prevent, as much as may be, the importation of foreign manufactures.

6. The Venetians being a people that take from us very little of our manufactures, have prohibited our English cloth; and from whose territories we receive great quantities of currants, purchased with our ready money; it seems to me advantageous for England, that *that* importation, as well as the importation of wrought-glass, drinking-glasses, and other manufactures from thence, should be discouraged, it being supposed we can now make them as well ourselves in England.

The trade for Canary wines I take to be a most pernicious trade to Enland, because those islands consume very little of our manufactures, fish, or other English commodities; neither do they furnish us with any commodities to be further manufactured here or re-exported; the wines we bring from thence being for the most part purchased with ready money. . . .

The Exclusion of Slavery from England

On December 3, 1771, two Englishmen and an Englishwoman filed an affidavit in the court of King's Bench that James Sommersett was being held in irons aboard a ship lying in the Thames, bound for Jamaica to be sold as a slave. Habeas corpus was obtained, Sommersett was brought before the court, and there he was represented by the most eminent counsel of the day. Francis Hargrave, a noted legal antiquary, put the historical case against slavery. His argument went well beyond narrow legal precedent, however, in its citation of Locke and a list of eminent European jurists and theorists, including the great French philosophe Montesquieu. His argument was that slavery was evil per se. The court agreed, and Lord Chief Justice Mansfield gave judgment for the freeing of Sommersett and the exclusion of slavery from England. The decision in Sommersett's Case was the first victory for the movement that four decades later secured the outlawing of the slave trade.

"The Case of James Sommersett, a Negro, on a Habeas Corpus," 1772

In truth, as I have already hinted, the variety of forms, in which slavery appears, makes it almost impossible to convey a just notion of it in the way of definition. There are however certain properties, which have accompanied slavery in most places; and by attending to these, we may always distinguish it, from the mild species of domestic service so common and well known in our own country. I shall shortly enumerate the most remarkable of those properties; particularly, such as characterize the species of slavery adopted in our *American* colonies, being that now under the consideration of this court. This I do, in order that a just conception may be formed, of the propriety with which I shall impute to slavery the most pernicious effects. Without such a previous explanation, the most solid objections to the permission of slavery will have the appearance of unmeaning, though specious, declamation.

Slavery always imports an obligation of perpetual service; an obligation, which only the consent of the master can dissolve. It generally gives to the master, an arbitrary power of administering every sort of correction, however inhuman, not immediately affecting the life or limb of the slave: sometimes even these are left exposed to the arbitrary will of the master; or they are protected by fines, and other slight punishments, too inconsiderable to restrain the master's inhumanity. It creates an incapacity of acquiring, except for the master's benefit. It allows the master to alienate the person of the slave, in the same manner as other property. Lastly, it descends from parent to child, with all its severe appendages. On the most accurate comparison, there will be found nothing exaggerated in this representation of slavery. The description agrees with almost every kind of slavery, formerly or now existing; except only that remnant of the ancient slavery, which still lingers in some parts of *Europe,* but qualified and moderated in favour of the slave by the humane provision of modern times.

From this view of the condition of slavery, it will be easy to derive its destructive consequences. It corrupts the morals of the master, by freeing him from those restraints with respect to his slave, so necessary for controul of the human passions, so beneficial in promoting the practice and confirming the habit of virtue. It is dangerous to the master; because his

From Francis Hargrave, *State-Trials,* vol. 11 (London, 1781), pp. 340–41.

oppression excites implacable resentment and hatred in the slave, and the extreme misery of his condition continually prompts him to risque the gratification of them, and his situation daily furnishes the opportunity. To the slave it communicates all the afflictions of life, without leaving for him scarce any of its pleasures; and it depresses the excellence of his nature, by denying the ordinary means and motives of improvement. It is dangerous to the state, by its corruption of those citizens on whom its prosperity depends; and by admitting within it a multitude of persons, who, being excluded from the common benefits of the constitution, are interested in scheming its destruction. Hence it is, that slavery, in whatever light we view it, may be deemed a most pernicious institution: immediately so, to the unhappy person who suffers under it; finally so, to the master who triumphs in it, and to the state which allows it. . . .

The great origin of slavery is captivity in war, though sometimes it has commenced by contract. It has been a question much agitated, whether either of these foundations of slavery is consistent with natural justice. It would be engaging in too large a field of enquiry, to attempt reasoning on the *general lawfulness* of slavery. I trust too, that the liberty, for which I am contending, doth not require such a disquisition; and am impatient to reach that part of my argument, in which I hope to prove slavery reprobated by the law of *England* as an *inconvenient* thing. Here therefore I shall only refer to some of the most eminent writers, who have examined, how far slavery founded on captivity or contract is conformable to the law of nature, and shall just hint at the reasons, which influence their several opinions. The ancient writers suppose the right of killing an enemy vanquished in a just war; and thence infer the right of enslaving him. In this opinion, founded, as I presume, on the idea of punishing the enemy for his injustice, they are followed by *Albericus Gentilis, Grotius, Puffendorf, Bynkershoek,* and many others. But in *The Spirit of Laws,*[1] the right of killing is denied, except in case of absolute necessity and for self-preservation. However, where a country is conquered, the author seems to admit the conqueror's right of enslaving for a short time, that is, till the conquest is effectually secured. Dr. *Rutherforth,* not satisfied with the right of killing a vanquished enemy, infers the right of enslaving him, from the conqueror's right to a reparation in damages for the expences of the war. I do not know, that this doctrine has been examined; but I must observe, that it seems only to warrant a temporary slavery, till reparation is obtained from the property or personal labour of the people conquered. The lawfulness of slavery by contract is assented to by *Grotius* and *Puffendorf,* who found themselves on the maintenance of the slave, which is the consideration moving from the master. But a very great writer of our own country,[2] who is now living, controverts the sufficiency of such a con-

[1] Written by Montesquieu. — T. G. B.
[2] Namely, William Blackstone. — T. G. B.

sideration. Mr. *Locke* has framed another kind of argument against slavery by contract; and the substance of it is, that a right of preserving life is unalienable; that freedom from arbitrary power is essential to the exercise of that right; and therefore, that no man can by compact enslave himself. Dr. *Rutherforth* endeavours to answer Mr. *Locke*'s objection, by insisting on various limitations to the despotism of the master; particularly, that he has no right to dispose of the slave's life at pleasure. But the misfortune of this reasoning is, that though the contract cannot justly convey an arbitrary power over the slave's life, yet it generally leaves him without a security against the exercise of that or any other power. I shall say nothing of slavery by birth; except that the slavery of the child *must* be unlawful, if that of the parent cannot be justified; and that when slavery is extended to the issue, as it usually is, it *may* be unlawful as to them, even though it is not so as to their parents. In respect to slavery used for the punishment of crimes against civil society, it is founded on the same necessity, as the right of inflicting other punishments; never extends to the offender's issue; and seldom is permitted to be domestic, the objects of it being generally employed in public works, as the galley-slaves are in *France*. Consequently this kind of slavery is not liable to the principal objections, which occur against slavery in general. Upon the whole of his controversy concerning slavery, I think myself warranted in saying, that the justice and lawfulness of every species of it, *as it is generally constituted,* except the limited one founded on the commission of crimes against civil society, is at least doubtful; that if in any case lawful, such circumstances are necessary to make it so, as seldom concur, and therefore render a just commencement of it barely possible; and that the oppressive manner in which it has generally commenced, the cruel means necessary to enforce its continuance, and the mischiefs ensuing from the permission of it, furnish very strong presumptions against its justice, and at all events evince the humanity and policy of those states, in which the use of it is no longer tolerated.

But however reasonable it may be to doubt the justice of domestic slavery, however convinced we may of its ill effects, it must be confessed, that the practice is ancient, and has been almost universal. Its beginning may be dated from the remotest period, in which there are any traces of the history of mankind. It commenced in the barbarous state of society, and was retained, even when men were far advanced in civilization. The nations of antiquity most famous for countenancing the system of domestic slavery were the *Jews,* the *Greeks,* the *Romans,* and the ancient *Germans;* amongst all of whom it prevailed, but in various degrees of severity. By the ancient *Germans* it was continued in the countries they over-ran; and so was transmitted to the various kingdoms and states, which arose in *Europe* out of the ruins of the *Roman* empire. At length however it fell into decline in most parts of *Europe;* and amongst the various causes, which contributed to this alteration, none were probably more effectual, than experience of the disadvantages of slavery; the difficulty of continuing it; and a persuasion that the cruelty and oppression almost necessarily incident to it were irreconcileable with the pure morality of the christian dispensation. The history of its decline in *Europe* has been traced by many eminent writers, particularly *Bodin, Albericus Gentilis, Potgiesserus,* Dr. *Robertson,* and Mr. *Millar.* It is sufficient here to say, that this great change began in *Spain,* according to *Bodin,* about the end of the eighth century, and was become general before the middle of the fourteenth century. *Bartolus,* the most famed commentator on the civil law in that period, represents slavery as in disuse; and the succeeding commentators hold much the same language. However they must be understood with many restrictions and exceptions; and not to mean, that slavery was completely and universally abolished in *Europe.* Some modern civilians, not sufficiently attending this circumstance, rather too hastily reprehend their predecessors for representing slavery as disused in *Europe.* The truth is, that the ancient species of slavery by frequent emancipations became greatly diminished in extent; the remnant of it was considerably abated in severity; the disuse of the practice of enslaving captives taken in the wars between christian powers assisted in preventing the future increase of domestic slavery; and in some countries of *Europe,* particularly *England,* a still more effectual method, which I shall explain hereafter, was thought of to perfect the suppression of it. Such was the expiring state of domestic slavery in *Europe* at the commencement of the sixteenth century, when the discovery of *America* and of the western and eastern coasts of *Africa* gave occasion to the introduction of a new species of slavery. It took its rise from the *Portuguese,* who, in order to supply the Spaniards with persons able to sustain the fatigue of cultivating their new possessions in *America,* particularly the islands, opened a trade between *Africa* and *America* for the sale of negro slaves. This disgraceful commerce in the human species is said to have begun in the year 1508, when the first importation of negro slaves was made into *Hispaniola* from the *Portuguese* settlements on the western coasts of *Africa.* In 1540 the emperor *Charles* the fifth endeavoured to stop the progress of the negro slavery, by orders that all slaves in the *American* isles should be made free; and they were accordingly manumitted by the governor of the country, on condition of continuing to labour for their masters. But this attempt proved unsuccessful, and on *Lagasca's* return to *Spain* domestic slavery revived and flourished as before. The expedient of having slaves for labour in *America* was not long peculiar to the *Spaniards;* being afterwards adopted by the other *Europeans,* as they acquired possessions there. In consequence of this general practice, negroes are become a very considerable article in the commerce between *Africa* and *America;* and domestic slavery has taken so deep a root in most of our own *American* colonies, as well as in those of other nations, that there is little probability of ever seeing it generally suppressed.

Here I conclude my observations on domestic slavery in general. I have exhibited a view of its nature, of its bad tendency, of its origin, of the arguments for and against its justice, of its decline in *Europe,* and the introduction of a new slavery by the *European* nations into their *American* colonies. I shall now examine the attempt to obtrude this new slavery into *England.* And here it will be material to observe that if on the declension of slavery in this and other countries of *Europe* where it is discountenanced, no means had been devised to obstruct the admission of a *new* slavery, it would have been vain and fruitless to have attempted superseding the *ancient* species. But I hope to prove, that our ancestors at least were not so short-sighted; and that long and uninterrupted usage has established rules, as effectual to prevent the revival of slavery as their humanity was successful in once suppressing it. I shall endeavour to shew, that the law of *England* never recognized any species of domestic slavery, except the *ancient* one of *villenage* [3] now expired, and has sufficiently provided against the introduction of a *new* slavery under the name of *villenage* or any other denomination whatever. . . .

Colonel Washington of the Virginia Militia Reports a Skirmish, 1754

In the spring of 1754, the governor of Virginia sent Lieutenant-Colonel George Washington with a small force to reconnoiter French military activity around the confluence of the Allegheny, Monongahela, and Ohio rivers.

Washington had earlier visited the area and recognized the excellent site for a fort on the point at the confluence (today, Pittsburgh, Pennsylvania). A small group of Virginia colonists under Captain Trent were already in occupation of the point when a French force arrived and compelled their withdrawal. The French commenced to build Fort Duquesne, the keystone of a line of forts stretching across the Ohio country to prevent English colonial penetration of the area. What happened next is recounted by Washington in dispatches to Governor Din-

[3] Serfdom. — T. G. B.

widdie and in letters to others. *Washington played the French game of using Indian allies to support and assist him, but to no avail. Having withdrawn from the skirmish with the French to "Great Meadow," he built a crude palisade, aptly dubbed Fort Neccessity, to await the French attack. After an adequate show of honorable resistance, he surrendered the fort on July 4, 1754, and returned to Virginia.*

To Governor Dinwiddie

Will's Creek, 15 April, 1754

Honble. Sir,

Captain Trent's ensign, Mr. Ward, has this day arrived from the Fork of the Monongahela, and brings the disagreeable account, that the fort, on the 17th instant, was surrendered at the summons of Monsieur Contrecoeur to a body of French, consisting of upwards of one thousand men, who came from Venango with eighteen pieces of cannon, sixty batteaux, and three hundred canoes. They gave him liberty to bring off all his men and working-tools, which he accordingly did the same day.

Immediately upon this information I called a council of war, to advise on proper measures to be taken in this exigency. A copy of their resolves, with the proceedings, I herewith enclose by the bearer, whom I have continued express to your Honor for more minute intelligence.

Mr. Ward has the summons with him, and a speech from the Half-King, which I also enclose, with the wampum. He is accompanied by one of the Indians mentioned therein, who were sent to see where we were, what was our strength, and to know the time to expect us out. The other young man I have prevailed upon to return to the Half-King with the following speech:

> Sachems, Warriors of the Six United Nations, Shawanese, and Delawares, our friends and brethren. I received your speech by the Buck's brother [Mr. Ward], who came to us with the two young men five sleeps after leaving you. We return you thanks from hearts glowing with affection for your steadfast adherence to us, for your kind speech, and for your wise counsels and directions to the Buck's brother.
>
> The young man will inform you where he met a small part of our army advancing towards you, clearing the road for a great number of our warriors, who are immediately to follow with our great guns, our ammunition, and our provisions.

From *The Writings of George Washington*, vol. 1, ed. W. C. Ford (New York, 1889), pp. 52–54. Reprinted by permission of G. P. Putnam's Sons.

I could not delay to let you know our hearts, and have sent back one of the young men with this speech to acquaint you with them. I have sent the other, according to your desire, to the governor of Virginia, with the Buck's brother, to deliver your speech and wampum, and to be an eyewitness of the preparations we are making to come in haste to support you, whose interest is as dear to us as our lives. We resent the usage of the treacherous French, and our conduct will henceforth plainly show you how much we have it at heart.

I cannot be easy without seeing you before our forces meet at the fork of the roads, and therefore I have the greatest desire that you and Escruniat, or one of you, should meet me on the road as soon as possible to assist us in council.

To assure you of the good will we bear you, and to confirm the truth of what has been said, I herewith present to you a string of wampum, that you may thereby remember how much I am your brother and friend.

I hope my proceedings in these affairs will be satisfactory to your Honor, as I have, to the utmost of my knowledge, consulted the interest of the expedition and good of my country; whose rights, while they are asserted in so just a cause, I will defend to the last remains of life. . . .

To Colonel Joshua Fry

23 May, 1754

Sir,

This day I returned from my discoveries down the Youghiogany, which, I am sorry to say, can never be made navigable. We traced the watercourse near thirty miles, with the full expectation of succeeding in the much desired aim; but, at length, we came to a fall, which continued rough, rocky, and scarcely passable, for two miles, and then fell, within the space of fifty yards, nearly forty feet perpendicular.

As I apprehended there would be difficulty in these waters, I sent the soldiers forward upon the road, when I left the camp, which was as soon as they could cross; therefore, no time has been lost; but the roads are so exceedingly bad, that we proceed very slow.

By concurring intelligence, which we received from the Indians, the French are not above seven or eight hundred strong, and by a late account we are informed, that one half of them were detached in the night, without even the Indians' knowledge, on some secret expedition; but the truth of this, though it is affirmed by an Indian lately from their fort, I cannot yet vouch for, nor tell where they are bound. . . .

From *The Writings of George Washington*, vol. 1, ed. W. C. Ford (New York, 1889), p. 68. Reprinted by permission of G. P. Putnam's Sons.

To Governor Dinwiddie

From our Camp at the Great Meadows, 29 May, 1754

Honble. Sir,

In answering your Honor's letter of ye 25th by Mr. Burney, I shall begin with assuring you, that nothing was farther from my intention than to recede, tho I then pressed, and still desire, that my services may be voluntary, rather than on the present pay. . . . [Colonel Washington complains for another five pages about his and his troops' pay being less than that of British regulars in the expedition.

Almost casually, he goes on to relate that on 27 May] I set out with forty men before ten, and [it] was from that time till near sunrise before we reached the Indians' camp, having marched in [a] small path, through a heavy rain, and night as dark as it is possible to conceive. We were frequently tumbling one over another, and often so lost, that fifteen or twenty minutes' search would not find the path again.

When we came to the Half-King, I counselled with him, and got his assent to go hand-in-hand and strike the French. Accordingly, himself, Monacatoocha, and a few other Indians set out with us; and when we came to the place where the tracks were, the Half-King sent two Indians to follow their tracks, and discover their lodgement, which they did about half a mile from the road, in a very obscure place surrounded with rocks. I thereupon, in conjunction with the Half-King and Monacatoocha, formed a disposition to attack them on all sides, which we accordingly did, and, after an engagement of about fifteen minutes, we killed ten, wounded one, and took twenty-one prisoners. Amongst those that were killed was Monsieur Jumonville, the commander; principal officers taken is Monsieur Drouillon and Mons'r La Force, who your Honour has often heard me speak of as a bold enterprising man, and a person of great subtlety and cunning. With these are two cadets. These officers pretend they were coming on an embassy; but the absurdity of this pretext is too glaring, as your Honour will see by the Instructions and Summons enclosed. These instructions were to reconnoitre the country, roads, creeks, &c., to Potomack, which they were about to do. These enterprising men were purposely choose out to get intelligence, which they were to send back by some brisk despatches, with mention of the day that they were to serve the summons; which could be through no other view, than to get a sufficient reinforcement to fall upon us immediately after. This, with several other reasons, induced all the officers to believe firmly, that they were sent as spies, rather than any thing else, and has occasioned my sending them as prisoners, tho they expected, or at least had some faint hope, of being continued as ambassadors. . . . In this engagement we

From *The Writings of George Washington*, vol. 1, ed. W. C. Ford (New York, 1889), pp. 76–77, 82–83, 85–87. Reprinted by permission of G. P. Putnam's Sons.

had only one man killed and two or three wounded, among which was Lieutenant Waggener slightly — a most miraculous escape, as our right wing was much exposed to their fire and received it all. The Half-King received your Honour's speech very kind, but desired me to inform you, that he could not leave his people at this time, thinking them in great danger. He is now gone to the Crossing for their families, to bring to our camp; and desired I would send some men and horses to assist them up, which I have accordingly done; sent 30 men and upwards of twenty horses. . . .

As these [1] runners went off to the fort [2] on Sunday last, I shall expect every hour to be attacked, and by unequal numbers, which I must withstand if there are five to one; or else I fear the consequence will be, that we shall lose the Indians, if we suffer ourselves to be drove back. I despatched an express immediately to Colonel Fry with this intelligence, desiring him to send reinforcements with all imaginable despatch.

Your Honor may depend I will not be surprised, let them come at what hour they will; and this is as much as I can promise. But my best endeavours shall not be wanting to deserve more. I doubt not, but if you hear I am beaten, but you will, at the same [time] hear that we have done our duty, in fighting as long [as] there was a possibility of hope.

I have sent Lieutenant West, accompanied with Mr. Splitdorph and a guard of 20 men, to conduct the prisoners in, and I believe the officers have acquainted him what answer to return your Honour. Monsieur La Force and Monsieur Drouillon beg to be recommended to your Honour's notice, and I have promised they will meet with all the favour due to imprisoned officers. I have show'd all the respect I could to them here, and have given some necessary cloathing, by which I have disfurnished myself; for, having brought no more than two or three shirts from Will's Creek, that we might be light, I was ill provided to furnish them. I am, &c.

P.S. I have neither seen nor heard any particular account of the Twigtwees since I came on these waters. We have already begun a palisadoed fort, and hope to have it up to-morrow. I must beg leave to acquaint your Honour, that Captain Vanbraam and Ensign Peyrouny has behaved extremely well since they came out, and I hope will meet with your Honour's favor.

[1] Two French. — T. G. B.
[2] Duquesne. — T. G. B.

To His Brother

Camp at Great Meadow, 31 May, 1754

Since my last we arrived at this place, where three days ago we had an engagement with the French, that is, a party of our men with one of theirs. Most of our men were out upon other detachments, so that I had scarcely 40 men remaining under my command, and about 10 or 12 Indians; nevertheless we obtained a most signal victory. The battle lasted about 10 or 13 minutes, with sharp firing on both sides, till the French gave ground and ran, but to no great purpose. There were 12 of the French killed, among whom was Mons. de Jumonville, their commander, and 21 taken prisoners, among whom are Mess. La Force and Drouillon, together with two cadets. I have sent them to his honour the Governor, at Winchester, under a guard of 20 men, conducted by Lieutenant West. We had but one man killed, and two or three wounded. Among the wounded on our side was Lieutenant Waggener, but no danger, it is hoped, will ensue. We expect every hour to be attacked by superior force, but, if they forbear one day longer, we shall be prepared for them. We have already got entrenchments, and are about a pallisado, which I hope will be finished to-day. The Mingoes have struck the French and I hope will give a good blow before they have done. I expect 40 odd of them here to-night, which, with our fort and some reinforcements from Col. Fry, will enable us to exert our noble courage with spirit.

P.S. I fortunately escaped without any wound, for the right wing, where I stood, was exposed to and received all the enemy's fire, and it was the part where the man was killed, and the rest wounded. I heard the bullets whistle, and, believe me, there is something charming in the sound.

From *The Writings of George Washington,* vol. 1, ed. W. C. Ford (New York, 1889), pp. 89–90. Reprinted by permission of G. P. Putnam's Sons.

SCIENCE: THE SEARCH FOR ORDER
Chapter 6

"Their first purpose was no more than only the satisfaction of breathing a freer air, and of conversing in quiet one with another, without being ingag'd in the passions and madness of that dismal age." Thus Bishop Sprat described the coming together in Oxford in the 1650's of the "virtuous and learned men" who would found the Royal Society of England in 1662. The "dismal age" was of course the period of the English civil wars, for Englishmen, though it might as well have been the Thirty Years' War for Europeans generally, or the Fronde for Frenchmen. Sprat's remark points to the stormy political backdrop against which there emerged one of the intellectually most creative epochs in history, the two generations of scientific endeavor from 1650 to 1720 that have been called the "scientific revolution." The term itself requires a gloss. "Scientific" cannot be confined to the work in the natural sciences only, though they — especially physics — were the pacesetters. Development in the social sciences was more uneven but it was just slightly less productive and original. "Science" is best understood in its traditional Latin root of *scientia,* knowledge. As for "revolution," the qualities of precipitateness, suddenness, and massive new departures that are usually connoted by the word are not so marked in the intellectual developments of the epoch. The foundations went back at least as far as the early sixteenth century, and the threshold for the spurt forward from 1650 to 1720 was the solid achievement of the preceding half-century of intellectual endeavor. Newton's gracious bow to the "giants" upon whose shoulders he stood was neither false modesty nor academic conventionalism; it was a statement of fact.

In two ways the "dismal age" of Europe, the early seventeenth century, contributed to the intellectual flowering of the second half of the century. First, dissonance and disorder in politics and society moved men of intelligence and sensitivity to seek order, especially order under law. Much of this quest operated at the level of the provocation itself, in jurisprudence and history, political theory and theology. Much of it was directed toward understanding the "natural laws," which had long been postulated as universally binding but which received direct applicability to physical phenomena in a systematic way only with Descartes. In the seventeenth century, law in all its forms became something of a panacea to the most extreme and unquestioning of its admirers; as a notion it was ubiquitous even among the most critical and perceptive intellects. Second, as individual spirits in hope of order recoiled from the brutality, meanness, and destructiveness of passion, they sought the company of like-minded men of reason in a mutually sustaining confederation of intellects. The great age of 1650 to 1720 was great not merely because of the commanding genius of a Newton or Leibniz but because of the community of intellect that gathered up the efforts and commitments of a myriad of lesser minds in a wide diversity of interests in search of knowledge and a rational meaning for man and matter. This was the age of virtuosi, men of extraordinary capacity because of the accident of individual ability, and of extraordinary curiosity and confidence because of the community of intellect to which they gave a primary allegiance. Thomas Sprat's description of the early Royal Society depicts a unique institution in the history of man's search for knowledge.

Sir Isaac Newton (1642–1727) was, as his French contemporary Fontenelle wrote, "revered to so great a degree that death could not procure him new honours, and he himself saw his own apotheosis." His achievement was worthy of the praise. In postulating gravity, Newton demonstrated that it is a single universal force that acts on heavenly bodies and terrestrial objects in motion. In the *Principia Mathematicae* (1687), Newton ordered the universe, joining the astronomical physics of Kepler and the dynamics of Galileo. Complex, couched in the theorems of classical geometry (rather than in the more manageable calculus that Newton made public only later, though he appears to have used it to work out and test the theorems), and bulky, the *Principia* challenged the scientific community for a half-century and finally displaced Descartes's theories as the commanding explanation of the physical world. Newtonian mechanics, the most enduring scientific work of the post-Copernican age, remained unchallenged until the twentieth century.

Newton's other contributions, the calculus (an honor shared with Leibniz) and his theoretical and practical work in optics, were hardly less significant. Yet the order of their magnitude is closer to the labor of other figures in the epoch's endeavor in the natural sciences. Robert Boyle laid the foundations of modern chemistry and William Harvey, Jan Swammerdam, and Anton van Leeuwenhoek accomplished the transition from the statics of anatomy to the dynamics of physiology in the study of the biological form. Significantly, biology and geology remained the preserve of the naturalist rather than of a theoretical genius such as Newton — Darwin was almost two centuries away. Spurred by the Cartesian conception of man as a machine, both Locke and Leibniz made fundamental though opposing constructs of the operation of the human mind. Their work remained epistemology (the philosophy of knowledge) rather than psychology, and their mechanistic conception of the operation of the human mind, derived from their physics, hindered the development of modern psychology.

The problem faced by the virtuosi of the social sciences was essentially the same as that of the naturalists: a great deal of data largely unclassified or otherwise poorly arranged. Systematization was the order of the day, and in economics it progressed far enough in the work of men such as Sir William Petty to constitute the foundation of modern economics. Petty's contributions were both to the theory of economics, particularly the labor theory of value, and to the methodology of the discipline, especially in comparative social statistics as a science. Although Petty had no developed social theory, his work abounds in brilliant social insights, observational and empirical rather than conventional and derivative as in Bacon.

As in economics, so too in history was there an abundance of unclassified data. The first stage of economics — systematization of the data — was, however, the second stage in history and came only in the late eighteenth century. Indeed, history almost did not survive the first stage: the critical dismantling of previous historical authority. The demolition was done by Pierre Bayle in the *Historical and Critical Dictionary* (1697). The authority dismantled was less secular history than the Christian pseudo-historical construct derived from the literal interpretation of Scripture and the uncritical acceptance of dogma. Bayle's disclaimer that his work "can do no prejudice to Religion" was philosophically valid, but his work effectually proved to be highly prejudicial to accepted orthodoxy, which faced the necessity of an accommodation to the new knowledge of the physical world raised by Newtonian mechanics and the conversion of God from the Final Cause into merely the First Cause in the "natural religion" of Newton and his contemporaries.

Science, represented in the accomplishments of the virtuosi, by the second decade of the eighteenth century had become the new order of the European intellect. Its successors and imitators were the philosophes of the Enlightenment. Like the stereotypical heir, there was something prodigal, insensitive, and uncreative about the way some of the philosophes employed their inheritance.

The Virtuosi Found the Royal Society

Thomas Sprat studied at Wadham College at Oxford in the 1650's, under its head John Wilkins and thereby was a member of the circle he describes as the founders of the Royal Society of London for Improving Natural Knowledge, chartered by Charles II shortly after the Restoration. Tolerance, commitment, balance between pure and applied science, a certain functional egalitarianism, comprehensiveness of interest — all the marks of the virtuosi — are reflected in this excerpt from Sprat's history of the Society.

Thomas Sprat's *History of the Royal Society*

It was therefore some Space after the End of the Civil Wars at *Oxford,* in Doctor [1] *Wilkins* his Lodgings, in *Wadham College,* which was then the Place of Resort for virtuous and learned Men, that the first Meetings were made, which laid the Foundation of all this that follow'd. The *University* had at that time many Members of its own, who had begun a *free way* of Reasoning; and was also frequented by some *Gentlemen* of Philosophical Minds, whom the Misfortunes of the Kingdom, and the Security and Ease of a Retirement amongst Gown-men, had drawn thither.

Their first Purpose was no more than only the Satisfaction of breathing a freer Air, and of conversing in Quiet one with another, without being ingag'd in the Passions and Madness of that dismal Age. And from the Institution of that *Assembly,* it had been enough if no other Advantage had come but this: That by this means there was a Race of young Men provided against the next Age, whose Minds receiving from them their first Impressions of *sober* and *generous Knowledge,* were invincibly arm'd against all the Inchantments of *Enthusiasm.* But what is more, I may venture to affirm, that it was in good Measure by the Influence which these Gentlemen had over the rest, that the *University* it self, or at least, any Part of its Discipline and Order, was sav'd from Ruin. And from hence we may conclude, that the same Men have now no Intention of sweeping away all the Honor of Antiquity in this their new Design; seeing they imploy'd so much of their Labor and Prudence in preserving that *most venerable Seat* of ancient Learning, when their shrinking from its Defence would have been the speediest Way to have destroy'd it. For

---

From Thomas Sprat, *History of the Royal Society of London for the Improving of Natural Knowledge,* 3d ed. (London, 1722), pp. 53–55, 61–68.

[1] John. — T. G. B.

the Truth of this, I dare appeal to all uninterested Men, who knew the Temper of that Place; and especially to those who were my own Cotemporaries there; of whom I can name very many, whom the happy Restoration of the Kingdom's Peace found as well inclin'd to serve their *Prince* and the *Church,* as if they had been bred up in the most prosperous Condition of their Country. This was undoubtedly so: Nor indeed could it be otherwise; for such *Spiritual Frensies,* which did then bear Rule, can never stand long, before a clear and a *deep Skill* in *Nature.* It is almost impossible, that they, who converse much with the Subtilty of *Things,* should be deluded by such *thick Deceits.* There is but one better Charm in the World, than *real Philosophy,* to allay the Impulses of the *false Spirit;* and that is, the blessed Presence and Assistance of the *true.*

Nor were the good Effects of this Conversation only confin'd to *Oxford:* But they have made themselves known in their printed Works, both in our own, and in the learned Language; which have much conduc'd to the Fame of our Nation *abroad,* and to the spreading of profitable Light *at home.* This, I trust, will be universally acknowledg'd, when I shall have nam'd the Men. The principal and most constant of them were Doctor *Seth Ward,* then Lord Bishop of *Exeter,* Mr.[2] *Boyle,* Dr. *Wilkins,* Sir *William Petty,* Mr. *Matthew Wren,* Dr. *Wallis,* Dr. *Goddard,* Dr. *Willis,* Dr. *Bathurst,* Dr. *Christopher Wren,* Mr. *Rook,* besides several others, who join'd themselves to them, upon Occasions. . . .

I will here, in the first place, contract into few Words, the whole *Sum* of their *Resolutions;* which I shall often have occasion to touch upon in *Parcels.* Their Purpose is, in short, to make faithful *Records* of all the Works of *Nature,* or *Art,* which can come within their Reach; that so the present Age, and Posterity, may be able to put a Mark on the Errors, which have been strengthened by long Prescription; to restore the Truths, that have lain neglected; to push on those, which are already known, to more various Uses; and to make the way more passable, to what remains unreveal'd. This is the Compass of their Design. And to accomplish this, they endeavour'd, to separate the Knowledge of *Nature,* from the Colours of *Rhetorick,* the Devices of *Fancy,* or the delightful Deceit of *Fables.* They have labor'd to inlarge it, from being confin'd to the Custody of a few, or from Servitude to private Interests. They have striven to preserve it from being over-press'd by a confus'd Heap of vain and useless Particulars; or from being streitghned and bound too much up by general Doctrines. They have tried to put it into a Condition of perpetual Increasing; by settling an inviolable Correspondence between the Hand and the Brain. They have studied, to make it not only an Enterprise of one Season, or of some lucky Opportunity; but a Business of Time; a steady, a lasting, a popular, an uninterrupted Work. They have attempted, to free it from the Artifice, and Humors, and Passions of Sects;

2 Robert. — T. G. B.

to render it an Instrument, whereby Mankind may obtain a Dominion over *Things,* and not only over one another's *Judgments:* And lastly, they have begun to establish these Reformations in Philosophy, not so much, by any solemnity of Laws, or Ostentation of Ceremonies, as by solid Practice and Examples; not by a glorious Pomp of Words; but by the silent, effectual, and unanswerable Arguments of real Productions. . . .

As for what belongs to the *Members* themselves that are to constitute the *Society:* It is to be noted, that they have freely admitted Men of different Religions, Countries, and Professions of Life. This they were oblig'd to do, or else they would come far short of the Largeness of their own Declarations. For they openly profess, not to lay the Foundation of an *English, Scotch, Irish, Popish,* or *Protestant* Philosophy; but a Philosophy of *Mankind.*

By their *naturalizing* Men of all Countries, they have laid the Beginnings of many great Advantages for the future. For by this Means, they will be able, to settle a *constant Intelligence,* throughout all civil Nations, and make the *Royal Society* the general *Bank* and Free-port of the World: A Policy, which whether it would hold good in the *Trade* of *England,* I know not; but sure it will in the *Philosophy.* We are to overcome the Mysteries of all the Workers of Nature; and not only to prosecute such as are confin'd to one Kingdom, or beat upon one Shore: We should not then refuse to list all the Aids, that will come in, how remote soever. . . .

By their Admission of Men of all *Professions,* these *two* Benefits arise: The *one,* that every *Art,* and every Way of Life already establish'd, may be secure of receiving no Damage by their Counsels. A Thing which all new Inventions ought carefully to consult. . . . But the other Benefit is, that by this equal Balance of all Professions, there will no one Particular of them overweigh the other, or make the *Oracle* only speak their *private* Sense; which else it were impossible to avoid. It is natural to all Ranks of Men, to have some one Darling, upon which their care is chiefly fix'd. If *Mechanicks* alone were to make a Philosophy, they would bring it all into their Shops, and force it wholly to consist of Springs, and Wheels, and Weights; if *Physicians,* they would not depart far from their Art; scarce any Thing would be consider'd, besides the *Body of Man,* the *Causes, Signs,* and *Cures* of Diseases. So much is to be found in Men of all Conditions, of that which is call'd *Pedantry* in Scholars; which is nothing else but an obstinate Addiction to the Forms of some private Life, and not regarding general Things enough. This Freedom therefore, which they use, in embracing all Assistance, is not advantageous to them; which is the more remarkable, in that they diligently search out, and join to them, all extraordinary Men, though but of ordinary Trades. And that they are likely to continue this comprehensive Temper hereafter, I will shew by one Instance; and it is the Recommendation which the

King[3] himself was pleased to make, of the judicious Author of *the Observations on the Bills of Mortality:* In whose Election, it was so far from being a Prejudice, that he was a Shop keeper of *London;*[4] that his Majesty gave this particular Charge to his Society, that if they found any more such Tradesmen, they should be sure to admit them all, without any more ado. From hence it may be concluded, what is their Inclination towards the manual Arts; by the careful Regard which their *Founder* and *Patron,* has engag'd them to have for all Sorts of *Mechanick Artists.*

But, though the *Society* entertains very many Men of *particular Professions,* yet the far greater Number are *Gentlemen,* free and unconfin'd. By the Help of this there was hopeful Provision made against *two Corruptions* of Learning, which have been long complain'd of, but never remov'd: The *one,* that *Knowledge* still degenerates to consult *present Profit* too soon; the *other,* that *Philosophers* have been always *Masters* and *Scholars;* some imposing, and all the other submitting; and not as equal Observers without Dependence.

The first of these may be call'd, the *marrying* of *Arts too soon;* and putting them to Generation before they come to be of Age; and has been the Cause of much Inconvenience. It weakens their Strength; it makes an unhappy Disproportion in their Increase; while not the *best,* but the *most gainful* of them flourish: But above all, it diminishes that very Profit for which Men strive. It busies them about possessing some petty Prize; while Nature it self, with all its mighty Treasures, slips from them. . . .

The second Error, which is hereby endeavour'd to be remedied, is, that the Seats of Knowledge have been for the most part heretofore, not *Laboratories,* as they ought to be; but only *Schools,* where some have *taught,* and all the rest *subscrib'd.* The Consequences of this are very mischievous. For first, as many *Learners* as there are, so many Hands and Brains may still be reckon'd upon as useless. It being only the *Master's* part to examine, and observe; and the Disciples, to submit with Silence to what they conclude. But besides this, the very Inequality of the Titles of *Teachers* and *Scholars,* does very much suppress and tame Men's Spirits; which though it should be proper for Discipline and Education; yet is by no means consistent with a free philosophical Consultation. . . .

---

[3] Charles II. — T. G. B.
[4] John Graunt (1620–1674); *Observations on the Bills of Mortality,* 1661. — T. G. B.

Newton Orders the Universe

The Principia Mathematicae *is peculiarly intractable for editorial and excerpting purposes. The few pages provided here reproduce four rules "of reasoning in philosophy" (science), which precede the Third Book, and the "General Scholium" (an additional note on the whole subject), which follows the Third Book. Neither is of the substance of the Third Book, which develops the Newtonian conception of the universe, but both do reflect the main ideas propounded there. These selections provide as much insight into Newton's scientific method as can be readily obtained. In his methodology, Newton, the perfecter of Galileo's methodology, stands in bold contrast to Descartes and his disciples. In another context, Newton had set out the three steps of his method: (1) investigate properties of things, (2) establish them by experimentation, and (3) seek hypotheses to explain them. Hypothesis, then, is the last stage in the process of inductive reasoning from evidence. For Newton it is the opposite of the Cartesian hypothesis, which Newton rejects in Rule IV and in the next to the last paragraph in the General Scholium as either an explicit fiction to evade experiment or an objection to experimentally founded laws derived by deduction from first principles not established inductively. Newton did not, as the Cartesians accused him, interest himself only with description of and prediction from phenomena; he was equally interested in explaining phenomena, but only by as rigid an inductive method as he used to determine the "laws" of phenomena.*

Rules of Reasoning in Philosophy

RULE I

We are to admit no more causes of natural things than such as are both true and sufficient to explain their appearances.

To this purpose the philosophers say that Nature does nothing in vain, and more is in vain, when less will serve; for Nature is pleased with simplicity, and affects not the pomp of superfluous causes.

RULE II

Therefore to the same natural effects we must, as far as possible, assign the same causes.

From Sir Isaac Newton, *Mathematical Principles of Natural Philosophy*, vol. 2, trans. Andrew Motte (London, 1729), pp. 202–05.

As to respiration in a man and in a beast; the descent of stones in *Europe* and in *America;* the light of our culinary fire and of the Sun; the reflection of light in the Earth, and in the Planets.

RULE III

The qualities of bodies, which admit neither intensification nor remission of degrees, and which are found to belong to all bodies within the reach of our experiments, are to be esteemed the universal qualities of all bodies whatsoever.

For since the qualities of bodies are only known to us by experiments, we are to hold for universal all such as universally agree with experiments; and such as are not liable to diminution can never be quite taken away. We are certainly not to relinquish the evidence of experiments for the sake of dreams and vain fictions of our own devising; nor are we to recede from the analogy of Nature, which uses [1] to be simple, and always consonant to itself. We no other way know the extension of bodies, than by our senses, nor do these reach it in all bodies; but because we perceive extension in all that are sensible, therefore we ascribe it universally to all others also. That abundance of bodies are hard, we learn by experience. And because the hardness of the whole arises from the hardness of the parts, we therefore justly infer the hardness of the undivided particles not only of the bodies we feel but of all others. That all bodies are impenetrable, we gather not from reason, but from sensation. The bodies which we handle we find impenetrable, and thence conclude impenetrability to be an universal property of all bodies whatsoever. That all bodies are movable, and endowed with certain powers (which we call the *vires inertiae*) of persevering in their motion, or in their rest, we only infer from the like properties observed in the bodies which we have seen. The extension, hardness, impenetrability, mobility, and *vis inertiae* of the whole, result from the extension, hardness, impenetrability, mobility, and *vires inertiae* of the parts; and thence we conclude the least particles of all bodies to be also all extended, and hard and impenetrable, and movable, and endowed with their proper *vires inertiae*. And this is the foundation of all philosophy. Moreover, that the divided but contiguous particles of bodies may be separated from one another, is matter of observation; and, in the particles that remain undivided, our minds are able to distinguish yet lesser parts, as is mathematically demonstrated. But whether the parts so distinguished, and not yet divided, may, by the powers of Nature, be actually divided and separated from one another, we cannot certainly determine. Yet, had we the proof of but one experiment that any undivided particle, in breaking a hard and solid body, suffered

---

[1] That is, is wont. — T. G. B.

a division, we might by virtue of this rule conclude that the undivided as well as the divided particles may be divided and actually separated to infinity.

Lastly, if it universally appears, by experiments and astronomical observations, that all bodies about the Earth gravitate towards the Earth, and that in proportion to the quantity of matter which they severally contain; that the Moon likewise, according to the quantity of its matter, gravitates toward the Earth; that, on the other hand, our Sea gravitates towards the Moon; and all the Planets mutually one towards another; and the Comets in like manner towards the Sun; we must, in consequence of this rule, universally allow that all bodies whatsoever are endowed with a principle of mutual gravitation. For the argument from the appearances concludes with more force for the universal gravitation of all bodies than for their impenetrability; of which, among those in the celestial regions, we have no experiments, nor any manner of observation. Not that I affirm gravity to be essential to bodies. By their *vis insita* I mean nothing but their *vis inertiae*. This is immutable. Their gravity is diminished as they recede from the Earth.

RULE IV

In experimental philosophy we are to look upon propositions inferred by general induction from phenomena as accurately or very nearly true, notwithstanding any contrary hypotheses that may be imagined, till such time as other phenomena occur, by which they may either be made more accurate, or liable to exceptions.

This rule we must follow, that the argument of induction may not be evaded by hypotheses.

General Scholium

The hypothesis of Vortices is pressed with many difficulties. That every Planet by a radius drawn to the Sun may describe areas proportional to the times of description, the periodic times of the several parts of the Vortices should observe the duplicate proportion [1] of their distances from the Sun; but that the periodic times of the Planets may obtain the sesquiplicate proportion [2] of their distances from the Sun, the periodic times of the parts of the Vortex ought to be as the sesquiplicate proportion of

From Sir Isaac Newton, *Mathematical Principles of Natural Philosophy*, vol. 2, trans. Andrew Motte (London, 1729), pp. 387–93.
 [1] That is, the square of the distances. — T. G. B.
 [2] That is the 3/2th power. — T. G. B.

Isaac Newton

their distances. That the smaller Vortices may maintain their lesser revolutions about Saturn, Jupiter, and other Planets, and swim quietly and undisturbed in the greater Vortex of the Sun, the periodic times of the parts of the Sun's Vortex should be equal. But the rotation of the Sun and Planets about their axes, which ought to correspond with the motions of their Vortices, recede far from all these proportions. The motions of the Comets are exceeding regular, are governed by the same laws with the motions of the planets, and can by no means be accounted for by the hypothesis of Vortices. For Comets are carried with very eccentric motions through all parts of the heavens indifferently, with a freedom that is incompatible with the notion of a Vortex.

Bodies projected in our air suffer no resistance but from the air. Withdraw the air, as is done in Mr. *Boyle*'s vacuum, and the resistance ceases. For in this void a bit of fine down and a piece of solid gold descend with equal velocity. And parity of reason must take place in the celestial spaces above the Earth's atmosphere; in which spaces, where there is no air to resist their motions, all bodies will move with the greatest freedom; and the Planets and Comets will constantly pursue their revolutions in orbits given in kind and position, according to the laws above explained. But though these bodies may, indeed, persevere in their orbits by the mere laws of gravity, yet they could by no means have at first derived the regular position of the orbits themselves from those laws.

The six primary Planets are revolved about the Sun in circles concentric with the Sun, and with motions directed towards the same parts, and almost in the same plane. Ten moons are revolved about the Earth, Jupiter, and Saturn, in circles concentric with them, with the same direction of motion, and nearly in the planes of the orbits of those Planets. But it is not to be conceived that mere mechanical causes could give birth to so many regular motions, since the Comets range over all parts of the heavens in very eccentric orbits. For by that kind of motion they pass easily through the orbs of the Planets, and with great rapidity; and in their aphelions, where they move the slowest, and are detained the longest, they recede to the greatest distance from each other, and thence suffer the least disturbance from their mutual attractions. This most beautiful System of the Sun, Planets, and Comets, could only proceed from the counsel and dominion of an intelligent and powerful being. And if the fixed Stars are the centres of other like systems, these being formed by the like wise counsel, must be all subject to the dominion of One; especially since the light of the fixed Stars is of the same nature with the light of the Sun, and from every system light passes into all the other systems: and lest the systems of the fixed Stars should, by their gravity, fall on each other, he hath placed those Systems at immense distances from one another.

This Being governs all things, not as the soul of the world, but as Lord over all; and on account of his dominion he is wont to be called

Lord God παντοκράτωρ,[3] or *Universal Ruler;* for *God* is a relative word, and has a respect to servants; and *Deity* is the dominion of God, not over his own body, as those imagine who fancy God to be the soul of the world, but over servants. The supreme God is a Being eternal, infinite, absolutely perfect; but a being, however perfect, without dominion, cannot be said to be Lord God; for we say, my God, your God, the God of *Israel,* the God of Gods, and Lord of Lords; but we do not say, my Eternal, your Eternal, the Eternal of *Israel,* the Eternal of God; we do not say, my Infinite, or my Perfect: these are titles which have no respect to servants. The word God usually signifies *Lord;* but every lord is not a God. It is the dominion of a spiritual being which constitutes a God; a true, supreme, or imaginary dominion makes a true, supreme or imaginary God. And from his true dominion it follows that the true God is a Living, Intelligent, and Powerful Being; and, from his other perfections, that he is Supreme, or most Perfect. He is Eternal and Infinite, Omnipotent and Omniscient; that is, his duration reaches from Eternity to Eternity; his presence from Infinity to Infinity; he governs all things, and knows all things that are or can be done. He is not Eternity and Infinity, but Eternal and Infinite; he is not Duration or Space, but he endures and is present. . . . We know him only by his most wise and excellent contrivances of things, and final causes; we admire him for his perfections; but we reverence and adore him on account of his dominion. For we adore him as his servants; and a God without dominion, providence, and final causes, is nothing else but Fate and Nature. Blind metaphysical necessity, which is certainly the same always and everywhere, could produce no variety of things. All that diversity of natural things which we find, suited to different times and places, could arise from nothing but the ideas and will of a Being necessarily existing. But, by way of allegory, God is said to see, to speak, to laugh, to love, to hate, to desire, to give, to receive, to rejoice, to be angry, to fight, to frame, to work, to build. For all our notions of God are taken from the ways of mankind by a certain similitude, which, though not perfect, has some likeness however. And thus much concerning God; to discourse of whom from the appearances of things, does certainly belong to Natural Philosophy.

Hitherto we have explained the phenomena of the heavens and of our sea by the power of Gravity, but have not yet assigned the cause of this power. This is certain, that it must proceed from a cause that penetrates to the very centres of the Sun and Planets, without suffering the least diminution of its force; that operates not according to the quantity of the surfaces of the particles upon which it acts (as mechanical causes use to do), but according to the quantity of the solid matter which they contain, and propagates its virtue on all sides to immense distances, decreasing

---

[3] "Lord God Almighty." — T. G. B.

always in the duplicate proportion [4] of the distances. Gravitation towards the sun is made up out of the gravitations towards the several particles of which the body of the sun is composed; and in receding from the sun decreases accurately in the duplicate proportion of the distances, as far as the orbit of Saturn, as evidently appears from the quiescence of the aphelions of the Planets; nay, and even to the remotest aphelions of the Comets, if those aphelions are also quiescent. But hitherto I have not been able to discover the cause of those properties of gravity from phenomena, and I frame no hypotheses. For whatever is not deduced from the phenomena is to be called an hypothesis; and hypotheses, whether metaphysical or physical, whether of occult qualities or mechanical, have no place in experimental philosophy. In this philosophy particular propositions are inferred from the phenomena, and afterwards rendered general by induction. Thus it was that the impenetrability, the mobility, and the impulsive force of bodies, and the laws of motion and of gravitation, were discovered. And to us it is enough that gravity does really exist, and act according to the laws which we have explained, and abundantly serves to account for all the motions of the celestial bodies, and of our sea.

And now we might add something concerning a certain most subtle Spirit which pervades and lies hid in all gross bodies; by the force and action of which Spirit, the particles of bodies mutually attract one another at near distances, and cohere, if contiguous; and electric bodies operate to greater distances, as well repelling as attracting the neighboring corpuscles; and light is emitted, reflected, refracted, inflected, and heats bodies; and all sensation is excited, and the members of animal bodies move at the command of the will, namely, by the vibrations of this Spirit, mutually propagated along the solid filaments of the nerves, from the outward organs of sense to the brain, and from the brain into the muscles. But these are things that cannot be explained in few words, nor are we furnished with that sufficiency of experiments which is required to an accurate determination and demonstration of the laws by which this electric and elastic spirit operates.

[4] That is, the inverse square of the distances. — T. G. B.

William Petty on Land Tax in Ireland

William Petty (1623–1687) was a founding member of the Royal Society and earlier, as an anatomy professor at Oxford, a member of Wilkins' circle. The dismalness of the "dismal age" was relieved for him by his fortune made in Irish lands granted Cromwell's soldiers during the 1650's. He surveyed the lands — the first scientific survey on such a scale — for a proportion of the final grants. For Petty, the value of land was measured not in acreage or even declared value of rentals; it was determined by what the land could produce, in agriculture, mining, manufacturing, and retailing. His functional interest was how to increase land values (understandably, in Ireland) and how to tax with maximum return and optimum encouragement for increased production. His A Treatise of Taxes . . . Applied to . . . Ireland *(1662) was only one of several studies, but it shows him at the height of his powers. Notice especially the "labor theory of value" in paragraphs 13 to 16.*

Value in Adversity

CHAPTER IV. OF THE SEVERAL WAYES OF TAXE, AND FIRST, OF SETTING A PART, A PROPORTION OF THE WHOLE TERRITORY FOR PUBLICK USES, IN THE NATURE OF CROWN LANDS; AND SECONDLY, BY WAY OF ASSESSEMENT, OR LAND-TAXE

But supposing, that the several causes of Publick Charge are lessened as much as may be, and that the people be well satisfied, and contented to pay their just shares of what is needfull for their Government and Protection, as also for the Honour of their Prince and Countrey: It follows now to propose the several wayes, and expedients, how the same may be most easily, speedily, and insensibly collected. . . .

2. Imagine then, a number of people, planted in a Territory, who had upon Computation concluded, that two Millions of pounds *per annum*, is necessary to the publick charges. Or rather, who going more wisely to work, had computed a twenty-fifth part of the proceed of all their Lands and Labours, were to be the *Excisium* or the part to be cut out, and laid aside for publick uses. Which proportions perhaps are fit enough to the affairs of *England*, but of that hereafter.

From William Petty, *A Treatise of Taxes and Contributions . . . Applied to . . . Ireland* (London, 1662), pp. 20–28.

3. Now the question is, how the one or the other shall be raised. The first way we propose, is, to Excize the very Land it self in kinde; that is, to cut out of the whole twenty-five Millions, which are said to be in *England* and *Wales,* as much Land *in specie,* as whereof the Rack-rent would be two Millions, *viz.* about four Millions of Acres, which is about a sixth part of the whole. . . .

4. This way in a new State would be good, being agreed upon, as it was in *Ireland,* before men had even the possession of any Land at all. . . .

5. But if the same were propounded in *England, viz.* if an aliquot part [1] of every Landlords Rent were excinded or retrenched, then those whose Rents were settled, and determined for long times to come, would chiefly bear the burthen of such an Imposition, and others have a benefit thereby. For suppose A and B have each of them a parcel of Land, of equal goodness and value; suppose also that A hath let his parcel for twenty-one years at twenty pound *per annum,* but that B is free; now there comes out a Taxe of a fifth part; hereupon B will not let under 25 pounds, that his remainder may be twenty, whereas A must be contented with sixteen neat; nevertheless the Tenants of A will sell the proceed of their bargain at the same rate, that the Tenants of B shall do. The effect of all this is; First, that the Kings fifth part of B his Farm shall be greater then before. Secondly, that the Farmer to B shall gain more then before the Taxe. Thirdly, that the Tenant or Farmer of A shall gain as much as the King and Tenant to B both. Fourthly, the Tax doth ultimately light upon the Landlord A and the Consumptioners. From whence it follows, that a Land-taxe resolves into an irregular Excize upon consumptions, that those bear it most, who least complain. And lastly, that some Landlords may gain, and onely such whose Rents are predetermined shall loose; and that doubly, *viz.* one way by the raising of their revenues, and the other by exhausting [2] the prices of provisions upon them.

6. Another way is an *Excisium* out of the Rent of Houseing, which is much more uncertain then that of Land. For an House is of a double nature, *viz.* one, wherein it is a way and means of expence; the other, as 'tis an Instrument and Tool of gain. . . . Now the way [of a] Land-taxe rates housing, as of the latter nature, but the Excize, as of the former.

7. We might sometimes adde hereunto, that housing is sometimes disproportionately taxed to discourage Building, especially upon new Foundations, thereby to prevent the growth of a City; suppose *London,* such excessive and over-grown Cities being dangerous to Monarchy, though the more secure when the supremacy is in Citizens of such places themselves, as in *Venice.*

---

[1] That is, some part contained within the whole and dividing it without a remainder. — T. G. B.

[2] "Enhancing" rather than "exhausting" makes sense; "exhausting" makes no sense in any context. — T. G. B.

8. But we say, that such checking of new Buildings signifies nothing to this purpose; forasmuch as Buildings do not encrease, until the People already have increased: but the remedy of the above mentioned dangers is to be sought in the causes of the encrease of People, the which if they can be nipt, the other work will necessarily be done. . . .

9. . . . Men are unwilling to build new houses at the charge of pulling down their old, where both the old house it self, and the ground it stands upon do make a much dearer ground-plot for a new house, and yet far less free and convenient; wherefore men build upon new free foundations, and cobble up old houses, until they become fundamentally irreparable, at which time they become either the dwelling of the Rascality, or in process of time return to waste and Gardens again, examples whereof are many even about *London*.

Now if great Cities are naturally apt to remove their Seats, I ask which way? I say, in the case of *London,* it must be Westward, because the Windes blowing near ¾ of the year from the West, the dwellings of the West end are so much the more free from the fumes, steams, and stinks of the whole Easterly Pyle; which where Seacoal is burnt is a great matter. Now if it follow from hence, that the Pallaces of the greatest men will remove Westward, it will also naturally follow, that the dwellings of others who depend upon them will creep after them. . . .

10. This digression I confess to be both impertinent to the business of Taxes, and in it self almost needless; for why should we trouble our selves what shall be five hundred years hence, not knowing what a day may bring forth; and since 'tis not unlikely, but that before that time we may be all transplanted from hence into *America,* these Countreys being overrun with Turks, and made waste, as the Seats of the famous Eastern Empires at this day are. . . .

13. Suppose a man could with his own hands plant a certain scope of Land with Corn . . . I say, that when this man hath subducted his seed out of the proceed of his Harvest, and also, what himself hath both eaten and given to others in exchange for Clothes, and other Natural necessaries; that the remainder of Corn is the natural and true Rent of the Land for that year; and the *medium* [3] of seven years, or rather of so many years as makes up the Cycle, within which Dearths and Plenties make their revolution, doth give the ordinary Rent of the Land in Corn.

14. But a further, though collaterall question may be, how much English money this Corn or Rent is worth? I answer, so much as the money, which another single man can save, within the same time, over and above his expence, if he imployed himself wholly to produce and make it; *viz.,* let another man go travel into a Countrey where is Silver, there Dig it,

---

[3] Average. — T. G. B.

William Petty

Refine it, bring it to the same place where the other man planted his Corn; Coyne it, &c. the same person, all the while of his working for Silver, gathering also food for his necessary livelihood, and procuring himself covering, &c. I say, the Silver of the one, must be esteemed of equal value with the Corn of the other: the one being perhaps twenty Ounces and the other twenty Bushels. From whence it follows, that the price of a Bushel of this Corn to be an Ounce of Silver.

15. And forasmuch as possibly there may be more Art and Hazzard in working about the Silver, then about the Corn, yet all comes to the same pass; for let a hundred men work ten years upon Corn, and the same number of men, the same time, upon Silver; I say, that the neat proceed of the Silver is the price of the whole neat proceed of the Corn, and like parts of the one, the price of like parts of the other. . . .

16. This, I say, to be the foundation of equallizing and ballancing of values; yet in the superstructures and practices hereupon, I confess there is much variety, and intricacy; of which hereafter.

17. The world measures things by Gold and Silver, but principally the latter; for there may not be two measures. . . .

18. Our Silver and Gold we call by severall names, as in *England* by pounds, shillings, and pence, all which may be called and understood by either of the three. But that which I would say upon this matter is, that all things ought to be valued by two natural Denominations, which is Land and Labour; that is, we ought to say, a Ship or garment is worth such a measure of Land, with such another measure of Labour; forasmuch as both Ships and Garments were the creatures of Lands and mens Labours thereupon: This being true, we should be glad to finde out a natural Par between Land and Labour, so as we might express the value by either of them alone as well or better then by both, and reduce one into the other as easily and certainly as we reduce pence into pounds. Wherefore we would be glad to finde the natural values of the Fee simple [4] of Land, though but no better then we have done that of the *usus fructus* [5] above-mentioned, which we attempt as followeth.

19. Having found the Rent or value of the *usus fructus per annum*, the question is, how many years purchase (as we usually say) is the Fee simple naturally worth? If we say an infinite number, then an Acre of Land would be equal in value to a thousand Acres of the same Land; which is absurd, an infinity of unites being equal to an infinity of thousands. Wherefore we must pitch upon some limited number, and that I apprehend to be the number of years, which I conceive one man of fifty years old, another of twenty-eight, and another of seven years old, all being alive together may be thought to live; that is to say, of a Grandfather,

[4] Full ownership. — T. G. B.
[5] Right to the product of the land. — T. G. B.

Father, and Childe; few men having reason to take care of more remote Posterity. . . .

20. Wherefore I pitch the number of years purchase, that any Land is naturally worth, to be the ordinary extent of three such persons their lives. Now in *England* we esteem three lives equal to one and twenty years, and consequently the value of Land, to be about the same number of years purchase. . . .

21. This I esteem to be the number of years purchase where Titles are good, and where there is a moral certainty of enjoying the purchase. But in other Countreys Lands are worth nearer thirty years purchase, by reason of the better Titles, more people, and perhaps truer opinion of the value and duration of three lives.

22. And in some places, Lands are worth yet more years purchase by reason of some special honour, pleasures, priviledge or jurisdiction annexed unto them.

23. On the other hand, Lands are worth fewer years purchase (as in *Ireland*) for the following reasons, which I have here set down, as unto the like whereof the cause of the like cheapness in any other place may be imputed.

First, In *Ireland,* by reason of the frequent Rebellions, (in which if you are conquered, all is lost; or if you conquer, yet you are subject to swarms of thieves and robbers) and the envy which precedent missions of English have against the subsequent, perpetuity it self is but forty years long, as within which time some ugly disturbance hath hitherto happened almost ever since the first coming of the English thither.

24. 2. The Claims upon Claims which each hath to the others Estates, and the facility of making good any pretence whatsoever by the favour of some one or other of the many Governours and Ministers which within forty years shall be in power there; as also by the infrequency of false testimonies, and abuse of solemn Oaths.

25. 3. The paucity of Inhabitants, there being not above the $\frac{1}{5}$th part so many as the Territory would maintain, and of those but a small part do work at all, and yet a smaller work so much as in other Countreys.

26. 4. That a great part of the Estates, both real and personal in *Ireland,* are owned by Absentees, and such as draw over the profits raised out of *Ireland* refunding nothing; so as *Ireland* exporting more then it imports doth yet grow poorer to a paradox.

27. 5. The difficulty of executing justice, so many of those in power being themselves protected by Offices, and protecting others. . . . But all this with a little care in due season might remedy, so as to bring *Ireland* in a few years to the same level of values with other places. . . .

Strong Medicine for Clio's Malady

Pierre Bayle (1647–1706) was a French Huguenot converted to Catholicism by the Jesuits and reconverted to Calvinism, a refugee in Holland from persecution in France for his Calvinism. Ultimately he was driven from his chair in the Calvinist university of Rotterdam because of his religious skepticism. His massive Historical and Critical Dictionary (1697) was uncompromisingly critical, and its author thrived on controversy. Bayle's muse was Clio, the muse of history; his medicine for the banishing of myth from her was the pure light of reason. His life's work was constructive only in clearing the ground for a sounder reconstruction of history. Henceforth, history would be almost entirely a secular study for secular ends. History tinged by faith never recovered from Bayle's therapy. Giambattista Vico's Principles of the New Science . . . Concerning the Common Nature of Nations (1725) was the theoretical construct built on the ground cleared by Bayle. German historians of the late eighteenth and early nineteenth centuries rewrote the history of ancient, medieval, and modern man within Vico's framework but on that same cleared ground. History owes a profound, though mixed, debt of gratitude to Bayle.

Bayle's *Dictionary, Historical and Critical*

CAIN, the eldest son of Adam and Eve, was an Husband-man. He offered to God the fruits of the earth, at the same time that his brother Abel, who was a Shepherd, offered up the firstlings of his flock. God was well-pleased with the offerings of Abel, but had no regard for those of Cain; upon which the latter was so highly exasperated, that without having the least respect for the remonstrance, which God made to him, he killed his brother. By the sentence, which God pronounced against him, he was condemned to banishment and a vagabond state of life; which made him apprehensive, that every one who found him should kill him. But to calm this fear, God had the goodness to set a mark on him, to prevent those who should find him from killing him. Cain retired to the land of Nod on the East of Eden, and built a city, to which he gave the name of his son Enoch. This is all that can be said of him with any certainty, there being no more concerning him in the Book of Genesis. The other things which are related of him in abundance are no other

From Pierre Bayle, *A General Dictionary, Historical and Critical*, trans. J. P. Bernard et al. (London, 1734–1741), vol. 4, pp. 16–19; vol. 10, pp. 409–10, 412–14.

than conjectures, or imaginary fancies, or traditions of the utmost uncertainty. We have elsewhere mentioned several things of this nature which relate to him; but we should never have done, if we were to set down the rest. What has there not been said as to the reasons for which it is pretended his offering was rejected by God? Who would believe Josephus capable of giving this reason, viz. that Cain offered not, as his brother did, things which are produced naturally, that is to say animals, but things which the labour and avarice of man cause to be produced forcibly, that is to say grain and fruits? Does not a Jew, who reasons in this manner, seem to have forgotten the grounds of his Religion? Were not the offerings of the first-fruits ordained by the Law of Moses? If the reasons alledged by Philo were a fact well supported, they would be preferable to the reason given by Josephus. This last Author tells one thing which is very probable; that Cain did not amend his life in his exile, but on the contrary grew more wicked: he satisfied his passions at the expence of others, and enriched himself by the spoil of his neighbour with a thousand acts of violence. Josephus attributes to him the invention of measures, weights, and boundaries. All this was very seasonable among people whom Cain's example accustomed to all sorts of injustice. We cannot tell precisely how many brothers and sisters he had, when he killed Abel; however it is not to be doubted but those who say there were then no more than four persons in the world, are mistaken; for though it were true, as some suppose, that Cain was but thirty years old when he committed that murder, there would be no room to doubt but that Eve had already lain in several times. I shall conclude with an old tradition concerning Cain's death. Being decrepit and blind, say they, he sate down one day among some very thick bushes; Lamech, who was then hunting, having notice that something stirred in that place, ran thither, and thinking that a wild beast was lying there, let fly an arrow, and slew Cain. Some place this event about the year of the world 701; and others in the year 875. Salianus the Jesuit embraces this last opinion, which he says is that of Pererius and Torniellus; whence we conclude, by the way, that Moreri is in the wrong to say, that according to Torniellus and Salianus, the murder of Cain by Lamech happened in the 688th year of the world. Tostatus makes Cain to have lived near eight hundred years. There are some who place his death under the year 931, and pretend that he was buried under the ruins of a house. Paulus Burgensis, who makes him perish in the deluge, did not mind what he was saying: this is to make him live almost 1656 years. There are some also who say he slew himself; and have the impertinence to conclude from thence, that God did not keep his word with him; because he had promised him, say they, that no man should kill him. It is false that God's promise was so expressed; it regarded only those whom Cain seemed to be so much afraid of, that is to say, the men who should light on him in his banishment.

Pierre Bayle

AN ILLUSTRATION OF CERTAIN PARTICULARS
INTERSPERSED IN THIS DICTIONARY

EXPLICATION III: THAT THE SCEPTICAL PARTICULARS,
WHICH HAVE BEEN ADVANCED IN THIS DICTIONARY,
CAN DO NO PREJUDICE TO RELIGION

I. I lay down, as the basis of this third explication, the following certain and undoubted maxim, *that the Christian Religion is of a supernatural order or kind, and that the solution of it is the supreme authority of God proposing mysteries to us, not with the design that we should comprehend, but that we may believe them, with all the humility due to the infinite being, who cannot deceive nor be deceived*. This is the polar-star of all discussions and controversies, in the articles of Religion which God has revealed to us thro' Jesus Christ.

This necessarily shews the insufficiency of the tribunal of Philosophy for the judging of controversies between Christians, since they ought to be carried to no other tribunal but that of Revelation.

Every dispute concerning the question of right, or reasonableness of the thing, ought to be instantly rejected. No one should be admitted to examine, if we ought to believe what God commands us to believe. This ought to be considered as a first principle in the affair of Religion. It is the business of the Metaphysicians to examine whether there is a God, and if he be infallible; but Christians, as such, ought to suppose this a matter already judged.

The question therefore is only about matter of fact, viz. whether God requires us to believe this or that. Two sorts of people may doubt of this, some because they do not look upon the Scriptures as coming from heaven, and the others because they do not believe the sense of the Revelation to be such as some sects interpret it.

The only dispute therefore that Christians can engage in with Philosophers is, on the matter of fact following, whether the Scriptures were wrote by persons inspired by God. If the proofs urged by the Christians on this occasion do not convince Philosophers, the controversy ought to be discontinued; since it would be to no purpose to descend to examine, in detail, the doctrine of the Trinity, &c. with persons who should not acknowledge the Divinity of the Scriptures, the only way to judge who is right or wrong is such controversies. Revealed authority ought to be the common principle of the disputants on this occasion, and consequently the dispute ought to be discontinued, when one part admits this principle, and the other denies it: *Adversus negantem principia non est disputandum.* I.e., "It is to no purpose to dispute with a person who denies the principles." . . .

Divines should not be ashamed to confess, that they cannot enter the lists, with such antagonists, and will not expose the Gospel truths to such a combat. The ship of Christ Jesus was not built in order to fail on that stormy sea, but to secure itself from tempest in the haven of faith. The Father, Son and Holy Ghost (ought the Christians to say), have thought proper to lead us by the paths of faith, and not by that of science or disputation. They are our doctors and directors; we cannot lose our way when conducted by such guides, and reason itself commands us to prefer them to its direction.

But was it not shocking, will some say, for me to have told, without confessing it, the confession made by an Abbé, viz. that the Sceptics find many arguments in the doctrines of the Christians, which make the first mentioned more formidable than ever? Here I answer, that this circumstance can shock such persons only, as have not sufficiently examined the character of the Christian belief. It would be a very false supposition, to imagine that Christ designed in any manner to favour directly or indirectly any one sect of Philosophers in their contests with others. His intention was rather to confound all Philosophy, and shew its vanity. He would have his Gospel interfere, not only with the religion of the heathens, but likewise the aphorisms of their wisdom; and that notwithstanding this opposition between its principles and those of the world, it yet should triumph over the Gentiles by the ministry of a few ignorant persons, who did not make use of eloquence, logic, nor any of the instruments necessary for all other revolutions. He would have his disciples to be so diametrically opposite to the wise men of this world, that they should call one another fools; he required, that as his Gospel appeared a folly to Philosophers, the knowledge of these, in its turn, should appear folly to the Christians. . . .

(4.) A true believer, a Christian, who is well acquainted with the spirit of his Religion, does not expect to find it agree with the maxims of the Lycaeum, nor capable of refuting, merely by the strength of reason, the difficulties of reason. He is very sensible, that natural things bear no proportion to such as are supernatural; and that if a Philosopher was desired to adjust the mysteries of the Gospel to the axioms of the Peripatetics, this would be requiring from him what is not consistent with the nature of things. A man must necessarily make an option between Philosophy and the Gospel. If such a one is resolved to believe nothing but what is evident, and conformable to received truths, he then should embrace Philosophy, and leave the Christian principles; but if he is for believing the incomprehensible mysteries of Religion, he then must adhere to the Christian Religion and leave Philosophy; for to enjoy, at the same time, evidence and incomprehensibility; can never be; the conjunction of these two things is almost as impossible, as the conjunction of the properties of a square and of a circle. . . . Every Christian who suffers himself to be startled, and take offence at the objections of unbelievers, is partly in the same sad condition with them. . . .

Nothing is more necessary than faith; nor is any thing of higher importance, than to be duly sensible of the virtue of this theological virtue. But what can contribute more to make us know it, than to mediate on the attribute, which distinguishes it from the rest of the acts of the understanding? Its essence consists, in imprinting on our minds a strong persuasion of revealed truth, and this solely from the motive of God's authority. Those who believe the immortality of the soul, from philosophical reasons, are orthodox; but so far they have no share in the faith we are speaking of. They have no share in it, but only as they believe this doctrine, because God revealed it to us, and because they humbly submit, to God's will, the most plausible arguments, which Philosophy suggests to them, in favour of the soul's mortality. Thus the merit of faith is greater, in proportion as revealed truth, which is the object of it, surpasses all the powers of our understanding; for, in proportion as the incomprehensibility of this object increases, by the great number of maxims of the light of nature which oppose it, we must sacrifice to the authority of God a stronger reluctance of reason, and consequently we shew a greater submission to God, and give him stronger testimonies of the veneration we bear him, than if the thing required but a moderate degree of belief. Wherefore, was the faith of the Father of the Faithful of such very great merit, but because *against hope he believed in hope?* [1] There would have been no very great merit in hoping, on God's promise, for a thing that was very probable naturally; the merit therefore consisted in this, that the hope of this promise was combated by all kinds of appearances. It may also be said, that that faith is of the highest merit, which, on the divine testimony, admits of such truths as are most repugnant to reason. . . .

[1] Romans IV:18.

THE ENLIGHTENMENT
Chapter 7

The parallels between the Renaissance of the fifteenth century and the Enlightenment of the eighteenth are striking. Each was strongly influenced by Platonism and derived from that indestructible philosophy the notion of perfectibility, along with great certainty and arrogance. They had similar material bases in the patronage of newly monied grandees, institutionalized in the Renaissance court and in the salon of the Enlightenment. The focus of each was in a specific geographic center, from which emanated the cultural influence in a continuing stream during the whole life of the movement — the northern Italian cities (particularly Florence) in the case of the Renaissance and northern France (particularly Paris) in the case of the Enlightenment. Each was secular and involved a modish imitativeness of the true, creative individual in a vulgarization highly attractive to the socially aspiring and the parvenu. Each was "art," in the sense of form — preeminently the plastic arts for the Renaissance, letters for the Enlightenment — and in the sense of a self-conscious channeling of knowledge and skill to a creative end. From each emerged a particular conception of the man of the age — the Renaissance man of *virtù*, the Enlightenment man of reason — and the ideal of each was epitomized in statecraft in a Platonic philosopher-king — the Renaissance prince, the Enlightened despot. Each had substantial intellectual foundations — the Renaissance in Classical learning, the Enlightenment in the new science — and were pitted against dominant intellectual traditions. Although each respected existing institutions, their object was to banish the old ways of making them work and replace those ways with new procedures, whether the institution was the Church of the fifteenth century or the absolutist monarchy of the eighteenth. Perhaps most striking, each contributed to the coming of cataclysmic ideological struggles that neither survived: the Reformation and the French Revolution.

Parallels can never go far enough and are always pushed too far. So with this one. Yet one attribute common to both epochs is compelling: For all their naïveté and ultimate ineffectualness, transitoriness, and unrealized aspiration, the Renaissance and the Enlightenment left indelible tokens of their passing in the humanistic commitment that survived the ideological civil wars that destroyed them.

The Enlightenment had two roots, and, somewhat surprisingly for a movement so tenaciously focused in France, each of them was largely English. The intellectual root was dual: the epistemology of John Locke's *Essay Concerning Human Understanding* (1690) and Newton's mechanics. The former work posited the environmentalism that, being conditioned by reason, determined experience and hence the condition of man. The environment could be changed by reason, and, though man's mind had no innate ideas, a change in the environment would make innate in man's mind experiences that would condition generations yet unborn. The philosophes built for the ages, and the environment was the determinant of the ages. Newton's mechanics, far more adequately and convincingly than the mechanics of Descartes, propounded "laws" of the operation of the physical world. His immense achievement invited the philosophes to propound laws of the operation of the social world. They were not averse to such an exercise, and the Enlightenment's certainty of progress and even ultimate perfectibility of man and the human condition by the operation of reason received much of its most persuasive manifestation in the propositions of general laws of human behavior, individual and collective.

The other predominantly English root of the Enlightenment was the political example of the constitutionalist oligarchy of eighteenth-century England. The philosophes stood in respectful though not affectionate awe of an England that was as powerful as ancient Rome and a replica of Athenian democracy in its golden age of Pericles. Voltaire's *English Letters* render due homage to the English model. And it is impossible to conceive of Montesquieu's brilliant exposition of good government by laws in the interest of oligarchy, *The Spirit of Laws* (1748), without the explicit model of the eighteenth-century English "constitution" (no matter how mistakenly he interpreted it).

The skepticism of traditional religion, implicit in Newton and the other virtuosi of the preceding scientific epoch and their "natural religion," was made more explicit in the deism of the philosophes. God as the great watchmaker starting the operation of the universe by law, as the retired Supreme Being overseeing but not intervening, was, after all, the logical result of the translation of God the Final Cause to God the First Cause.

The great cooperative venture of the philosophes, the *Encyclopédie* (28 volumes, 1751–1772), epitomized the ideas, outlook, and aspiration of the Enlightenment. The desire for progress and the optimism that accompanied it, the belief that men everywhere are the same and that only irrational customs and unjustifiable, restrictive laws account for differences among nations and discrepancies in the human condition, the commitment to useful knowledge as the purgative of the old irrationalities and the vehicle for the implementation of the new reason — all are evident in the *Encyclopédie*.

As a movement transcending the boundaries of its homeland, the Enlightenment made itself felt all over Europe, from the Atlantic to the Urals, and in North America. Its most influential foreign thinker — one of the most original anywhere — was the Italian jurist Caesare Beccaria. His pioneering work in penology reflected the ideas and aspirations of the entire movement but had a particularly rigorous intellectual quality sometimes lacking in the writing of the philosophes. Interestingly enough, the Enlightenment made less impact in England than anywhere else so potentially fertile for the reception of its ideas, and its best home in the British Isles was Scotland.

The first blow from within the Enlightenment at its underlying assumptions and its hitherto unabashed optimism came from a Scottish philosophe, David Hume, in 1739. To Hume, man's nature could not be explained by reason or reduced to universal natural laws. His argument was picked up, expanded, and conditioned by the brilliant German philosopher Immanuel Kant, in the *Critique of Pure Reason* (1781). But between Hume and Kant, the counter-Enlightenment set in in force with the vivid prose of the epoch's premier misanthrope, Jean Jacques Rousseau.

Rousseau was the seminal figure in the reaction against rationalism. In 1750 he won the prize of the Academy of Dijon for his *Discourse on the Moral Effects of the Arts and Sciences*. "Full of warmth and force, it is wholly without logic or order; . . . weakest in argument and the least harmonious" — so Rousseau characterized the *Discourse* thirty years later. Yet it was just these qualities, so opposed to those gracing the prose of the Enlightenment, that made Rousseau the lion of the salons of Paris, moved philosophes to wrath, and even provoked a rebuttal from the king of Poland. Rousseau's greatest and most ominous works were ahead. Political theory has not yet recovered from *The Social Contract* (1762) or biography from the *Confessions* (1784). In retrospect, however, there was nothing in these, or in his nature-loving novels, not presaged in the *Discourse* of 1750. The salon-philosophes who lionized the unsmiling Rousseau did not detect the rising force of the hot wind of passion and romanticism in him that would blow out the still cool air of reason, progress, optimism, perfectibility, and, in the political dress of revolution, snuff out the lives of more than one of them.

Voltaire Admires the English "Constitution"

François Marie Arouet, "Voltaire" (1694–1778), was the undisputed master philosophe, the darling of the salons, for a while the palace philosopher of Frederick II of Prussia, and the sparkling correspondent of Catherine II of Russia. His writings were voluminous, varied, and profound. His literary gift above all others was satire, which he turned on most institutions of his day and on numerous individuals. Voltaire's most persistent target was the Church and the clergy, and he managed almost singlehandedly to give to the Enlightenment its complexion of anticlericalism. As early as 1717 he was in prison for his satirical attacks. On his second sojourn in the Bastille he was released on the condition that he leave France. From 1726 to 1729 he lived in England, and the English Letters (London, 1733; Paris, 1734) were the product of his close look at English institutions and manners. Their publication caused such a furor that for fifteen years he was forced into seclusion in eastern France with a highly intellectual mistress who exercised great influence over him. This period was most productive of his fictional and dramatic works, all bent to the ideas of the Enlightenment.

On the Parliament

The members of the Parliament of England are fond of comparing themselves to the ancient Romans whenever the occasion arises.

Not long ago Mr. Shippen [1] began a speech in the House of Commons with these words: "The majesty of the English people would be wounded. . . ." The oddness of this expression raised a great shout of laughter; but without embarrassment Mr. Shippen repeated his words firmly, and the House was quiet. I confess that I see no resemblance between the majesty of the English people and that of the Roman, and even less between their governments. There is a senate in London, some of whose members are under suspicion, doubtless unjustly, of selling their votes on occasion, as was done in Rome: this is the only similarity. Otherwise, the two nations seem to me quite different as to both good and evil. Among the Romans

---

From Voltaire, *Philosophical Letters*, Letter 8, ed. and trans. Ernest Dilworth (© 1961 by Bobbs-Merrill Company, Inc.), (Indianapolis, 1961), pp. 30–33. Reprinted by permission of Bobbs-Merrill Company, Inc.

[1] A Tory and Jacobite, adversary of Walpole.

the horrible madness of religious wars was unknown; that abomination was reserved for pious preachers of humility and patience. Marius and Sulla, Pompey and Caesar, Antony and Augustus did not fight over the question whether the Flamen should wear his shirt over his robe or his robe over his shirt; or whether, for auspices to be taken, the sacred chickens must both eat and drink or simply eat.[2] The English have in the past reciprocally hanged one another at their Assizes and destroyed one another in pitched battle over matters of this kind. Episcopalianism and Presbyterianism have turned these grave heads for a time. I suppose that no such foolishness will get control of them again, however, for they appear to me to have grown wiser at their own expense, and I see in them no longer any inclination to cut one another's throats over syllogisms.

There is a more essential difference between Rome and England which gives all the advantage to the latter, and that is that in Rome the fruit of civil wars was slavery, whereas in England it was freedom. The English are the only people on earth who have managed to prescribe limits to the power of kings by resisting them, and who by long endeavor have at last established that wise form of government in which the prince, all-powerful to do good, is restrained from doing evil;[3] in which the nobles are great without insolence or feudal power, and the people take part in the government without disorder.

The House of Lords and that of the Commons are the arbiters of the nation, and the king is umpire. This balance the Romans lacked; there was always discord in Rome between the nobles and the common people, and no intermediary with power to reconcile them. The Senate of Rome, which had the unjust, the criminal arrogance to refuse to share anything with the plebeians, knew no other trick for keeping government out of their reach than to busy them continually with foreign wars. They regarded the People as a ferocious animal that had better be let loose upon the neighbors than kept at home to devour its master. Thus the greatest weakness in the government of the Romans made conquerors of them; it is because they were unhappy at home that they became the masters of the world — until domestic discord turned them into slaves.

The government of England was not made for such a burst of grandeur, nor for so disastrous an end. Its purpose is not the splendid folly of making conquests but to prevent its neighbors from making them. This people is not only jealous of its liberty, it is at the same time concerned about the liberty of others. The English were implacably opposed to Louis XIV for the sole reason that they thought him ambitious. They waged war against him with a light heart and surely without self-interest.

---

[2] It was by the appetite of these birds that the augurs interpreted the divine will.
[3] See Fénelon's *Télémaque* (Book V), where the old Cretan is defining the royal authority. Voltaire has borrowed this particular antithesis almost word for word.

It has doubtless cost a good deal to establish liberty in England; the idol of arbitrary power was drowned in seas of blood. But the English do not believe that for good laws too high a price has been paid. Other nations have not had fewer troubles nor poured out less blood, but the blood they shed for liberty has only hardened their bondage.

What becomes a revolution in England is only a mutiny in other countries. In Spain, in Barbary, or in Turkey a city will take to arms to defend its privileges, and immediately it is subjugated by mercenary soldiers, and punished by executioners, and the rest of the nation kisses its chains. The French think that the government of this island is stormier than the sea that surrounds it, and so it is; but that is when the king provokes the tempest, when he wants to make himself master of the ship of which he is only the pilot. The civil wars of France have been longer, more ruthless, more productive of crimes than those of England, but not one of all these civil wars had a wise liberty for its object.

In the detestable days of Charles IX and Henri III [4] the only question was whether one was going to be the slave of the Guise family. As for the last war of Paris, it deserves only catcalls. I seem to see a crowd of schoolboys rioting against their headmaster, and being whipped for it. Cardinal de Retz, a man who had much wit and courage and used them badly, a rebel without a cause, a dissident without a plan, head of a faction without an army, intrigued for the sake of intrigue, and seemed to foment civil war for his own pleasure. The Parlement knew neither what it had in mind nor what it didn't have in mind. It raised troops by decree and discharged them; it threatened, it apologized; it put a price on the head of Cardinal Mazarin and then came to compliment him in state. Our civil wars under Charles VI had been savage; those of the Ligue were abominable; that of the Fronde was ridiculous.

What the French chiefly reproach the English for is the execution of Charles I, who was treated by his vanquishers as he would have treated them if he had been lucky.

After all, consider on the one hand Charles I defeated in pitched battle, made prisoner, tried, sentenced at Westminister; and on the other hand the emperor Henry VII [5] poisoned by his chaplain while receiving the sacrament; Henri III killed by a monk, minister to the fury of a whole faction; thirty plots to assassinate Henri IV, several set going, and the last one depriving France of that great king forever. Weigh these outrages, and then judge.

---

[4] 1560–1589. — T. G. B.

[5] Thirty-first Holy Roman Emperor; of the house of Luxembourg, he died near Siena in 1313. The crime, as Voltaire says in *Annals of the Empire,* is difficult to prove. But that does little harm to the argument.

On the Government

This happy mixture in the government of England, this union of commons, lords, and king, has not always been in effect. England was long a slave; it was enslaved to the Romans, the Saxons, the Danes, the French. William the Conqueror, more than others, governed with an iron scepter; he disposed of the property and the life of his new subjects like some Oriental monarch. He forbade, on pain of death, any Englishman to be so presumptuous as to have any fire or light in his house after eight in the evening — either expecting by such measures to prevent their assembling at night, or else wishing to discover, by so bizarre a prohibition, just how far the power of one man over other men could go.

It is true that before and after William the Conqueror the English had parliaments; they boast about it, as if the assemblies then called parliaments, composed as they were of ecclesiastical tyrants and of plunderers known as barons — as if those assemblies were the guardians of liberty and public bliss.

The barbarians, who from the shores of the Baltic Sea poured into the rest of Europe, brought with them the custom of these legislative bodies or parliaments that so much fuss is made about and are so little known. The kings at the time were not despotic, it is true, but the people only groaned the more for it in a wretched state of bondage. The chiefs of these savages who had devastated France, Italy, Spain, and England made themselves kings; their captains shared among themselves the lands of the conquered: hence these margraves, these lairds, these barons, these under-tyrants who often squabbled with their king over what they had plundered from the peoples. They were birds of prey battling an eagle to suck the blood of doves. Each people had a hundred tyrants instead of one master. The priests soon joined the party. It had always been the fate of the Gauls, the Germans, and the islanders of England to be ruled by their druids and by the chiefs of their villages, an ancient species of baron, less tyrannical than what came after. These druids professed to be mediators between the deity and mankind; they made laws, they excommunicated people, they condemned people to death. The bishops gradually succeeded to their temporal authority in the Goth and Vandal governments. The popes put themselves at the head of them, and with breves, bulls, and monks, made kings tremble, deposed them, had them assassinated, and drew to themselves as much of the money of Europe as they could. The imbecile Ina, one of the tyrants of the English Heptarchy, was the first who on a pilgrimage to Rome consented to pay Peter pence (which would amount to about an *écu* in our money) for every house in

From Voltaire, *Philosophical Letters*, Letter 9, ed. and trans. Ernest Dilworth (© 1961 by Bobbs-Merrill Company, Inc.), (Indianapolis, 1961), pp. 34–38. Reprinted by permission of Bobbs-Merrill Company, Inc.

his lands. The whole island promptly followed his example, England little by little became a province of the pope, and the Holy Father sent his legates there from time to time to levy exorbitant taxes. At last, John Lackland, following regulations, ceded his realm to His Holiness, who had excommunicated him; and the barons, who found that not exactly to their interest, drove out their miserable king. They put in his place Louis VIII, the father of St. Louis of France, but they soon sickened of this newcomer and sent him back across the water.

While barons, bishops, and popes were in this way pulling apart an England of which they all wanted control, the people, the most numerous, the most virtuous even, and consequently the most respectable class of men, composed of those who devote themselves to the laws and the sciences of merchants, of craftsmen — in a word, of all that was not tyrannical — the people, I say, were regarded by them as animals on a plane below the human. The commons were then far from having any part in the government; they were villeins: their labor, their blood belonged to their masters, who were called nobles. Most men were, throughout Europe then, what they still are in several parts of the North, serfs of a lord, a species of cattle bought and sold with the land. It has taken centuries to do justice to humanity, to feel it was horrible that the many should sow and the few should reap. And isn't it a good thing for the human race that the authority of those little brigands was stamped out in France by the legitimate power of our kings, and in England by the legitimate power of the kings and the people?

Fortunately, in the shaking that the strife between kings and nobles gave to empires, the chains of the nations have been more or less loosened. Liberty was born in England of the quarrels between tyrants. The barons forced John Lackland and Henry III to grant that famous Charter whose main purpose was really to make the kings subordinate to the lords, but in which the rest of the nation was favored a little, so that when the occasion arose they would range themselves on the side of their pretended protectors. That Great Charter, which is regarded as the consecrated source of English liberty, shows very clearly in itself how little liberty was known. The title alone proves that the King thought himself absolute by right, and that the barons and even the clergy were able to force him to relax his hold on this pretended right only by being stronger than he.

This is how the Great Charter begins: "We grant of our own free will the following rights to archbishops, bishops, abbots, priors, and barons of our realms," etc.[1]

In the articles of that Charter not a word is said about the House of Commons, which is proof that it did not yet exist, or that it existed in

[1] Voltaire's information about the charter comes from the condensation of Rapin de Thoyras.

impotence. The "freemen" of England are specified there, sad evidence that there were some who were not that. It is clear by Article 32 that these supposedly free men owed services to their lord. Such liberty had a remarkable resemblance to slavery.

In Article 21 the king orders that his officers no longer be permitted to seize by force the horses and carts of free men unless payment is made, and this regulation struck the people as true liberty, because it removed a greater kind of tyranny.

Henry VII, a successful usurper and great politician, who pretended to love the barons but who hated and feared them, had the idea of securing the alienation of their lands. As a result, as time went on, the villeins who by means of hard work had acquired some capital, bought the castles of the noble peers, who had ruined themselves through their own folly. Little by little all the lands changed masters.

The House of Commons became daily more powerful; the older noble families in time died out; and since in England according to the rigor of the law only peers are noble, there would be no more nobility in that country at all if the kings had not created new lords from time to time, and preserved the order of peers, which they once had been so much afraid of, so as to oppose it to that of the commons now grown too formidable.

All these new peers who compose the upper house receive from the king their title and nothing more; hardly any of them owns the land whose name he bears. One is Duke of Dorset and hasn't an inch of ground in Dorsetshire. Another is Earl of a village and scarcely knows where the village is situated. They have power in parliament but nowhere else.

You hear no talk in this country of high, middle, and low justice, nor of the right of hunting over the property of a citizen who himself has not the liberty of firing a shot in his own field.

A man is not exempt here from paying certain taxes because he is a nobleman or a priest. All taxes are levied by the House of Commons, which, though second in rank, is first in importance.

It is quite within the power of the lords and bishops to reject a tax bill presented by the Commons, but they are not permitted to alter it in any way; they must either pass it or throw it out altogether and without reserve. When a bill is confirmed by the Lords and approved by the king, then everyone pays, each giving not according to his rank (which is absurd) but according to his income: there is no *taille* or arbitrary poll tax, but a real tax on lands, all of which were evaluated under the famous King William III and classified accordingly.

The tax rate remains the same as it was, though the revenues from land have gone up, and so nobody is downtrodden and nobody complains. The feet of the peasant are not tortured by wooden shoes, he eats white bread, he is well clothed, and he is not afraid to increase the number of his cattle or to cover his roof with tile, lest his taxes be raised next year. There are many peasants here who own property amounting to some 200,000 francs, and who do not disdain to keep on cultivating the soil that enriched them and on which they live free.

Instruction in the Spirit of the Age of Reason

The subtitle of the Encyclopédie, *published between 1751 and 1772, was "An Analytical Dictionary of the Sciences, Arts, and Trades" — a fair description as far as it goes. Eleven of the twenty-eight volumes contained beautiful plates illustrating arts, crafts, and science, and a number of the articles were succinct résumés of technical developments. However, much of the work was pure propaganda from a consistently orthodox Enlightenment viewpoint, dissembled in indirectness and innuendo in order to skirt censorship. The following excerpts tend to convey this quality perhaps more than is warranted, but it was precisely this quality that gave the work its remarkable circulation and wide influence. Denis Diderot was the guiding spirit and editor of the project, assisted for a while by the mathematician Jean d'Alembert. The contributors included most of the eminent philosophes, including Voltaire.*

The *Encyclopédie*

CONSECRATED BREAD (*Eccles. hist.*) is the *bread* that one blesses every Sunday at the parish mass and then distributes to the faithful.

The custom, in the first centuries of Christianity, was that all those who attended the celebration of the holy mysteries participated in the communion of the bread that had been consecrated; but the Church, having found an objection to this practice, because Christians could be in a bad mood, restricted the sacramental communion to those who were duly prepared. Nevertheless, in order to preserve the memory of the early communion that was extended to everybody, one continued the distribution of ordinary *bread* that was blessed, as we do today.

From *Denis Diderot's The Encyclopedia: Selections* (© 1967 by Stephen J. Gendzier), ed. and trans. Stephen J. Gendzier (New York, 1967), pp. 79–81, 133–36, 169–70, 212–14. Reprinted by permission of Harper & Row, Publishers, Inc.

Moreover, the taste for luxury and a magnificence onerous to many people having slipped even into the practice of religion, the custom was introduced in the cities to give more or less dainty cake instead of *bread,* and to add some other costly and burdensome trimmings; which gives to poor families an inconvenient expense that would be more profitably used for real needs. If it were not demonstrated by an exact calculation, one would not believe what this single article cost the nation every year.

We know that in the nation there are forty thousand parishes where *consecrated bread* is distributed, sometimes at even two high masses in one day, without counting those of the brotherhood, those of the different art and business groups. I saw twenty-two of them provided for a celebration by new master craftsmen in a Parisian community. We are astonished that there is so much misery around us; and I for one, when I see all our extravagance and folly, am even more astonished that there does not exist much more.

However that may be, I believe that all told one can estimate the expense of *consecrated bread,* including paraphernalia and chapels, at about forty sous each time it is offered. If it costs a little less in the country, it costs much more in the city, and many people will find my estimate too low. Nevertheless forty thousand wafers of *bread* at forty sous apiece equals eighty thousand pounds, a sum which, multiplied by fifty-two Sundays, adds up to more than four million per year, or 4,000,000 pounds.

What prevents us from sparing the public this expense? It has already been said elsewhere: *bread* does not carry more of a blessing than the water used to bless it; and consequently one could be satisfied with just the water, which costs nothing, and do away with the expense of the *bread,* which becomes a real loss. . . .

Religion does not consist in decorating temples, in delighting the eyes or the ears, but in paying sincere reverence to the Creator and in making ourselves conform to the example set by Jesus Christ. Let us love God by preference, and let us fear to displease Him by violating His commandments; let us love our neighbor as ourselves, and let us consequently always be careful to do him good, or at least always be on guard not to do him evil; finally, let us fulfill our duties to the state. This is precisely the religion that God has prescribed for us and the very one which men do not practice. But they try to compensate for these failures in another manner: they bear the expenses, for example, of the decorations for the altars and of the pomp for the ceremonies: the ornaments, the lights, the chants, the bells are not spared. Strictly speaking, all of this constitutes the soul of their religion, and most of them know nothing beyond. Vulgar and deceitful piety, so little in accordance with the spirit of Christianity, which inspires only charity and brotherly love!

How many more important deeds of good will must be done that are much more worthy of the followers of Jesus Christ! How many unfortunate, crippled, and infirm people without help and without consolation! How many uncomplaining poor without any chance and without any work! How many poor families overburdened with children! In fact, how many wretched souls of every description, whose relief and comfort should be the great object of Christian commiseration! An object consequently to which we should assign as many sums of money as we fruitlessly and unnecessarily squander elsewhere.

HISTORY, is the recital of facts represented as true. Fable, on the contrary, is the recital of facts represented as fiction. There is the *history* of human opinions, which is hardly anything more than a compilation of human errors. The *history* of the arts may be the most useful of all, when to a knowledge of their invention and progress it adds a description of their techniques. *Natural history,* improperly called *history,* is an essential part of natural philosophy.

The *history* of events has been divided into sacred and profane. Sacred *history* is a succession of divine and miraculous operations by which it has pleased God formerly to guide the Jewish nation and in the present day to test our faith. I shall not discuss this worthy subject. . . .

On the usefulness of history. The advantage consists of the comparison that a statesman or a citizen can make of foreign laws, morals, and customs with those of his country. This is what stimulates modern nations to surpass one another in the arts, in commerce, and in agriculture. The great mistakes of the past are useful in all areas. We cannot describe too often the crimes and misfortunes caused by absurd quarrels. It is certain that by refreshing our memory of these quarrels, we prevent a repetition of them. . . .

Finally the great usefulness of modern *history* and the advantage that it has over ancient *history* is to teach all potentates that since the fifteenth century people have always united against overly preponderant power. This system of equilibrium, or balance of power, has always been unknown to the ancients, and it is the reason for the success of the Romans, who, having created an army superior to those of other nations, subjugated them one after the other from the Tiber to the Euphrates.

On the certainty of history. All certainty that does not consist of mathematical demonstration is nothing more than the highest probability. There is no other historical certainty. . . .

Uncertainty of history. We have distinguished between fabulous and historical periods of time. But even in historical times themselves we should distinguish truths from fables. I am not here speaking of fables now admitted to be such. There is no question, for example, about the prodigies with which Livy embellished or marred his *History.* But in regard to the most universally admitted facts, how many reasons exist for doubt!

On the method and manner of writing history and of style. . . . But while he models himself in general on these great masters [1] the modern historian has a heavier burden than his predecessors. We demand today of historians more minute details, facts more completely authenticated, exact dates, precise authorities, more attention to customs, laws, manners, commerce, finance, agriculture, and population: it is the same with *history* as it is with mathematics and natural philosophy. The field of knowledge has been enormously increased. The easier it is to compile a list of newspapers today, the more difficult it is today to write *history*.

The *history* of a foreign country should not be formed on the same model as that of our own.

These rules are sufficiently known, but the art of writing *history* well will always be rather uncommon. It certainly requires a dignified, pure, varied, and pleasant style. But in regard to the laws of writing *history*, like those of all the intellectual arts, there are many precepts and few great masters.

(Voltaire)

HUMANITY (*Morality*) is a benevolent feeling for all men, which hardly inflames anyone without a great and sensitive soul. This sublime and noble enthusiasm is troubled by the pains of other people and by the necessity to alleviate them. With these sentiments an individual would wish to cover the entire universe in order to abolish slavery, superstition, vice, and misfortune.

A sense of humanity conceals from us the flaws of our fellow men or prevents us from being conscious of them, but it makes us stern judges of crime. It snatches from the hands of a scoundrel the weapon that would be deadly to a virtuous man. It does not impel us to free ourselves of particular bonds: on the contrary, it makes us better friends, better citizens, and better spouses. It takes pleasure in showering good deeds upon those beings that nature has placed near us. I have seen this virtue, the source of so many others, in many minds but in very few hearts.

(Unsigned in the *Encyclopedia*,
but included in Diderot's complete works,
edited by Assézat and Tourneux)

NATURAL EQUALITY (*Nat. Law*) is that which is found among all men solely by the constitution of their nature. This *equality* is the principle and foundation of liberty.

Natural or *moral equality* is therefore based on the constitution of human nature common to all men, who are born, grow, live, and die in the same way.

[1] Livy, Tacitus, Polybius, Dionysius of Halicarnassus. — T. G. B.

Since human nature is the same in all men, it is clear according to natural law that each person must value and treat other people as so many individuals who are naturally equal to himself, that is to say, as men like himself.

Several consequences ensue from this principle of the *natural equality of men*. I shall rapidly examine the principal ones.

1. It follows from this principle that all men are naturally free and that the faculty of reason could only make them dependent for their own welfare.

2. That in spite of all the inequalities produced in the political government by the differences in station, by nobility, power, riches, etc., those who have risen the most above others must treat their inferiors as being naturally equal to them by avoiding any insults, by demanding nothing beyond what is required, and by demanding with humanity only what is unquestionably due.

3. That whoever has not acquired a particular right by virtue of which he can demand preferential treatment, must not claim more than others but, on the contrary, allow them to enjoy equally the same rights that he assumes for himself.

4. That anything which is a universal right must be either universally enjoyed or alternately possessed, or divided into equal portions among those who have the same right, or allotted with equitable and regulated compensation; or finally if this is possible, the decision should be made by lot: a quite suitable expedient that removes any suspicion of contempt and partiality without diminishing in any way the esteem of those people not immediately favored.

(De Jaucourt)

REASON (*Logic*). [The author first provides various definitions of reason, and then attempts to state the precise limits of reason and faith.]

Everything within the province of revelation must prevail over our opinions, our prejudices, and our interests, and is entitled to demand complete assent from the mind. But such submission of our *reason* to faith does not thereby reverse the limits of human knowledge and does not shake the foundations of *reason;* it allows us the freedom to employ our faculties in the areas of application for which they were given to us.

If we are not careful in distinguishing between the different jurisdictions of faith and *reason* by means of these limits, *reason* will have no place in matters of religion, and we shall have no right to mock the extravagant opinions and ceremonies that we notice in most religions of the world. Who does not see that this opens a wide field to the most excessive fanaticism and the most insane superstition? With such a principle there is nothing so absurd that will not be believed. Hence it happens that religion, which is to the credit of humanity and the most excellent prerogative of our nature over the animals, is often the area in which men seem to be the most irrational.

(Unsigned in the *Encyclopedia,*
but included in Diderot's complete works,
edited by Assézat and Tourneux)

Reason Brought to Bear on Law

An Essay on Crimes and Punishments (1764) by Caesare Bonesana, Marchese di Beccaria, ranks with Montesquieu's Spirit of Laws *(1748) as one of the two most influential works of the Enlightenment. Beccaria (1738–1794) was a professor of jurisprudence at Milan, an avid philosophe, and an original mind. Penology and prison reform began with the* Essay, *and Beccaria's ideas caught hold particularly in England, though it required two generations for them to work massive changes in the English criminal law. Their first fame was in the influence they had on Catherine II's instructions for the reform of Russian law, and they later exerted considerable influence on Napoleon's reform of the criminal code in France. Note the reflection of Locke's ideas in Chapter I.*

Caesare Beccaria's
Essay on Crimes and Punishments

CHAPTER I. OF THE ORIGIN OF PUNISHMENTS

Laws are the conditions, under which men, naturally independent, united themselves in society. Weary of living in a continual state of war, and of enjoying a liberty, which became of little value, from the uncertainty of its duration, they sacrificed one part of it, to enjoy the rest in peace and security. The sum of all these portions of the liberty of each individual constituted the sovereignty of a nation; and was deposited in the hands of the sovereign, as the lawful administrator. But it was not sufficient only to establish this deposite; it was also necessary to defend it from the usurpation of each individual, who will always endeavour to take away from the mass, not only his own portion, but to encroach on

From Caesare Beccaria, *An Essay on Crimes and Punishments* (London, 1767), pp. 5–7, 9–12, 98–101, 120–21.

that of others. Some motives, therefore, that strike the senses, were necessary, to prevent the despotism of each individual from plunging society into its former chaos. Such motives are the punishments established against the infractors of the laws. I say, that motives of this kind are necessary; because, experience shews, that the multitude adopt no established principle of conduct; and because, society is prevented from approaching to that dissolution (to which, as well as all other parts of the physical, and moral world, it naturally tends) only by motives, that are the immediate objects of sense, and which being continually presented to the mind, are sufficient to counterbalance the effects of the passions of the individual, which oppose the general good. Neither the power of eloquence, nor the sublimest truths, are sufficient to restrain, for any length of time, those passions, which are excited by the lively impression of present objects.

CHAPTER II. OF THE RIGHT TO PUNISH

Every punishment, which does not arise from absolute necessity, says the great *Montesquieu,* is tyrannical. A proposition which may be made more general, thus. Every act of authority of one man over another, for which there is not an absolute necessity, is tyrannical. It is upon this then, that the sovereign's right to punish crimes is founded; that is, upon the necessity of defending the public liberty, entrusted to his care, from the usurpation of individuals; and punishments are just in proportion, as the liberty, preserved by the sovereign, is sacred and valuable. . . .

Observe, that by *justice* I understand nothing more, than that bond, which is necessary to keep the interest of individuals united; without which, men would return to their original state of barbarity. All punishments, which exceed the necessity of preserving this bond, are in their nature unjust. We should be cautious how we associate with the word *justice,* an idea of any thing real, such as a physical power, or a being that actually exists. I do not, by any means, speak of the justice of God, which is of another kind, and refers immediately to rewards and punishments in a life to come.

CHAPTER III. CONSEQUENCES OF THE FOREGOING PRINCIPLES

The laws only can determine the punishment of crimes; and the authority of making penal laws can only reside with the legislator, who represents the whole society, united by the social compact. No magistrate then (as he is one of the society) can, with justice, inflict on any other member of the same society, punishment, that is not ordained by the laws. But as a punishment, increased beyond the degree fixed by the law, is the just punishment, with the addition of another; it follows, that no magistrate, even under a pretence of zeal, or the public good, should increase the punishment already determined by the laws.

If every individual be bound to society, society is equally bound to him, by a contract, which from its nature, equally binds both parties. This obligation, which descends from the throne to the cottage, and equally binds the highest, and lowest of mankind, signifies nothing more, than that it is the interest of all, that conventions, which are useful to the greatest number, should be punctually observed. The violation of this compact by any individual, is an introduction to anarchy.

The sovereign, who represents the society itself, can only make general laws, to bind the members; but it belongs not to him to judge whether any individual has violated the social compact, or incurred the punishment in consequence. For in this case, there are two parties, one represented by the sovereign, who insists upon the violation of the contract, and the other is the person accused, who denies it. It is necessary then that there should be a third person to decide this contest; that is to say, a judge, or magistrate, from whose determination there should be no appeal; and this determination should consist of a simple affirmation, or negation of fact.

If it can only be proved, that the severity of punishments, though not immediately contrary to the public good, or to the end for which they were intended, viz. to prevent crimes, be useless; then such severity would be contrary to those beneficent virtues, which are the consequence of enlightened reason, which instructs the sovereign to wish rather to govern men in a state of freedom and happiness, than of slavery. It would also be contrary to justice, and the social compact. . . .

CHAPTER XXVII. OF THE MILDNESS OF PUNISHMENTS

The course of my ideas has carried me away from my subject, to the elucidation of which I now return. Crimes are more effectually prevented by the *certainty,* than the *severity* of punishment. Hence in a magistrate, the necessity of vigilance, and in judge, of implacability, which that it may become an useful virtue, should be joined to a mild legislation. The certainty of a small punishment will make a stronger impression, than the fear of one more severe, if attended with the hopes of escaping; for it is the nature of mankind to be terrified at the approach of the smallest inevitable evil, whilst hope, the best gift of heaven, hath the power of dispelling the apprehension of a greater; especially if supported by examples of impunity, which weakness, or avarice too frequently afford.

If punishments be very severe, men are naturally led to the perpetration of other crimes, to avoid the punishment due to the first. The countries and times most notorious for severity of punishments, were always those in which the most bloody and inhuman actions and the most atrocious crimes were committed; for the hand of the legislator and the assas-

Caesare Beccaria

sin were directed by the same spirit of ferocity; which, on the throne, dictated laws of iron to slaves and savages and, in private, instigated the subject to sacrifice one tyrant, to make room for another.

In proportion as punishments become more cruel, the minds of men, as a fluid rises to the same height with that which surrounds it, grow hardened and insensible; and the force of the passions still continuing, in the space of an hundred years, the *wheel* terrifies no more than formerly the *prison*. That a punishment may produce the effect required, it is sufficient that the *evil* it occasions should exceed the *good* expected from the crime; including in the calculation the certainty of the punishment, and the privation of the expected advantage. All severity beyond this is superfluous, and therefore tyrannical. . . .

CHAPTER XXVIII. OF THE PUNISHMENT OF DEATH

The useless profusion of punishments, which has never made men better, induces me to enquire, whether the punishment of *death* be really just or useful in a well-governed state? What *right*, I ask, have men to cut the throats of their fellow-creatures? Certainly not that on which the sovereignty and laws are founded. The laws, as I have said before, are only the sum of the smallest portions of the private liberty of each individual, and represent the general will, which is the aggregate of that of each individual. Did any one ever give to others the right of taking away his life? Is it possible, that in the smallest portions of the liberty of each, sacrificed to the good of the public, can be contained the greatest of all good, life? If it were so, how shall it be reconciled to the maxim which tells us, that a man has no right to kill himself? Which he certainly must have, if he could give it away to another.

But the punishment of death is not authorised by any right; for I have demonstrated that no such right exists. It is therefore a war of a whole nation against a citizen, whose destruction they consider as necessary, or useful to the general good. But if I can further demonstrate, that it is neither necessary nor useful, I shall have gained the cause of humanity. . . .

CHAPTER XXX. OF PROSECUTION AND PRESCRIPTION

The proofs of the crime being obtained, and the certainty of it determined, it is necessary to allow the criminal, time and means for his justification; but a time so short, as not to diminish that promptitude of punishment, which, as we have shewn, is one of the most powerful means of preventing crimes. A mistaken humanity may object to the shortness of the time, but the force of the objection will vanish, if we consider that the danger of the innocent increases with the defects of the legislation.

The time for inquiry and for justification should be fixed by the laws, and not by the judge, who, in that case, would become legislator. With regard to atrocious crimes, which are long remembered, when they are once proved, if the criminal have fled, no time should be allowed; but in less considerable and more obscure crimes, a time should be fixed, after which the delinquent should be no longer uncertain of his fate. For in the latter case, the length of time, in which the crime is almost forgotten, prevents the example of impunity, and allows the criminal to amend, and become a better member of society. . . .

"Virtue! Sublime Science of Simple Minds"

The Social Contract of Jean Jacques Rousseau (1712–1778), published in 1762, has had an extraordinary fascination for generations, though it attracted little contemporaneous attention. It became the ostensible model for Robespierre's Republic of Virtue during the most extreme phase of the French Revolution, and it enjoyed an unusual vogue in the 1930's when Mussolini's Italy and Hitler's Germany seemed the marching manifestation of the "general will." The Social Contract alone assures Rousseau his niche in history. But his most immediate and ultimately most enduring success through Romanticism was as the herald of the counter-Enlightenment. Rousseau maintained that the natural, good qualities of man stem from his emotions, the evil qualities from his reason. In nature, "virtue," that "sublime science of simple minds," as this excerpt from the Discourse on the Moral Effects of the Arts and Sciences *(1750) puts it, could be recaptured.*

Rousseau's *Discourse on the Moral Effects of the Arts and Sciences*

The question before me is: "Whether the Restoration of the arts and sciences has had the effect of purifying or corrupting morals." Which side am I to take? That, gentlemen, which becomes an honest man, who is sensible of his own ignorance, and thinks himself none the worse for it.

I feel the difficulty of treating this subject fittingly, before the tribunal which is to judge of what I advance. How can I presume to belittle the sciences before one of the most learned assemblies in Europe, to commend

From Jean Jacques Rousseau, *The Social Contract and Discourses,* ed. and trans. G. D. H. Cole (New York, 1950), pp. 145–47, 159, 164–65, 173–74. Reprinted from the Everyman's Library Edition by permission of E. P. Dutton & Co., Inc., and J. M. Dent & Sons Ltd.

Jean Jacques Rousseau

ignorance in a famous Academy, and reconcile my contempt for study with the respect due to the truly learned?

I was aware of these inconsistencies, but not discouraged by them. It is not science, I said to myself, that I am attacking; it is virtue that I am defending, and that before virtuous men — and goodness is ever dearer to the good than learning to the learned.

What then have I to fear? The sagacity of the assembly before which I am pleading? That, I acknowledge, is to be feared; but rather on account of faults of construction than of the views I hold. Just sovereigns have never hesitated to decide against themselves in doubtful cases; and indeed the most advantageous situation in which a just claim can be, is that of being laid before a just and enlightened arbitrator, who is judge in his own case.

To this motive, which encouraged me, I may add another which finally decided me. And this is, that as I have upheld the cause of truth to the best of my natural abilities, whatever my apparent success, there is one reward which cannot fail me. That reward I shall find in the bottom of my heart.

THE FIRST PART

It is a noble and beautiful spectacle to see man raising himself, so to speak, from nothing by his own exertions; dissipating, by the light of reason, all the thick clouds in which he was by nature enveloped; mounting above himself; soaring in thought even to the celestial regions; like the sun, encompassing with giant strides the vast extent of the universe; and, what is still grander and more wonderful, going back into himself, there to study man and get to know his own nature, his duties and his end. All these miracles we have seen renewed within the last few generations.

Europe had relapsed into the barbarism of the earliest ages; the inhabitants of this part of the world, which is at present so highly enlightened, were plunged, some centuries ago, in a state still worse than ignorance. A scientific jargon, more despicable than mere ignorance, had usurped the name of knowledge, and opposed an almost invincible obstacle to its restoration.

Things had come to such a pass, that it required a complete revolution to bring men back to common sense. This came at last from the quarter from which it was least to be expected. It was the stupid Mussulman, the eternal scourge of letters, who was the immediate cause of their revival among us. The fall of the throne of Constantine brought to Italy the relics of ancient Greece; and with these precious spoils France in turn was enriched. The sciences soon followed literature, and the art of thinking joined that of writing: an order which may seem strange, but is perhaps only too natural. The world now began to perceive the principal advantage of an intercourse with the Muses, that of rendering mankind more sociable by inspiring them with the desire to please one another with performances worthy of their mutual approbation.

The mind, as well as the body, has its needs: those of the body are the basis of society, those of the mind its ornaments.

So long as government and law provide for the security and well-being of men in their common life, the arts, literature, and the sciences, less despotic though perhaps more powerful, fling garlands of flowers over the chains which weigh them down. They stifle in men's breasts that sense of original liberty, for which they seem to have been born; cause them to love their own slavery, and so make of them what is called a civilized people.

Necessity raised up thrones; the arts and sciences have made them strong. Powers of the earth, cherish all talents and protect those who cultivate them.[1] Civilized peoples, cultivate such pursuits: to them, happy slaves, you owe that delicacy and exquisiteness of taste, which is so much your boast, that sweetness of disposition and urbanity of manners which make intercourse so easy and agreeable among you — in a word, the appearance of all the virtues, without being in possession of one of them. . . .

THE SECOND PART

What a variety of dangers surrounds us! What a number of wrong paths present themselves in the investigation of the sciences! Through how many errors, more perilous than truth itself is useful, must we not pass to arrive at it? The disadvantages we lie under are evident; for falsehood is capable of an infinite variety of combinations; but the truth has only one manner of being. Besides, where is the man who sincerely desires to find it? Or even admitting his good will, by what characteristic marks is he sure of knowing it? Amid the infinite diversity of opinions where is the criterion [2] by which we may certainly judge of it? Again, what is still more difficult, should we even be fortunate enough to discover it, who among us will know how to make right use of it? . . .

We cannot reflect on the morality of mankind without contemplating

[1] Sovereigns always see with pleasure a taste for the arts of amusement and superfluity, which do not result in the exportation of bullion, increase among their subjects. They very well know that, besides nourishing that littleness of mind which is proper to slavery, the increase of artificial wants only binds so many more chains upon the people. Alexander, wishing to keep the Ichthyophagi in a state of dependence, compelled them to give up fishing, and subsist on the customary food of civilized nations. The American savages, who go naked, and live entirely on the products of the chase, have been always impossible to subdue. What yoke, indeed, can be imposed on men who stand in need of nothing?

[2] The less we know, the more we think we know. The Peripatetics doubted of nothing. Did not Descartes construct the universe with cubes and vortices? And is there in all Europe one single physicist who does not boldly explain the inexplicable mysteries of electricity, which will, perhaps, be for ever the despair of real philosophers?

with pleasure the picture of the simplicity which prevailed in the earliest times. This image may be justly compared to a beautiful coast, adorned only by the hands of nature; towards which our eyes are constantly turned, and which we see receding with regret. While men were innocent and virtuous and loved to have the gods for witnesses of their actions, they dwelt together in the same huts; but when they became vicious, they grew tired of such inconvenient onlookers, and banished them to magnificent temples. Finally, they expelled their deities even from these, in order to dwell there themselves; or at least the temples of the gods were no longer more magnificent than the palaces of the citizens. This was the height of degeneracy; nor could vice ever be carried to greater lengths than when it was seen, supported, as it were, at the doors of the great, on columns of marble, and graven on Corinthian capitals.

As the conveniences of life increase, as the arts are brought to perfection, and luxury spreads, true courage flags, the virtues disappear; and all this is the effect of the sciences and of those acts which are exercised in the privacy of men's dwellings. When the Goths ravaged Greece, the libraries only escaped the flames owing to an opinion that was set on foot among them, that it was best to leave the enemy with a possession so calculated to divert their attention from military exercises, and keep them engaged in indolent and sedentary occupations. . . .

But so long as power alone is on one side, and knowledge and understanding alone on the other, the learned will seldom make great objects their study, princes will still more rarely do great actions, and the peoples will continue to be, as they are, mean, corrupt, and miserable.

As for us, ordinary men, on whom Heaven has not been pleased to bestow such great talents; as we are not destined to reap such glory, let us remain in our obscurity. Let us not covet a reputation we should never attain, and which, in the present state of things, would never make up to us for the trouble it would have cost us, even if we fully qualified to obtain it. Why should we build our happiness on the opinions of others, when we can find it in our own hearts? Let us leave to others the task of instructing mankind in their duty, and confine ourselves to the discharge of our own. We have no occasion for greater knowledge than this.

Virtue! sublime science of simple minds, are such industry and preparation needed if we are to know you? Are not your principles graven on every heart? Need we do more, to learn your laws, than examine ourselves and listen to the voice of conscience, when the passions are silent?

This is the true philosophy, with which we must learn to be content, without envying the fame of those celebrated men, whose names are immortal in the republic of letters. Let us, instead of envying them, endeavour to make, between them and us, that honourable distinction which was formerly seen to exist between two great peoples, that the one knew how to speak, and the other how to act, aright.

THE CRISIS OF ABSOLUTISM
Chapter 8

"Man is born free and his happiness depends on justice." This is not the cry of Voltaire, Montesquieu, or Rousseau, not words from a speech in the National Assembly after the beginning of the French Revolution. It is a sentence from a solemn remonstrance of the high court of Paris to Louis XVI, condemning arbitrary arrest by *lettres de cachet,* in January, 1788, sixteen months before the convention of the Estates-General, eighteen months before the storming of the Bastille. It suffices to indicate what was the crisis of absolutism, though not to explain it. The crisis of absolutism was the rapidly accelerating erosion of the credibility of the monarch and of the viability of monarchy in the face of a challenge by a class and its institutions, which had been tamed at the outset of absolutism. The institutions were the high courts, the parlements, of France; the class was the nobility, which composed the magistrature of the parlements. In short, the crisis of absolutism was the noble reassertion of the late years of Louis XV and the reign of Louis XVI, the four decades that preceded the coming of revolution.

The phenomenon was not peculiar to France, although it wrecked absolutism there. Everywhere it was intimately linked to the shift from the old concept of divine-right absolutist monarchy to the new secular notion of enlightened despotism, a shift that was nearly complete by 1750, even in states — notably France — where the monarch made no pretense of being enlightened. Enlightened despotism became the norm for absolutism. Yet its appeal to reason and the direction of policy to utilitarian ends as the justification for absolute power in the monarch constituted a threat to absolutism. Divine-right justification had raised an inscrutable otherworldly God as master over the monarch. The early absolutists had faced a long, hard struggle to get God's terrestial agent, the priest, off their backs. Enlightened despotism substituted the philosophe for the priest, and there was nothing inscrutable or otherworldly about Enthroned Reason. It led to continuous superintendence of the monarch by "reasonable men," and to some extent at least made the monarch sensitive to a variety of public opinion even less controllable and more critical than had been the estates of pre-absolutist days.

Enlightened despotism raised the expectation of reform from above, even though few absolutist monarchs were prepared to attempt, or even saw much need for, any systematic reform. One monarch, Emperor Joseph II, did see this need and from remarkably pure motives. While reforming, however, he almost destroyed the already tenuous ligatures holding the Austrian Empire together, and he had to face a noble reassertion that not only vitiated most of his reforms but threatened incipient insurrection. More cynical enlightened despots used discrete ideas of the philosophes as it suited their purposes, while rejecting the system of the Enlightenment. Generally, they also appreciated the publicity value of a reputation for being "enlightened".

In the France of Louis XV and Louis XVI, the noble reassertion began well before the advent of enlightened despotism as the norm of absolutist conduct. It began with the regency of Louis XV's early years, with the fatigue caused by Louis XIV's wars, and at the moment when there was really no monarch on the throne. It began when the parlement of Paris annulled Louis XIV's will and proclaimed the duc d'Orléans regent. In return, Orléans restored to the parlement the right of remonstrance against the king's acts and legislation as it had existed in 1673, before Louis XIV's stringent limitation on this last, but important, vestige of the parlement's once-extensive power in making law. Literally from the morrow of Louis XIV's death, the parlements, especially the premier one of Paris, began to assert the claims of privilege and to seek greater influence on royal policy. The power of the parlement was essentially negative. It could not prevent legislation by the king's will. But it could serve as a sounding-board of opposition, harass the king's ministers, disrupt the orderly operation of the bureaucracy, and for a time impede the implementation of law.

The history of monarchical response to the parlements' assertiveness is a dreary tale of continuous decline in the king's capacity and willingness to withstand the parlements, broken by spasms of attempted repression of the parlements and the noble-magistrates that composed them, no repression lasting long enough to do more than allow the restoration of the parlements to appear as a triumph over the king. Louis XV's one eloquent and vigorous handling of a confrontation with the parlement of Paris indicates how far the parlement had gone in its assertions and how inflated were its claims — and how potentially dangerous were those claims to the continuation of absolutism.

The parlements' assertiveness was often in defense of bread-and-butter interests of noble privilege such as attempts to tax the nobility. But the parlement always claimed to be upholding legal due process and defending the privileges of all classes. This was more than self-serving hyperbole. It was the Enlightenment, however, that gave force to the claim. After 1750 the rhetoric and, increasingly, the notions of the Enlightenment crept into the remonstrances of parlement, culminating in the quotation that begins this chapter. This absorption of the Enlightenment into the parlements' rhetoric constituted the acceptance of "enlightened despotism" as the norm for absolutism in France, not by the absolutist monarch but by the entrenched opposition to absolutism. With this rhetorical weapon, parlements struck a responsive chord in the entire body politic, enjoying a popularity forfeited only on the eve of the Revolution when the parlement of Paris, having played the principal role in summoning the Estates-General, attempted to retain the old system of voting in it by orders.

The failure of both Louis XV and Louis XVI to overcome the challenge of the parlements explains the erosion of the monarch's credibility. The monarchy's viability was eroded by the growing fiscal feebleness of French absolutism, which ultimately compelled Louis XVI to summon the Estates-General and so set in train the Revolution. The physiocrats, philosophes who were particularly interested in economics, could number some disciples among the finance ministers of the king, but Jacques Necker was not among them, though he was articulate and clever. He was a master of financial deception, a floater of loans at ruinous rates of interest. Yet he was the only politically capable finance minister of Louis XVI, and politics rather than fiscal ability was the determinant of such success as any minister enjoyed in staying in power in the last decades of the Old Regime. The ablest French statesman the Old Regime produced in its last years entered the service of the state only with the Revolution, but Talleyrand's after-the-fact analysis of the crisis of absolutism in the 1780's is telling.

The quotation that opens this chapter, Louis XV's reply to the Paris parlement in 1766, Necker's glib treatise, and the substance of Talleyrand's analysis, all point to a great truth about the crisis of absolutism and hence the coming of the Revolution. As the distinguished British historian of the era, Alfred Cobban, put it: French opinion began "to talk republican language even before it had thought republican thoughts."

The Model "Enlightened Despot": Joseph II

Empress Maria Theresa (1740–1780) was one of the most remarkable rulers of the century. The first eight years of her rule were dedicated to a desperate defense of Austria against Frederick II, and throughout her reign he remained the cloud on her horizon. Without pretense of intellectuality, she never made the roster of enlightened despots. But she was intelligent, dutiful, resourceful, courageous, and genuinely dedicated to her country. The results were modest but continuous programs of reform in administration, education, law, military service, taxes, and agriculture, undertaken by ministers whose thinking was more advanced than their mistress' but who were allowed by her the initiative for change. From 1765 until her death in 1780, Maria Theresa's co-ruler was her son, Joseph II. Spoiled and headstrong, over-infatuated with the notions of the Enlightenment, Joseph proved a trial to his more pragmatic mother. His chance came in 1780 with his succession as sole ruler. His decade of unimpeded rule was a whirlwind of change that ended in failure and a reaction by his successor, a reaction that forestalled almost certain rebellion by whole provinces, the nobility, and even the peasantry who were the intended beneficiaries of Joseph's liberalization.

The following selections — Maria Theresa's instructions to the tutor of ten-year-old Joseph, a revealing letter of 1775, extracts from Joseph's letters, and a paean of praise for Joseph's emancipation of the serfs in a lecture by Joseph von Sonnenfels, Joseph II's principal academic adviser and a professor at the academy founded by Maria Theresa — afford insight into the most devout enlightened despot, Joseph II.

Instructions of the Empress Maria Theresa for the Tutor of Her Son Joseph, Field-Marshal Count Batthyány, 1751

After having committed and entrusted my eldest Archduke to Count Batthyány to be educated, and thereby having manifested sufficiently my good opinion created by him, I find it necessary to impart to him some knowledge of my son's qualities, which have been observed in him throughout his childhood years, in order to make it easier for Batthyány

From *Letters of an Empress*, ed. G. Pusch, trans. Eileen R. Taylor (London, 1939), pp. 26–31.

and to clear the way or ways, for his zealous and reliable, faithful and well-meaning intentions thereby devoted to us.

As my son has been tended from the cradle up with great tenderness and love as so dear and important a pledge, it is certain that his wishes and desires were too much yielded to in many points, and in especial, that his attendants misled him, not only through open flattery, but also several untimely representations of his exalted rank, to love seeing himself obeyed and honoured, to find, on the other hand, opposition unpleasant and almost insupportable, to deny himself nothing, but to act towards others lightly, without kindness, and roughly.

Although, indeed, these tendencies have been in some part corrected by the care and teaching directed thereto by his zealous Abbé, and my son, also, shows many signs of a good heart, it is yet sure that his great vivacity, which was not formerly expected in him, from which, however, people will be able to profit in many things to their best advantage, is at present notably increasing, from which arise, in the first place, strong desires to fulfil his will in all small fancies, and to be so occupied by them that he seldom hears admonitions such as most young people often forget a thousand times, and it is often hard to bring him to the necessary application, but least of all, through the lengthy or, so to say, dry severity and manner of which most masters make use in school, for thereby he will only fall into a forbearance, which certainly makes him obey, but never makes him succeed, which has been often and many times put to the test; on the contrary, through one or two varying plans of recreations suitable to him, and several encouragements to honour and the like, he has often done more than was required of him.

What must be observed, however, in such cases and throughout, is that the man on whom he depends entirely, must make himself feared and respected by him. I do not also say loved, for this is in no doubt between my son, who has a good heart, and Batthyány. The indispensable necessity is that the Ajo [1] possess the trust of the child. . . . The Ajo must irrevocably keep to the punishment or privation which he may have threatened, and the child must be so assured of his firmness, that this too must serve him as a stimulus and to the fulfilment of his obligation. . . .

It will be observed in him that it comes hard to him to acknowledge his faults. He is ashamed of them, and tries to cloak them with other conversation or digressions, so that he is delivered from confessing them or humbling himself for them. He often shows a similar shame when there is required of him some loud talk, a compliment, or grave ceremony in conversation, or deference, wherefore it must be constantly attempted to tame him, so that he should partly confess his faults with greater uprightness, and seek pardon, and partly should entirely lose an embarrassment so unbecoming a great gentleman.

---

[1] That is, tutor. — T. G. B.

One of the tendencies which must be most contested, and which it must be attempted to prevent, is the desire arising out of his lively mind, to watch in everyone the outward and even inward faults, to let himself be prejudiced by them, to mock at them, which so sorely hinders not only the love of our neighbors, but also a sensible judgment, so that he remains preoccupied by a figure, or face, or the speech of a person, and can no more recognise their true qualities, and in this manner is often led astray in conversation, which leads up to all kinds of bad effects. . . .

Lament of a Mother and Co-Ruler: Maria Theresa to Joseph, December 24, 1775

There is a great misfortune existing between us; with the best will in the world we do not understand each other. It may be that I am too much overcome with concern at being met with neither the confidence nor the frankness which I believe I have deserved, that makes my lasting disappointment. I can truly say that, for thirty-six years, I have been preoccupied only with you. Twenty-six of them have been happy, but I could not say as much now, since I cannot consent to loose principles, too lax in religion and morals. You let be seen too clearly your antipathy to all the old customs and all the clergy, and principles too free in the matter of morals and conduct. This is reason enough to alarm my heart concerning your delicate situation and makes me tremble for the future. All this has become only too well known, and advantage will be taken of it. This night and these days are too glorious to spend in considering such a resolution [1] as you have demanded of me; I will give it you after the new year. You can well believe that my heart is more than affected by it, seeing yours so little in agreement, and preferring its former prejudices. I hope they will make you happier than I am.

Joseph on Privilege, Inequality, and Reform

How wonderful is the career of an aristocrat; the insignia of a chamberlain, a position in the government are ready for him. He will use them by never entering his office. After all, such a position is the least that the government owes to his beautiful name, his ancestors or his family. Even

From *Letters of an Empress*, ed. G. Pusch, trans. Eileen R. Taylor (London, 1939), pp. 13–14.

[1] Joseph wished to resign from the co-regency of Austria.

From E. M. Link, *The Emancipation of the Austrian Peasant, 1740–1798* (New York, 1949), pp. 95–97, 116–18, 135–36. Reprinted by permission of Columbia University Press.

if he and his brothers are recognized fools, they cannot be absent from the privy councillor's table because once upon a time their family produced a single honest and sensible man. The court must be happy when, without the slightest merit, such a man allows it to hang the ribbon of St. Stephan's Cross around his neck. If he goes on vegetating for a while after that, he can even become a Knight of the Golden Fleece.

[I would] accord liberty of marriage without distinction, even to those marriages which are today considered *mésalliances*.[1] I know of no law, divine or natural, which would oppose them. It is only the law of prejudice which would make us believe that I am worth more because my grandfather was already a count, and because I own a parchment signed by Charles the Fifth. At birth we inherit nothing from our parents but animal life. Thus king, count, burgher or peasant, there is not the slightest difference.

I begin with education. It is much neglected here. All the parents want is to see their children adopt certain attitudes which are in conformity with their own. The good souls believe that they have obtained everything and have made a great man for the state if their son attends mass, confesses every fortnight, prays his rosary, and reads only what the limited mind of his father confessor allows him to read. Provided then that he does not lift up his eyes or blush in society, that he keeps one hand on his belt and the other on his waistcoat, that he knows how to bow gracefully or to ask politely: "what time is it?" or "how are you?," who would be bold enough not to say, "what a nice boy, how well educated!" Yes, I would reply, if our state were a monastery and our neighbors chaplains.

[*To Count Kolowrat, Vice-Chancellor, on bureaucratic recalcitrance to putting into operation the tax reform law of 1785*]: All this is empty blabber and superfluous waste of time. These phrases are nothing but ghosts by which one wishes to frighten people and to awaken their dissatisfaction. My principles are unshaken: everyone must pay according to his income . . . I shall not stoop to investigate what is to the advantage of this or that person. To whoever wins, I wish success with all my heart, just as I regret those who lose under the new regulation.

All beginning is difficult, especially when human beings are awakened and torn from their prejudices, from the slow pace which has become their second nature, and from the routine in which they have slept calmly, easily and blissfully and which has brought them honors, titles, status, and financial compensation as well.

[1] That is, mixed-marriages, either from differences in religion or from social status. — T. G. B.

[*To the Imperial civil service, 1783*]: Three years have passed since I was forced to take over the administration of the state. I have during that period made known my principles, thoughts and intentions, with great difficulty, care and patience.

I have not stopped at ordering a matter once I have worked it out and explained it. I have corrected conditions arising from deep-seated prejudices, and have fought old customs by enlightenment . . . I have sought to instill into every official the love I feel for the general welfare and my zeal for its service. I have given confidence to the heads of departments, in order that they may influence the thoughts and actions of their subordinates . . . I therefore find it part of my duty, and of the complete loyalty which I have given to the state all my life, to insist with the utmost seriousness upon the fulfillment of the orders and principles which, to my utmost regret, I have seen very much neglected. I see that a great deal is ordered, but that little attention is paid to execution. Orders must be given repeatedly since most matters are treated without real interest. In this mechanical, servile manner, it is impossible to carry on public administration . . . In all offices every single person must work with such zeal that he does not count hours, or days, or pages, but strains every nerve to the utmost in order to serve completely according to expectation and according to his duty.

Since the good can only be of one kind, namely that which serves all, or at least the greatest number . . . and since equally all provinces in the monarchy must constitute only one whole, all jealousy, all prejudice, which until now has existed frequently among nations must cease . . . Nation, religion, must not make the slightest difference, and as brothers in a monarchy all must strive to be useful to one another.

He who wishes to serve the state must think of himself last . . . Only one intention can guide his action, the greatest good and usefulness for the greatest number.

Joseph's "Palace Professor," Joseph von Sonnenfels, on the Emancipation of the Serfs, 1782

He [Joseph] has given to the useful agricultural population, whose happy condition wise princes have always considered the glory of their governments, and which is recognized by all men as the strength of states, as that class of subjects which is the mother and provider of all others, the original rights of humanity, the membership in civil society which had been denied to it. From the memorable moment of this decision, may

From E. M. Link, *The Emancipation of the Austrian Peasant, 1740–1798* (New York, 1949), pp. 113–14. Reprinted by permission of Columbia University Press.

the word "servitude" no longer be spoken among us! All of Joseph's subjects are citizens.

The despotism of oppressive princes over their peoples is an abomination. But the most abominable, the most unbearable despotism is that which citizens exercise over their fellow-countrymen. That was serfdom, that stain on any constitution wherein it is tolerated, the shame of the so-called sciences of law which argued human beings down to commodities, the disgrace of reason which thought up spurious grounds to defend oppression. Never has defenseless weakness given the stronger a right over it, except for the purpose of entrusting it with its own defense and best interest. Never has any confidence been more infamously violated than when the right to protection was turned into the right of the master, and creatures, which came from the hand of nature provided with the same strength of body and ability of spirit, were dragged down to be the property of their fellow creatures. How in the name of reason could men, even to protect their lives, have wished to sell that which constituted the greatest, the only value of life? How could a few thousand healthy, hard-working, vigorous creatures ever become the property of a weakling born of degenerate parents, or of a clever monk whose deputy today calls the father of the house for week work by impatiently knocking at the same door where only yesterday one of his order humbly begged for food?

But while philosophy fights such an absurd, revolting paradox with the superior power of victorious truth, while academies announce prizes for a plan detailing how sighing humanity can be freed from this yoke — *Joseph acts.*

Louis XV Lectures the Parlement of Paris, 1766

The provincial parlements, although neither so eminent as that of Paris nor possessing the parlement of Paris' role in legislation of recording the king's acts, were similar in composition and were guardians of noble privilege. After 1763, the provincial parlements, especially that of Rennes for the province of Brittany, became more bellicose. In 1765, Louis dissolved the parlement of Rennes and also declared vacant the seats of refractory magistrates in the parlement of Pau for the province of Béarn. The parlement of Paris intervened with a judgment of February 11, 1766, invoking the theory of "parlementary solidarity" garnished with the notion that all the parlements composed a "great council" of France. On March 3, 1766, Louis went in person to the parlement of

Paris and, in the strongest language of his reign, rejected the theories advanced by the parlement. His reply reflects the assertions advanced by the parlement. In evoking "the Nation," however, he is using the rhetoric of republicanism, though entirely unintentionally.

The Sovereign Power

[*After mounting the dais, the King addresses the president of the parlement*]: I understand that the present sitting raises nothing of consequence. Mr. President, assemble the Chambers [of the parlement].

[*The parlement is convened. The King says*]: Gentlemen, I have come myself to answer your remonstrances. . . . [*The King gives his speech to the count of Saint-Florentin, a councillor of state, who in turn passes it to Joly de Fleury, another councillor, who reads it.*]

That which has taken place in my parlements of Pau and Rennes is none of the business of my other parlements. I have done with respect to those two courts as it concerns my authority, and I owe no one an account.

I should have no other answer to make to so many remonstrances that have been made to me on this subject, if their gathering, the indecency of their style, the temerity of the most erroneous principles and the affectation of novel expressions for characterizing them did not manifest the pernicious consequences of this system of unity that I have already proscribed and which some would wish to establish in principle at the same time that they dare to put it into practice.

I shall not tolerate that there be formed in my kingdom an association which would make the natural bond of both duties and common obligations degenerate into a confederation of resistance, or which might introduce into the Monarchy an imaginary body that could only disturb harmony. The magistrature does not form a body, nor an order separate from the three orders of the realm. The magistrates are my officers, charged to relieve me of the truly royal duty of rendering justice to my subjects, a function that attached them to my person and which will always render them estimable in my eyes. I recognize the importance of their services. Therefore, it is an illusion, which tends only to shake confidence by false alarms, to imagine a project formed to destroy the magistrature and to infer that he [the King] has enemies close to the throne. His only, his true, enemies are those who, in his own bosom, use towards him a language opposed to his principles; who suggest to him that all the parlements make only one and the same body, divided into several classes; that this body, necessarily indivisible, is of the essence of Mon-

From *Remonstrances du Parlement de Paris au 18ème Siècle,* vol. 2, ed. J. Flammermont and M. Tourneux (Paris, 1895), pp. 555–60. Trans. Thomas G. Barnes.

archy and that it serves him [the King] as his base; that it is the seat, the tribunal, the organ of the Nation; that it is the protector and the essential trustee of its [the Nation's] liberty, its interests, its rights; that it answers him from this trust and would be a criminal against it [the Nation] if it was to abandon it; that it is accountable for all parts of the public good, not only to the King, but also to the Nation; that it is judge between the King and his people; that as respective custodian it maintains the equilibrium of government in reprimanding both excess of liberty and abuse of power; that the parlements cooperate with the sovereign power in the establishment of laws; that they are able sometimes by their sole effort to be freed of a law [duly] recorded and to regard a just right as non-existent; that they ought to raise an insurmountable barrier to decisions that they attribute to arbitrary authority and which they call illegal acts (as well as to orders to which they pretend surprise) and that, if there results a conflict of authority, it is their duty to abandon their functions and to resign their offices even though their resignations may not be accepted. To attempt to erect in principle novelties so pernicious is to injure the magistrature, to contradict their institution, to betray its interests and ignore the true fundamental laws of the State. As if it was allowed to be forgotten that it is in my sole person that the sovereign power resides, of which the characteristic attribute is the spirit of counsel, of justice and of reason; that it is from me alone that my courts hold their being and their authority; that the fullness of this authority, which they exercise only in my name, resides always in me, and that the use of it can never be turned against me; that the legislative power appertains to me alone, without dependence and without sharing; that it is by my sole authority that the officers of my courts proceed, not to the formation but to the recording, the publication, the execution of the law, and that it is permitted to them by me to remonstrate that which is of the duty of good and useful counsellors; that public order emanates entirely from me and that the rights and interests of the Nation, which some dare to make a body separate from the Monarch, are necessarily joined with my own and repose only in my hands.

I am persuaded that the officers of my courts will never lose sight of these sacred and unchangeable maxims, which are graven on the hearts of all faithful subjects, and that they will disavow strange notions, this spirit of independence and the errors, the consequences of which they would not know how to foresee without being dismayed in their loyalty.

Remonstrances will always be favorably received when they will breathe only that moderation which marks the magistrate and truth, when the secrecy thereof will preserve decency and usefulness, and when this way so wisely established will not be found travestied in libels, wherein the submission to my will is presented as a crime and the accomplishment of duties that I have prescribed [presented] as a subject of opprobrium, wherein some suppose that the whole Nation groans to see its rights, its liberty, its safety about to perish under the force of a terrible power, and wherein some announce that the bonds of obedience are about to be slackened. But if, after I have examined such remonstrances and in knowledge of the matter have persisted in my will, my courts should persevere in refusal to submit to it, instead of recording [the law] at the very positive command of the King (the usual form for expressing the duty of obedience), if they should attempt to destroy by their own effort laws solemnly recorded, if finally, when my authority has been forced to be unfolded in all its extent, they should dare still to fight in some way against it — by judgments of prohibition, by suspensive opposition, or by irregular ways of stopping service or resignations — confusion and anarchy would take the place of legitimate order and the scandalous spectacle of a rival contradiction to my sovereign power would reduce me to the sad necessity of employing all the power that I have received from God in order to preserve my people from the baneful results of these encroachments.

Let the officers of my courts weigh carefully, therefore, that which my favor is quite willing again to remind them of; that, listening only to their proper sentiments, they may banish all notions of association, all novel systems, and all these expressions invented to give credit to the most false and most dangerous ideas; that in their judgments and remonstrances they be contained within the bounds of reason and the respect due me; that their deliberations remain secret and that they be sensible of how indecent and undignified of their character it is to launch out in invectives against the members of my council whom I have charged with my orders and who have so worthily responded to my confidence. I shall not permit that there be given the least prejudice to the principles stated in this answer. I should expect to find them [the principles] in my parlement of Paris, even if they might be ignored in the others; that it [the parlement of Paris] never forget what it has done so many times to maintain them in all their purity, and that the court of Paris ought to set the example for the other courts of the realm.

[*Following the reading of his speech, the King says*]: The principles that you have just heard ought to be those of all my subjects and I shall not tolerate any deviation from them. As for the business of Pau and Rennes, I shall maintain with all my authority all that is being done by my orders. [*Louis then announces that he has annulled in his council the judgment of February 11 and directs the clerk of the parlement to strike out the minute of that judgment.*

Then, having descended from the dais, the King says to the president of the parlement]: Here is my answer: you shall record all that has passed.

The Financial Conjurer Preaches What He Does Not Practice

There is nothing profound about Jacques Necker's Treatise on the Administration of the Finances of France, *published in 1784, three years after his dismissal from office as minister of finance. It was self-serving in the extreme and was intended to polish his badly tarnished reputation as a financier and man of enlightened views and to keep him in the public eye. It served admirably and played a part in his recall to power in 1788 as the darling of the parlements and the hope of "the people." His dismissal — which did not prove long lasting — in July, 1789, provoked the storming of the Bastille.*

Necker's sentiments are those of pure "enlightened depotism." The thrust of his argument is admirable; his practice was something else; and his mode of expression at this critical point in French history was pernicious.

Jacques Necker's *Treatise on the Administration of the Finances of France*

INTRODUCTION

Retired to a private station, after a long series of labour and agitation of mind, I have not as yet been able to disengage myself from the great concerns, which have for so long a time engrossed all my thoughts; and by meditating on the past, and extending my views to future times, I have given way to the idea, that I might still be of some use to the public cause, even though it were only by communicating in a regular order, a great number of researches absolutely essential to the administration of the finances. I have myself experienced how difficult it was to unite those researches, almost all widely dispersed, and the greatest part of which had never been sought after: I have experienced how much time for reflection such a work required, which consequently retarded the hour, when I could act with security. Besides, I know not whether it be a vain illusion; but there have been moments in which I have flattered myself, that this last communication of a man who had shewn some zeal and application in an important career, would be favorably accepted and treated with indulgence. I have even dared to presume, that if the emotions of a mind still zealously disposed can supply the place of abilities, I should

From Jacques Necker, *A Treatise on the Administration of the Finances of France*, vol. 1, 2d ed., trans. Thomas Mortimer (London, 1786), pp. i–iii, 38–39, 44–45, 48–50.

Jacques Necker

perhaps be successful in strengthening the confidence that is due to those principles of administration which tend to the public happiness, and to the prosperity of an empire. But above all, I have persuaded myself, that if it was possible to demonstrate clearly to every one, the extent of the resources, and of the riches of France, it would be an efficacious way both to impress the enemies of that kingdom with more awe, and to moderate a little, in the minds of those who may be called to the government of it, those political jealousies which have been the source of so many evils. Lastly, either as a truth, or as a matter of consolation, I have cherished with rapture the hopes, that now, or hereafter, my works perhaps may be found to contain some sentiments, and some ideas which will enroll me, after my death, in the number of the well-wishers of France and of humanity. . . .

CHAPTER II. GENERAL REFLECTIONS ON THE EXTENT OF THE TAXES

I have now presented the statement of the taxes paid by the people; and I have shewn, that exclusive of the quartering of soldiers, of the obligation to cast lots for the militia, and of the sea service, these taxes amount to 585,000,000 [livres].

Indifferent men, and mere politicians, will only perceive, in this immensity of imposts, the great resources of France. No doubt, such an inference may be drawn from it; but I could wish that the first ideas and sentiments it occasions, were directed to another consideration. I could wish that the administration of the finances did not only see in that statement, the political power of the monarch, but that it could also perceive with heart-felt sorrow, the frightful extent of the self-denials that are required from the people: I could wish that it might be inspired with pity, by casting a look at the unhappy inhabitants of the country, and that giving way to a beneficent emotion it might consider, the immensity of the public charges, as a noble and wide field for the continual exercise of the wisdom and beneficence of the sovereign.

It is in vain that we endeavour to divert our thoughts from the enormity of the taxes; it is in vain that we listen to the hints of that class of men, who have connected the interest of self-love, and of their fortunes, with the extent of the collections, and their revenue knowledge; it is in vain that we seek, for an apology for our own administration, in the excessive taxes paid by the subjects of other countries. . . .

That which the good of the state requires: here lies the question, taxes that are proportioned to that public good of which the sovereign is the judge and the guardian, are just; but when they exceed that proportion, they cease to be equitable: therefore, no other difference exists between private acts of usurpation, and those of the sovereign, but that the injustice of the first is connected with a simple idea, which every one may distinguish, whilst the other being joined with combinations the extent of which is as immense as it is complicated, no one can form a judgment of their injustice, otherwise than by conjectures. But the principles of justice are not changed in a monarchical state, and the duties of the chief magistrate are not the less real, because he is the link of every political interest, and because under that form of government, he alone determines the measure of the sacrifices of his subjects, because he alone can decide on the exigencies of the state; because he alone commands, and has the sole power to enforce obedience!

These reflections give birth to a truth, that ought to terrify the consciences of soveigns; which is, that whilst they leave to courts of judicature, the decision of the common disputes that arise among their subjects, they remain sole arbiters of the greatest case, that can exist under the social compact: of that which should fix the bounds of the rights and claims of the royal exchequer, on the property of every member of society; and that in order to be well acquainted with this case in all its parts, and to be able to give judgment upon it, not only an honest heart, but likewise close study and great knowledge are necessary. In fact, if the sacrifices which the sovereign requires of his people become unjust; the moment they are unnecessary for the good of the state, how much attention does not that important consideration demand! He ought to have investigated every corrupt practice, and to have estimated every public expence, before he can say with certainty: this new tax which they propose to me as an addition to the public burthens, is an act of government which justice warrants. . . .

It is to avoid the consequences that result from these truths, that we often wish to consider the sovereign as the proprietor of an immense fortune, who disposes of his income according to his fancy, whilst, in fact, he is, or ought to be only a scrupulous distributor of the public treasures; and it is perhaps, a violation of the most sacred of all deposits, to employ the sacrifices of a whole nation in inconsiderate prodigalities, useless expences and undertakings foreign to the good of the state.

I have hitherto considered an unreasonable increase of taxes, so far as it is contrary only to justice; but we may likewise discover in such extensions, a continual source of evils and of vexations. In effect, as long as the total sum of the taxes is moderate, it is in the power of administration to regulate the disposal of them with prudence, their assessment with equity, and their collection with lenity; proportions may be established in which the difference of fortunes will be taken into consideration; the revenue officers may be narrowly watched, in short, the evils attending the imposts, may be confined to the imposts alone. But when the taxes are immoderate, when they even exceed a certain limit, the necessity of requiring great exactness, is augmented in proportion to the difficulty of collecting: it becomes necessary to give greater authority to the collectors; it becomes necessary to be insensible to complaints; and above all, we must venerate the science of finances, and honour all the professors of it without distinction; the very sources of the public prosperity must often be neglected, through the fear of constraining, by unskilful taxes, the encouragements of agriculture, the operations of commerce, and the efforts of industry. In short, when an immense debt, or ancient grants converted to pensions, are added to all the unjust, useless or extravagant expences of the present times, then the people no longer see a proportion between the sacrifices that are required from them, and the expences that appear necessary for the good of the state; and a diffidence and detestation of all fiscal operations, makes the nation lose the idea of the important affinity that ought to exist between the public exchequer, and the common interest of society. Let it not then be said, that excessive taxes, are not a great misfortune; they are too much so, for the people, the state and the sovereign: for, then, one of the greatest blessings of society is taken from the people, namely, the faculty of enjoying according to their inclinations, the fruits of their labours; part of the sources of its prosperity is likewise taken away from the state; and lastly, sovereigns sometimes lose that love and confidence of their subjects, the enjoyment of which is one of the greatest consolations, in the midst of the cares of government.

The Last Crisis of French Absolutism

Charles Maurice de Talleyrand-Perigord (1754–1838), sometime Bishop of Autun, Prince de Bénévent, served the Revolution and Napoleon Bonaparte, played a principal role in the restoration of Louis XVIII in 1814, and, as foreign minister of France at the Congress of Vienna, accomplished the spectacular feat of restoring France to a major place among the powers that had so recently defeated her. His Memoirs *were written late in his career from notes made at the time of the events recounted. In the 1780's, Talleyrand was a habitué of the salons of the Enlightenment and an aspiring prelate. Despite his cloth, he was anticlerical and played a prominent radical role in the National and Constituent Assemblies of the Revolution. There was a greater consistency in his position than his various life-roles would indicate. He was a French patriot and a committed rationalist. That consistency gives particular value, and not a little poignancy, to this excerpt.*

Talleyrand's Analysis

The importance which economic philosophers have enjoyed for nearly thirty years, demands that I should speak of them in a special manner.

The economists were a section of philosophers solely occupied in drawing from the administration all the means of amelioration of which they believed the social order was susceptible. They were divided into two classes: the one looked upon agriculture as the only creator of riches, and treated industrial labour and commerce as sterile, under the plea that they only created new forms and changes in the materials produced and created by agriculture. The doctrine of this first class of economists is called the doctrine of the net result, and is set forth in the *Tableau Économique*.[1] The object of this work is to show the distribution of the riches produced by agriculture, and spreading thence into all the arteries of the social body. The consequences of these doctrines following the circulation of wealth, end in the theory of taxation, which eventually saddles agriculture exclusively.

The liberty of commerce is almost the only point upon which this first class of economists is in harmony with the economists about whom I am going to speak. The latter did not adopt the division of sterile classes; they did not look upon the *Tableau Économique* as a strict or even sufficient demonstration of the phenomena of circulation. They restrict themselves in this respect to some truths of detail. Their great principle is the general liberty of trade in the most extended sense. As for taxation, they accept modifications — they are not absolute.

The government rejected the ideas of the economists of any school whatever; they preferred known and established principles. They feared changes which might interfere with the existing method of taxation, and with the regular flow of the revenue thus obtained into the royal treasury. Their fear of some diminution in the revenues of the State was such as to prevent their risking any means of increasing them. Such shortsighted and narrow views were necessarily prohibitive. . . .

The new spirit introduced into the *parlement* having sown the seeds of discontent and ambition amongst the members composing this ancient body, intrigue penetrated everywhere. M. Necker, M. de Calonne, M. de Breteuil [2] each had their creatures who defended or attacked the measures of the minister whom they wished to sustain or overthrow. Each day saw the great magistracy farther estranged from the royal authority, to which in the best times of the monarchy, it had been constantly attached.

From *Memoirs of the Prince de Talleyrand,* vol. 1, ed. Duc de Broglie, trans. R. L. de Beaufort (New York, 1891), pp. 66–67, 71–72, 89–93.
[1] The *Tableau Économique,* in which is set forth the physiocratic doctrine, is the work of the physician [François] Quesnay, 1694–1774, founder and head of that school.
[2] Successive finance ministers under Louis XVI from 1781 to 1788. — T. G. B.

Even *esprit de corps* no longer existed; the demand of the States-General, made a little more than a month afterwards, is a proof of this. An alarming number of scattered opinions which did not always take their stand under the colour of any party, caused anxiety to the ministry on the registering of each law that the needs of the State appeared to require. . . .

The State, although nominally divided into three orders, was really so only into two classes — the nobles and the plebeians; a portion of the clergy belonged to the first, and the rest to the second of these two classes.

[All pre-eminence in social order is founded on one of these four things — power, birth, riches, and personal merit.]

After the ministry of Cardinal de Richelieu and under Louis XIV, all the political power became concentrated in the hands of the monarch, and the orders of the State no longer possessed any.

Industry and commerce gave riches to the plebeian class, which developed all sorts of merit.

Only one title of pre-eminence thus remained: birth.

But, as nobility had been conferred for a long time on the purchasers of venal offices, birth itself could be obtained for money, thus lowering it to the level of riches.

The nobles themselves lowered it still more, by taking as wives the daughters of enriched *parvenus,* rather than poor girls of noble blood. Nobility could not fall below riches, without poverty degrading it; and the greater number of noble families were relatively or absolutely poor. Degraded by poverty, it was still more so by riches, when it had, as it were, sacrificed itself to them by these misalliances.

In the Church and episcopacy, the most lucrative dignities had become the almost exclusive portion of the aristocracy. In this respect, the principles constantly followed by Louis XIV had been abandoned. The plebeian, that is to say by far the most numerous section of the clergy, was therefore interested in seeing that, in its order, not only merit should always prevail over birth, but even that birth should count for nothing. In the noble class, there was no fixed hierarchy: the titles which ought to have served to indicate the rank had no constant value.

Instead of one nobility, there were seven or eight; that of the sword, and that of the magistracy, of the court, and the provincial nobility, the ancient and the recent nobility, the higher and lesser nobility. Each of these pretended to be superior to the others, which themselves claimed to be its equals. Besides these pretensions, the plebeian raised his own claims, almost equal to those of the simple gentleman seeing how easily he could obtain this title. Often quite superior to a gentleman in wealth and talents, the plebeian did not believe himself inferior to the nobles whom the simple gentleman considered as his equal.

The nobles no longer inhabited their feudal towers; war was no longer their sole occupation. They no longer lived exclusively with nobles like themselves, with their men-at-arms, or with the tenants of their estates. Another style of life had given them other tastes, and these tastes other needs. Often unoccupied, and making pleasure their only business, everything which was a resource against weariness, all that added to their enjoyment, became necessary to them. The plebeian, rich and enlightened, being no longer dependent upon them, having indeed no need of them, I have already said so, lived with them as with his equals.

When I spoke of the upper French society at the time of the Revolution, my object was to make known all the heterogeneous elements of which it was then composed, and to point out the results which such inconsistency of manners must necessarily bring about. I have reached the time when love of equality began to manifest itself without fear and with open face.

In polished times, the culture of letters, of the sciences, and of the fine arts, constitutes professions followed by men who generally belong, by their personal merit, to all that is most elevated; and, by their birth or fortune to all that is most inferior in civil society. A secret instinct must induce them to raise the advantages they possess to the level of, if not above, those of which they are deprived. Besides, their aim is, in general, to secure celebrity. The first condition for this is to please and to interest, to succeed in which there is no safer way for them than to flatter the ruling tastes and the prevailing opinions, which they strengthen by flattering. Manners and public opinion tended to equality; thus these men became its apostles.

While there were few other riches than landed property, and this was in the hands of the nobility, while industry and commerce were the callings of inferior men, the nobles scorned them, and, because they had once scorned them, they believed it their right and even their duty to scorn them always (even when relating themselves by marriage, which it shocked them to do, with the men who followed these callings), and by this, they incensed the pride of the plebeian class, who felt that one could not scorn their industry without scorning themselves.

From among the ruins of its former existence, the nobility had preserved certain privileges, which, in their origin, were only a compensation for charges which they alone supported, but which they had ceased to support. When the cause existed no longer, these privileges appeared unjust; but their injustice was not that which made them most odious, it was rather by reason of the fact that not on the quota but on the form of the tax, they established a distinction in which the plebeian class saw less a favour to the nobles than a slight to itself.

These sentiments in the plebeian class proceeded from the spirit of equality, and served to encourage it. He who would not be considered as an inferior, either claims or aspires to be treated on a footing of equality.

I ought to say besides, that that portion of the army so imprudently sent to the aid of the English colonies struggling against their mother-country, was imbued in the New World with the doctrines of equality. It returned full of admiration for these doctrines and perhaps with the desire also to put them into practice in France; and, by a sort of fatality, it was even this very time that Marshal de Ségur chose for reserving for the nobles all the officers' promotions in the army. A host of articles appeared denouncing the measure which closed to all who were not nobles, a career in which Fabert, Chevert, Catinat,[3] and others, plebeians like themselves, had covered themselves with glory. The lucrative professions being forbidden to the poor nobility, it had been thought advisable to offer them this compensation. Only this side of the question had been considered. But this measure, substituting evidently birth for personal merit, in what was the proper domain of merit, offended both reason and public opinion. For, in order to indemnify the nobles for the loss of advantages which the plebeian class already looked upon as a prejudice humiliating to them, on the latter were inflicted an injustice and an affront. This measure completed the estrangement of the troops already disaffected by the introduction of a foreign discipline which exposed them to a treatment, which, from the earliest times had been considered in France, as ignominious.[4] It seemed as though it were wished not to be able to depend on our brave soldiers at the time of the greatest danger, and, in fact, their assistance failed when it was most needed.

Thus all tended to injure the noble class: that which had been taken from it, and that which had been left to it, the poverty of some of its members, the wealth of the others, their vices and even their virtues.

But all this, as I have said before, when speaking of the second ministry of M. Necker,[5] was the work of the government, at least as much as the result of the general evolution of human things. It was not the work of the plebeian class, which merely profited by it. Equality had come, so to say, to meet the plebeians. To resist its advances would have required in the greater mass of men, a moderation and foresight of which but few privileged individuals are capable.

Equality once established between the two classes by new manners and accepted by public opinion, could not fail to be established by law as soon as the occasion should present itself.

[3] These three were all famous generals of the seventeenth and eighteenth centuries. — T. G. B.
[4] Lieutenant-General Comte de Saint-Germain, having been called to the Ministry of War, tried to re-establish discipline in the army. But he wished to introduce into France the corporal punishments in vogue with the Germans and the English. Public opinion was aroused against this innovation, and the Comte de Saint-Germain lost all the favour he commanded when he took office (1776).
[5] From 1788 to 1790. — T. G. B.

THE FRENCH REVOLUTION
Chapter 9

A revolution is many things. It is always success, for there is no revolution, only rebellion or insurrection, if those who seek change by force fail to achieve the power requisite to accomplish that change. It is always the legitimization of the force-that-succeeds. It is always the institutionalization of the change accomplished by the force-that-succeeds. Revolution is always in part symbolic, no matter how substantial its force, power, and change. Ultimately the success that is revolution depends upon a symbolic contrivance to represent the force, the power, and the change. For revolution does not last long; the excitation of a season cannot be sustained over more than a matter of years, counter-revolution saps the resolution of the opportunists, the excesses of revolution forfeit the allegiance of the conscientious, and the constant exhortation to greater effort, which alone affords continuation of the revolutionary impetus, falls on the increasingly deaf ears of the mass of the people whose indifference to all change is always considerable but whose sullen acquiescence in the use of force is essential to success. A revolution is in process of dissolution even as it begins. It is engaged in a grim race with time to create the symbols representing force, power, and change, and by those symbols to legitimize the force and institutionalize the change before its power disappears.

No analysis of a revolution that limited itself to the symbolic contrivance of the revolution would be complete. Yet no analysis that ignored the symbolic contrivance could wholly succeed in explaining how the revolution succeeded. Moreover, if an analyst is limited by time and effort, he will find an approach to the revolution through its symbolic contrivance at least a suggestive means toward understanding it. No revolution in history has been so well documented and so thoroughly studied as the French Revolution, which began with the convention of the Estates-General at Versailles on May 5, 1789, and ended with the Proclamation of the Consuls of the French Republic at Paris on 24 Frimaire, Year VIII (December 15, 1799). It remains to be seen whether any other revolution in history will have as profound effects as did the French Revolution.

The following documents have been chosen not for what they indicate factually about the Revolution — though there is plenty of fact in them — but for the insight they give into the French Revolution as a symbolic contrivance.

> [Louis XVI's] apprehension got the better of the party, who had for some days guided him; and he was thus induced to take this step, which is of such importance, that he will never more know where to stop, or what to refuse; or rather he will find, that in the future arrangement of the kingdom, his situation will be very nearly that of Charles I, a spectator, without power, of the effective resolutions of a long parliament. The joy this step occasioned was infinite; the assembly, uniting with the people, all hurried to the chateau [of Versailles]. *Vive le Roi* might have been heard at Marly: the King and Queen appeared in the balcony, and were received with the loudest shouts of applause; the leaders, who governed these motions, knew the value of the concession much better than those who made it.

Arthur Young's prophetic words of May 27, 1789, catch the opening success of the Revolution both as substance and as symbol.

Twenty Days That Shook the World: June 8–27, 1789

Arthur Young (1741–1820), an Englishman, was an astute observer, a journalist, and a highly original writer on agriculture. He was an admirer of the philosophes, especially the physiocrats because of their interest in agricultural economics. He was well connected in French circles and traveled extensively in France in 1787 and 1788, before arriving in Paris in early June, 1789. The Estates-General had convened a month before. Abbé Siéyès' "What is the Third Estate?" was the question of the moment, and Siéyès along with Mirabeau comprised the voice of change. Young was a good Whig, a respecter of constitutionalism, and no friend of absolutism. His position was suitably detached, though, and his sense of history, the keenness of his powers as an observer, and his articulateness provided him with an understanding of the situation that eluded the actors in it — especially the king and his advisers.

Account by Arthur Young, a Visiting Englishman

[June 8, 1789]. Paris is at present in such a ferment about the States General, now holding at Versailles, that conversation is absolutely absorbed by them. Not a word of any thing else talked of. Every thing is considered, and just so, as important in such a crisis of the fate of four-and-twenty millions of people. . . . The most prominent feature that appears at present is, that an idea of common interest and common danger does not seem to unite those, who, if not united, may find themselves too weak to oppose the common danger that must arise from the people being sensible of a strength the result of *their* weakness. The king, court, nobility, clergy, army, and parliament, are nearly in the same situation. All these consider, with equal dread, the ideas of liberty, now afloat; except the first, who, for reasons obvious to those who know his character, troubles himself little, even with circumstances that concern his power the most intimately. Among the rest, the feeling of danger is common, and they would unite, were there a head to render it easy, in order to do without the states at all. That the commons themselves look for some such hostile union as more than probable, appears from an idea which gains ground, that they will find it necessary should the other two orders continue to unite with them in one chamber, to declare themselves boldly the representatives of the kingdom at large, calling on the nobility and clergy to take their places — and to enter upon deliberations of business without them, should they refuse it. All conversation at present is on this topic, but opinions are more divided than I should have expected. There seem to be many who hate the clergy so cordially, that rather than permit them to form a distinct chamber would venture on a new system, dangerous as it might prove.

The 9th. The business going forward at present in the pamphlet shops of Paris is incredible. I went to the Palais Royal to see what new things were published, and to procure a catalogue of all. Every hour produces something new. . . . The spirit of reading political tracts, they say, spreads into the provinces, so that all the presses of France are equally employed. Nineteen-twentieths of these productions are in favour of liberty, and commonly violent against the clergy and nobility; I have to-day bespoken many of this description, that have reputation; but enquiring for such as had appeared on the other side of the question, to my astonishment I find there are but two or three that have merit enough to be known. Is it not wonderful, that while the press teems with the most levelling and even seditious principles, that if put in execution would

Arthur Young, *Travels During 1787, 1788, and 1789* (Bury St. Edmunds, 1792), pp. 102–07, 110–12, 114–16, 118–19, 122–24.

overturn the monarchy, nothing in reply appears, and not the least step is taken by the court to restrain this extreme licentiousness of publication. It is easy to conceive the spirit that must thus be raised among the people. But the coffee-houses in the Palais Royal present yet more singular and astonishing spectacles; they are not only crouded within, but other expectant crouds are at the doors and windows, listening *à gorge deployé* to certain orators, who from chairs or tables harrangue each his little audience: the eagerness with which they are heard, and the thunder of applause they receive for every sentiment of more than common hardiness or violence against the present government, cannot easily be imagined. I am all amazement at the ministry permitting such nests and hotbeds of sedition and revolt, which disseminate amongst the people, every hour, principles that by and by must be opposed with vigour, and therefore it seems little short of madness to allow the propagation at present.

The 10th. Every thing conspires to render the present period in France critical: the want of bread is terrible: accounts arrive every moment from the provinces of riots and calling in the military, to preserve the peace of the markets. The prices reported are the same as I found at Abbeville and Amiens 5 *sou* (2½ *d.*) a pound for white bread, and 3½ *sou* to 4 *sou* for the common sort, eaten by the poor: these rates are beyond their faculties, and occasion great misery. . . . It appears plain to me, that the violent friends of the commons are not displeased at the high price of corn, which seconds their views greatly, and makes any appeal to the common feeling of the people more easy, and much more to their purpose than if the price was low. Three days past, the chamber of the clergy contrived a cunning proposition; it was to send a deputation to the commons, proposing to name a commission from the three orders to take into consideration the misery of the people, and to deliberate on the means of lowering the price of bread. This would have led to the deliberation by order, and not by heads, consequently must be rejected, but unpopularly so from the situation of the people: the commons were equally dextrous; in their reply, they prayed and conjured the clergy to join them in the common hall of the states to deliberate, which was no sooner reported at Paris than the clergy became doubly an object of hatred; and it became a question with the politicians of the *Caffé de Toy*, whether it was not lawful for the commons to decree the application of their estates towards easing the distress of the people?

The 11th. I have been in much company all day, and cannot but remark, that there seem to be no settled ideas of the best means of forming a new constitution. Yesterday the Abbé Syeyes made a motion in the house of commons, to declare boldly to the privileged orders, that if they will not join the commons, the latter will proceed in the national business without them; and the house decreed it, with a small amendment.

This causes much conversation on what will be the consequence of such a proceeding; and on the contrary, on what may flow from the nobility and clergy continuing steadily to refuse to join the commons, and should they so proceed, to protest against all they decree, and appeal to the King to dissolve the states, and recal them in such a form as may be practicable for business. In these most interesting discussions, I find a general ignorance of the principles of government; a strange and unaccountable appeal, on one side, to ideal and visionary rights of nature; and, on the other, no settled plan that shall give security to the people for being in future in a much better situation than hitherto; a security absolutely necessary. But the nobility, with the principles of great lords that I converse with, are most disgustingly tenacious of all old rights, however hard they may bear on the people; they will not hear of giving way in the least to the spirit of liberty, beyond the point of paying equal land-taxes, which they hold to be all that can with reason be demanded. The popular party, on the other hand, seem to consider all liberty as depending on the privileged classes being lost, and outvoted in the order of the commons, at least for making the new constitution; and when I urge the great probability, that should they once unite, there will remain no power of ever separating them; and that in such case, they will have a very questionable constitution, perhaps a very bad one; I am always told, that the first object must be for the people to get the power of doing good; and that it is no argument against such a conduct to urge that an ill use may be made of it. But among such men, the common idea is, that any thing tending towards a separate order, like our house of lords, is absolutely inconsistent with liberty; all which seems perfectly wild and unfounded. . . .

[June 12]. The ideas of the public on the great business going on at Versailles change daily and even hourly. It now seems the opinion, that the commons, in their late violent vote, have gone too far; and that the union of the nobility, clergy, army, parliament, and King, will be by far too many for them; such an union is said to be in agitation; and that the count d'Artois, the Queen, and the party usually known by her name, are taking steps to effect it, against the moment when the proceedings of the commons shall make it necessary to act with unity and vigour. The abolition of the parliaments is common conversation among the popular leaders, as a step essentially necessary; because, while they exist, they are tribunals to which the court can have resort, should they be inclined to take any step against the existence of the states: those bodies are alarmed, and see with deep regret, that their refusal to register the royal edicts, has created a power in the nation not only hostile, but dangerous to their own existence. It is now very well known and understood on all hands, that should the King get rid of the states, and govern on any tolerable principles, all his edicts would be enregistered by all the parliaments. In the

June 8–27, 1789 181

dilemma and apprehension of the moment, the people look very much to the duc d'Orleans, as to a head; but with palpable and general ideas of distrust and want of confidence; they regret his character, and lament that they cannot depend on him in any severe and difficult trial: they conceive him to be without steadiness, and that his greatest apprehension is to be exiled from the pleasures of Paris, and tell of many littlenesses he practiced before, to be recalled from banishment. They are, however, so totally without a head, that they are contented to look to him as one; and are highly pleased with what is every moment reported, that he is determined to go at the head of a party of the nobility, and verify their powers in common with the commons. All agree, that had he firmness, in addition to his vast revenue of seven millions (306,250 *livres*) and four more (175,000 *livres*) in reversion, after the death of his father-in-law, the duc de Penthievre, he might, at the head of the popular cause do any thing.

The 15th. This has been a rich day, and such an one as ten years ago none could believe would ever arrive in France; a very important debate being expected on what, in our house of commons, would be termed the state of the nation. My friend Mons. Lazowski and myself were at Versailles by eight in the morning. We went immediately to the hall of the states to secure good seats in the gallery; we found some deputies already there, and a pretty numerous audience collected. The room is too large; none but stentorian lungs, or the finest clearest voices can be heard; however the very size of the apartment, which admits 2000 people, gave a dignity to the scene. It was indeed an interesting one. The spectacle of the representatives of twenty-five millions of people, just emerging from the evils of 200 years of arbitrary power, and rising to the blessings of a freer constitution, assembled with open doors under the eye of the public, was framed to call into animated feelings every latent spark, every emotion of a liberal bosom. To banish whatever ideas might intrude of their being a people too often hostile to my own country — and to dwell with pleasure on the glorious idea of happiness to a great nation — of felicity to millions yet unborn. Mons. l'Abbé Syeyes opened the debate. He is one of the most zealous sticklers for the popular cause; carries his ideas not to a regulation of the present government, which he thinks too bad to be regulated at all, but wishes to see it absolutely overturned; being in fact a violent republican: this is the character he commonly bears, and in his pamphlets he seems pretty much to justify such an idea. He speaks ungracefully, and uneloquently, but logically, or rather reads so, for he read his speech, which was prepared. His motion, or rather string of motions, was to declare themselves the representatives known and verified of the French nation, admitting the right of all absent deputies (the nobility and clergy) to be received among them on the verification of their powers. Mons. de Mirabeau spoke without notes, for near an hour, with a warmth, animation, and eloquence, that entitles him to the reputation of an undoubted orator. He opposed the words *known* and *verified,* in the proposition of Abbé Syeyes, with great force of reasoning; and proposed, in lieu, that they should declare themselves simply *Representatives du peuple Françoise:* that no *veto* should exist against their resolves in any other assembly: that all taxes are illegal, but should be granted during the present session of the states, and no longer: that the debt of the king should become the debt of the nation, and be secured on funds accordingly. Mons. de Mirabeau was well heard, and his proposition much applauded. . . .

In regard to their general method of proceedings, there are two circumstances in which they are very deficient: the spectators in the galleries are allowed to interfere in the debates by clapping their hands, and other noisy expressions of approbation: this is grossly indecent; it is also dangerous; for, if they are permitted to express approbation, they are, by parity of reason, allowed expressions of dissent; and they may hiss as well as clap; which, it is said, they have sometimes done: this would be, to overrule the debate, and influence the deliberations. Another circumstance, is the want of order among themselves; more than once to-day there were an hundred members on their legs at a time, and Mons. Baillie absolutely without power to keep order. This arises very much from complex motions being admitted; to move a declaration relative to their title, to their powers, to taxes, to a loan, &c. &c. all in one proposition, appears to English ears preposterous, and certainly is so. Specific motions, founded on single and simple propositions, can alone produce order in debate; for it is endless to have five hundred members declaring their reasons of assent to one part of a complex proposition, and their dissent to another part. . . .

The 18th. Yesterday the commons decreed themselves, in consequence of the Abbé Syeyes's amended motion, the title of *Assembleé Nationale;* and also, considering themselves then in activity, the illegality of all taxes; but granted them during the session, declaring that they would, without delay, deliberate on the consolidating of the debt; and on the relief of the misery of the people. These steps give great spirits to the violent partizans of a new constitution, but amongst more sober minds, I see evidently an apprehension, that it will prove a precipitate measure. It is a violent step, which may be taken hold of by the court, and converted very much to the peoples disadvantage. . . .

The 20th. News! News! Every one stares at what every one might have expected. A message from the King to the presidents of the three orders, that he should meet them on Monday; and, under pretence of preparing the hall for the *seance royale,* the French guards were placed with bayonets to prevent any of the deputies entering the room. The circumstances of doing this ill-judged act of violence have been as ill-advised as the act itself. Mons. Bailly received no other notice of it than by a letter from the marquis de Brézé, and the deputies met at the door of the hall, without knowing that it was shut. Thus the seeds of disgust were sown wantonly in the manner of doing a thing, which in itself was equally impalatable and unconstitutional. The resolution taken on the spot was a noble and firm one; it was to assemble instantly at the *Jeu de paume,* and there the whole assembly took a solemn oath never to be dissolved but by their own consent, and consider themselves, and act as the national assembly, let them be wherever violence or fortune might drive them, and their expectations were so little favourable, that expresses were sent off to Nantes, intimating that the national assembly might possibly find it necessary to take refuge in some distant city. This message, and placing guards at the hall of the states, are the result of long and repeated councils, held in the king's presence at Marly, where he has been shut up for some days, seeing nobody; and no person admitted, even to the officers of the court, without jealousy and circumspection. The King's brothers have no seat in the council, but the count d'Artois incessantly attends the resolutions, conveys them to the Queen, and has long conferences with her. When this news arrived at Paris, the Palais Royal was in a flame, the coffee-houses, pamphlet-shops, corridores, and gardens were crouded — alarm and apprehension sat in every eye — the reports that were circulated eagerly, tending to shew the violent intentions of the court, as if it was bent on the utter extirpation of the French nation, except the party of the Queen, are perfectly incredible for their gross absurdity: but nothing was so glaringly ridiculous but the mob swallowed it with undiscriminating faith. It was, however, curious to remark, among people of another description (for I was in several parties after the news arrived), that the balance of opinions was clearly that the national assembly, as it called itself, had gone too far — had been too precipitate — and too violent — had taken steps that the mass of the people would not support. From which we may conclude, that if the court, having seen the tendency of their late proceedings, shall pursue a firm and politic plan, the popular cause will have little to boast.

The 21st. It is impossible to have any other employment at so critical a moment, than going from house to house demanding news; and remarking the opinions and ideas most current. The present moment is, of all others, perhaps that which is most pregnant with the future destiny of France. The step the commons have taken of declaring themselves the national assembly, independent of the other orders, and of the King himself, precluding a dissolution, is in fact an assumption of all the authority in the kingdom. They have at one stroke converted themselves into the long parliament of Charles I. It needs not the assistance of much penetration to see that if such a pretension and declaration are not done away, King, lords, and clergy are deprived of their shares in the legislature of France. So bold, and apparently desperate a step, full in the teeth of every other interest in the realm, equally destructive to the royal authority, by parliaments and the army, can never be allowed. If it is not opposed, all other powers will lie in ruins around that of the common. With what anxious expectation must one therefore wait to see if the crown will exert itself firmly on the occasion, with such an attention to an improved system of liberty, as is absolutely necessary to the moment! All things considered, that is, the characters of those who are in possession of power, no well digested system and steady execution are to be looked for. . . .

The 23d. The important day is over: in the morning Versailles seemed filled with troops: the streets, about ten o'clock, were lined with the French guards, and some Swiss regiments, &c.: the hall of the states was surrounded, and centinels fixed in all the passages, and at the doors; and none but deputies admitted. This military preparation was ill judged, for it seemed admitting the impropriety and unpopularity of the intended measure, and the expectation, perhaps fear of popular commotions. They pronounced, before the King left the chateau, that his plan was adverse to the people, from the military parade with which it was ushered in. The contrary, however, proved to be the fact; the propositions are known to all the world: the plan was a good one; much was granted to the people in great and essential points; and as it was granted before they had provided for those public necessities of finance, which occasioned the states being called together; and consequently left them at full power in future to procure for the people all that opportunity might present, they apparently ought to accept them, provided some security is given for the future meetings of the states, without which all the rest would be insecure; but as a little negotiation may easily secure this, I apprehend the deputies will accept them conditionally: the use of soldiers, and some imprudencies in the manner of forcing the King's system, relative to the interior constitution, and assembling of the deputies, as well as the ill-blood which had had time to brood for three days past in their minds, prevented the commons from receiving the King with any expressions of applause; the clergy, and some of the nobility, cried *vive le Roi!* but treble the number of mouths being silent, took off all effect.

The 24th. The ferment at Paris is beyond conception; 10,000 people have been all this day in the Palais Royal; a full detail of yesterday's proceedings was brought this morning, and read by many apparent leaders of little parties, with comments, to the people. To my surprise, the King's propositions are received with universal disgust. He said nothing explicit on the periodical meeting of the states; he declared all the old feudal rights to be retained as property. These, and the change in the balance of representation in the provincial assemblies, are the articles that give the greatest offence. But, instead of looking to, or hoping for further concessions on these points, in order to make them more consonant to the gen-

June 8–27, 1789

eral wishes; the people seem, with a sort of phrenzy, to reject all idea of compromise, and to insist on the necessity of the orders uniting, that full power may consequently reside in the commons, to effect what they call the regeneration of the kingdom, a favourite term, to which they affix no precise idea, but add the indefinite explanation of the general reform of all abuses. . . .

The 26th. Every hour that passes seems to give the people fresh spirit: the meetings at the Palais Royal are more numerous, more violent, and more assured; and in the assembly of electors, at Paris, for sending a deputation to the National Assembly, the language that was talked, by all ranks of people, was nothing less than a revolution in the government, and the establishment of a free constitution: what they mean by a free constitution, is easily understood — *a republic;* for the doctrine of the times runs every day more and more to that point; yet they profess, that the kingdom ought to be a monarchy too; or, at least, that there ought to be a king. In the streets one is stunned by the hawkers of seditious pamphlets, and descriptions of pretended events, that all tend to keep the people equally ignorant and alarmed. The supineness, and even stupidity of the court, is without example: the moment demands the greatest decision — and yesterday, while it was actually a question, whether he should be a doge of Venice, or a king of France, the King went a hunting! . . .

The 27th. The whole business now seems over, and the revolution complete. The King has been frightened by the mobs into overturning his own act of the *seance royale,* by writing to the presidents of the orders of the nobility and clergy, requiring them to join the commons — full in the teeth of what he had ordained before. It was represented to him, that the want of bread was so great in every part of the kingdom, that there was no extremity to which the people might not be driven: that they were nearly starving, and consequently ready to listen to any suggestions, and on the *qui vive* for all sorts of mischief: that Paris and Versailles would inevitably be burnt; and, in a word, that all sorts of misery and confusion would follow his adherence to the system announced in the *seance royale.* His apprehensions got the better of the party, who had for some days guided him; and he was thus induced to take this step, which is of such importance, that he will never more know where to stop, or what to refuse; or rather he will find, that in the future arrangement of the kingdom, his situation will be very nearly that of Charles I, a spectator, without power, of the effective resolutions of a long parliament. The joy this step occasioned was infinite; the assembly, uniting with the people, all hurried to the chateau. *Vive le Roi* might have been heard at Marly: the King and Queen appeared in the balcony, and were received with the loudest shouts of applause; the leaders, who governed these motions, knew the value of the concession much better than those who made it.

The Constitution of 1791 and Louis, "King of the French"

Having declared itself the National Assembly on June 17, 1789, the Estates-General ceased to exist. In its new role and later as the Constituent Assembly, this representative body dismantled the Old Regime and its absolutist forms in Church and state. At its back was the Paris mob, and after the mob brought the king and the royal family to Paris from Versailles in October, 1789, the Assembly moved too, and the mob was in its galleries.

The lengthy National Constitution promulgated on September 14, 1791, summed up the structural innovations of the Assembly in the preceding two years and the spirited Declaration of the Rights of Man and Citizen of August, 1789. It established a constitutional monarchy with the executive power vested in ministers responsible to a unicameral Legislative Assembly that could not be dissolved by the executive. It was a moderate, workable constitution. Louis — in his new style, "by the Grace of God and the constitutional law of the state, King of the French" — proclaimed his acceptance of it in the most touching document of the era. His intent to live with and by the new constitution was sincere, though his enthusiasm was forced.

The Constitution of September 14, 1791

PREAMBLE

The National Assembly, wishing to establish the French Constitution upon the principles it has just recognized and declared, abolishes irrevocably the institutions which wounded liberty and equality of rights.

There no longer exists nobility, or peerage, or hereditary distinctions, or distinctions of orders, or feudal regime, or patrimonial courts, or any titles, denominations, or prerogatives derived therefrom, or any order of knighthood, or any associations or decorations requiring proofs of nobility or implying distinctions of birth, or any superiority other than that of public functionaries in the exercise of their functions.

There no longer exists venality or inheritance of any public office.

There no longer exists for any part of the nation or any individual any privilege or exception to the law common to all Frenchmen.

From *Collection Générale des Lois*, vol. 5, part 2, August–September 1791 (Paris, 1792), pp. 1216–19, 1221–23, 1230–33. Trans. Thomas G. Barnes.

There no longer exists *jurandes* or associations of professions, arts and crafts.

The law no longer recognizes religious vows or any other obligation that would be contrary to natural rights or to the Constitution.

TITLE I. FUNDAMENTAL PROVISIONS GUARANTEED BY THE CONSTITUTION

The Constitution guarantees as natural and civil rights:

1st, That all citizens are admissible to offices and employments, without other distinction than virtues and talents;

2nd, That all taxes shall be apportioned equally upon all citizens, in proportion to their means;

3rd, That like offences shall be punished with like penalties, without any distinction of persons.

The Constitution guarantees likewise as natural and civil rights:

Liberty to every man to come, remain, and to go without being subject to arrest or detention, except according to the forms determined by the Constitution;

Liberty to every man to speak, write, print, and publish his thoughts without his writings being subject to any censorship or inspection before their publication, and to exercise the religion to which he is attached.

Liberty to citizens to assemble peaceably and without arms in accordance with police regulations;

Liberty to address individually signed petitions to the constituted authorities.

The legislative power may not make any laws which infringe upon or obstruct the exercise of the natural and civil rights recorded in the present title and guaranteed by the Constitution; but, since liberty consists of being able to do only that which does not injure the rights of others or public safety, the law can establish penalties for acts which, assailing either public safety or the rights of others, might be injurious to society.

The Constitution guarantees the inviolability of property, or just and prior indemnity for that of which a legally established public necessity requires the sacrifice.

Property intended for the expenses of worship and for all services of public benefit belongs to the nation, and is at its disposal at all times.

The Constitution guarantees transfers of property which have been or may be made according to the forms established by law.

Citizens have the right to elect or choose the ministers of their religions.

There shall be created and organized a general institution for *public relief* to raise foundlings, relieve the infirm poor, and furnish work for the able-bodied poor who have been unable to procure it for themselves.

There shall be created and organized *public instruction* for all citizens, free of charge, in those branches of education indispensable to all men, and the institutions thereof shall be distributed by a graduated scale, in accordance with the division of the kingdom.

There shall be established national festivals to preserve the memory of the French Revolution, to maintain fraternity among the citizens, and to bind them to the Constitution, the *Patrie,* and the laws.

There shall be made a code of civil law common to the entire kingdom. . . .

TITLE III. OF PUBLIC POWERS

1. Sovereignty is one, indivisible, inalienable, and imprescriptible. It appertains to the nation; no section of the people nor any individual may assume the exercise thereof.

2. The nation, from which alone all powers emanate, may exercise such powers only by delegation.

The French Constitution is representative; the representatives are the legislative body and the King.

3. The legislative power is delegated to a National Assembly, composed of temporary representatives freely elected by the people, to be exercised by it, with the sanction of the King, in the manner which will be hereinafter determined.

4. The government is monarchical; the executive power is delegated to the King, to be exercised, under his authority, by ministers and other responsible agents in the manner which will be hereinafter determined.

5. The judicial power is delegated to judges who are elected for a term by the people.

CHAPTER I. OF THE NATIONAL LEGISLATIVE ASSEMBLY

1. The National Assembly constituting the legislative body is permanent and is composed of only one chamber.

2. It shall be formed every two years by new elections.

Every period of two years shall constitute a legislature.

3. The provisions of the preceding article shall not apply to the next legislative body, the powers of which shall cease on the last day of April, 1793.

4. Renewal of the legislative body shall be done as of full right.

5. The legislative body may not be dissolved by the King. . . .

[Detailed specific provisions for the composition of, election to, and meetings of the National Legislative Assembly follow.]

CHAPTER II. OF MONARCHY, THE REGENCY, AND THE MINISTERS

Section 1. Monarchy and the King

1. Monarchy is indivisible, and is delegated hereditarily to the reigning

The Constitution of 1791

family, from male to male, by order of primogeniture, to the perpetual exclusion of women and their descendants.

(Nothing is presumed concerning the effect of renunciations in the present reigning family.)

2. The person of the King is inviolable and sacred; his only title is *King of the French*.

3. There is no authority in France superior to that of the law; the King reigns only thereby, and only in the name of the law may he exact obedience.

4. The King, on his accession to the throne, or as soon as he has attained his majority, shall take an oath to the nation, in the presence of the legislative body, *to be faithful to the nation and to the law, to employ all the power delegated to him to maintain the Constitution decreed by the National Constituent Assembly in the years 1789, 1790, and 1791, and to have the laws executed.* . . .

5. If, one month after the invitation of the legislative body, the King has not taken this oath, or if, after having taken it, he retracts it, he shall be deemed to have abdicated the throne.

6. If the King places himself at the head of an army and directs the forces thereof against the nation, or if he does not, by a formal act, oppose any such undertaking carried on in his name, he shall be deemed to have abdicated the throne.

7. If the King, having left the kingdom, does not return after invitation has been made to him by the legislative body, and within the period established by the legislative body's proclamation, which may not be less than two months, he shall be deemed to have abdicated the throne. . . .

8. After express or legal abdication, the King shall be classed as a citizen, and he may be accused and tried as one for acts subsequent to his abdication.

9. The private property which the King possesses upon his accession to the throne is irrevocably united with the national domain; he has disposition of property acquired by singular title; if he has not disposed thereof, it likewise is united at the end of the reign.

10. The nation provides for the splendor of the throne by a civil list, the sum of which shall be determined by the legislative body at each change of reign, for the entire duration of the reign.

11. The King shall appoint an administrator of the civil list, who shall undertake lawsuits on behalf of the King, and against whom all actions for debt against the King shall be directed and judgments pronounced. Condemnations obtained by creditors of the civil list shall be executory against the administrator personally, and upon his own property.

12. The King shall have apart from the guard of honor furnished him by the citizen National Guard of the place of his residence, a guard, paid out of funds of the civil list; it may not exceed the number of 1,200 infantry and 600 cavalry. . . .

Louis XVI's Proclamation of September 28, 1791

Louis, by the grace of God and the constitutional law of the state, King of the French, to all citizens, greeting:

I have accepted the Constitution; I shall exert every effort to maintain it and to have it executed.

The end of the revolution is come. It is time that order be re-established so that the constiution may receive the support now most necessary to it; it is time to settle the opinion of Europe concerning the destiny of France, and to show that Frenchmen are worthy of being free.

But my vigilance and care must be further seconded by the cooperation of all friends of the *Patrie* and of liberty. It is by submission to the laws, it is by abjuring partisan spirit and all the passions that accompany it, it is by a happy union of sentiments, desires, and efforts that the constitution will be secured, and that the nation will be able to enjoy all the advantages guaranteed by it.

Therefore, may every notion of intolerance be forever dispelled; may the thoughtless desire for independence be no longer confused with the love of liberty; may these injurious qualifications, with which some seek to agitate the people, be irrevocably banished; may religious opinions no longer be a source of persecution and hatred, that each, by observing the laws, may be able at his pleasure to practice the religion to which he is attached; and that on all sides one no longer abuses those who, following different opinions, believe that they are obeying their consciences.

But it is not sufficient to avoid the excesses into which the spirit of exaggeration might transport you; you must also fulfill the obligations which the public interest imposes upon you. One of the first, one of the most essential, is the payment of the taxes established by your representatives. It is for the fulfillment of promises which national honor has rendered sacred, for the internal tranquillity of the state and for its external security, it is for the very stability of the constitution that I remind you of this indispensable duty.

Citizens armed for the maintenance of the law, National Guards never forget that it is to "protect the security of persons and property, the collection of public taxes, the circulation of grain and provisions," that the arms you bear have been placed in your hands. It is for you to perceive that both justice and utility demand that among the inhabitants of one empire abundance comes to succor need, and that it is the responsibility of the armed forces to encourage the movement of commerce, as the means to remedy the immoderateness of the seasons, that redresses

From *Collection Générale des Lois*, vol. 5, part 2, August–September 1791 (Paris, 1792), pp. 1315–17. Trans. Thomas G. Barnes.

the inequality of crops, that binds all parts of the kingdom together, that makes common the various productions of soil and industry.

And you, whom the people have chosen to watch over its interests, you also have conferred upon you the awesome power to pronounce upon the property, the honor, and the lives of citizens; you moreover who have been instituted to conciliate their differences, members of the several administrative bodies, judges of the courts, justices of the peace, I enjoin you to become imbued with the importance and dignity of your functions; fulfill them with zeal, courage, and impartiality; work with me to restore peace and the rule of law; and, by thus assuring the happiness of the nation, prepare the return of those whose departure was motivated only by fear of disorders and violence.

And all you who for various motives have left your *Patrie,* your king recalls you to your fellow citizens; he bids you to defer to the public will and the national interest. Return with confidence, under the guarantee of the law, and this honorable return, at a time when the constitution has just been definitively decreed, will facilitate and hasten the re-establishment of peace and order.

And you, the French people, for so many centuries a celebrated nation, show that you are magnanimous and generous at the time of the establishment of your liberty; resume your happy character; may your moderation and wisdom effect among you a rebirth of the security which the tumults of revolution have banished therefrom, and may your king henceforth enjoy, without anxiety, without confusion, this testimony of love and fidelity which alone can assure his happiness.

Done at Paris, the twenty-eighth of September, one thousand, seven hundred and ninety-one.

Signed, Louis

Virtue Enthroned

Louis did not have long to live with the new constitution. His attempt to flee France even before the constitution was promulgated had made him suspect. The closing menace of foreign reaction to the Revolution, ostensibly to defend Louis and traditional monarchy, brought war. Neither the monarchy nor Louis survived the terrorism of the Paris mob led by the extreme radicals of the Revolution in August and September, 1792. A new, hastily elected, National Convention abolished monarchy and proclaimed a republic in September, 1792, and "Citizen Capet" — once Louis XVI — went to the guillotine on January 21, 1793.

The new republic aspired to be a "Republic of Virtue" in Rousseau's sense of virtue. Robespierre established the new cult of Worship of the Supreme Being as a means of strengthening national unity behind the republic. The step was characteristic of the extreme revolutionary phase of a revolution, when unity and legitimacy require a total ideological break with the past. One practical result of the Decree of the National Convention of 18 Floréal, Year II (May 7, 1794; the new revolutionary calendar was another such break), was fewer holidays than the old Christian faith had allowed and hence higher productivity. The seven-day week, with Sunday as the day of rest, by the new calendar became a ten-day week, with the tenth day (décade) a day of rest. There were only four annual holidays.

Institution of Tenth-Day Festivals

The National Convention, after having heard the report of the Committee of Public Safety decrees:

1. The French people recognize the existence of the Supreme Being and the immortality of the soul.
2. They recognize that the worship worthy of the Supreme Being is the observance of the duties of man.
3. They place in the forefront of such duties detestation of bad faith and tyranny, punishment of tyrants and traitors, succoring of unfortunates, respect of the weak, defence of the oppressed, doing to others all the good that one can, and being just towards everyone.
4. There shall be instituted festivals to remind man of the concept of the Divinity and of the dignity of his being.
5. They shall take their names from the glorious events of our Revolution, from the virtues most dear and most useful to man, and from the greatest benefits of nature.
6. The French Republic shall celebrate annually the festivals of 14 July, 1789, 10 August, 1792, 21 January, 1793, and 31 May, 1793.
7. On the days of *décade* it shall celebrate the following festivals:

To the Supreme Being and to nature; to the human race; to the French people; to the benefactors of humanity; to the martyrs of liberty; to liberty and equality; to the Republic; to the liberty of the world; to the love of the *Patrie;* to the hatred of tyrants and traitors; to truth; to justice; to modesty; to glory and immortality; to friendship; to frugality; to courage; to good faith; to heroism; to disinterestedness; to stoicism; to love; to conjugal love; to paternal love; to maternal tenderness; to filial

From *Collection Générale des Lois,* vol. 17 (Paris, 1794), pp. 769–71. Trans. Thomas G. Barnes.

piety; to infancy; to youth; to manhood; to old age; to misfortune; to agriculture; to industry; to our forefathers; to posterity; to happiness.

8. The Committees of Public Safety and Public Instruction are charged to present a plan of organization of these festivals.

9. The National Convention summons all talents worthy of serving the cause of humanity to the honor of concurring in their establishment by hymns and civic songs, and by every means which can contribute to their embellishment and usefulness.

10. The Committee of Public Safety shall single out the works which seem to it the most suitable to realize this objective, and shall compensate their authors.

11. Liberty of worship is maintained, in conformity with the decree of 18 Frimaire [December 8, 1793].

12. Every assembly which is aristocratic and contrary to public order shall be repressed.

13. In the event of disturbances whereof any worship whatever shall be the occasion or the motive whatsoever, those who instigate them by fanatical preachings or counter-revolutionary insinuations, those who provoke them by unjust and gratuitous violence, shall be uniformly punished according to the rigor of the laws.

14. There shall be made a particular report concerning the arrangements of detail relative to the present decree.

15. There shall be celebrated, on 20 Prairial next [June 8], a festival in honor of the Supreme Being.

David [1] is charged with presenting the plan thereof to the National Convention.

The National Convention decrees that the present decree and the report that has preceded it shall be printed and sent, in ordinary form and in poster, to all communities, armies, and popular associations of the Republic to be read and posted in all public places and in the army camps; it decrees as well that the report and the decree shall be translated into all languages, and six copies distributed to each of the members of the Convention.

---

[1] Jacques Louis David, the French classical painter, was court painter to Louis XVI, the Republic, and Napoleon, and he was a close friend of Robespierre — a politically extraordinary association. — T. G. B.

Terror Enthroned

The Terror of 1793 and 1794 was the systematic destruction of all opposition to the most extreme leadership in the Convention. It ended only when it became clear to his fellow radicals that Robespierre would ultimately destroy them. The Terror could be justified so long as France stood in imminent danger of external invasion and internal subversion, but by July, 1794, these dangers were no longer imminent. Robespierre was the only danger. His colleagues turned on him, the mob failed to heed his call, and on July 28 the dictator was guillotined. The Republic of Virtue died with him.

The Law of 22 Prairial, Year II (June 10, 1794), establishing the Revolutionary Tribunal, was the culmination of the steady growth of dictatorial power in the hands of Robespierre's Committee of Public Safety at the expense of the Convention itself. It was also the culmination of the Terror; almost no vestiges of due process in law were left in the broadened category of "counter-revolutionary crimes."

Establishment of the Revolutionary Tribunal

The National Convention, after having heard the report of the Committee of Public Safety, decrees:

1. In the Revolutionary Tribunal there shall be a president and four vice-presidents, one public prosecutor, four substitutes for the public prosecutor, and twelve judges.

2. The jurors shall be fifty in number.

3. The divers functions shall be performed by the citizens hereinafter named. . . .

The Revolutionary Tribunal shall divide itself into sections, composed of twelve members, to wit: three judges and nine jurors, which jurors may not pass judgment unless they are seven in number.

4. The Revolutionary Tribunal is instituted to punish the enemies of the people.

5. The enemies of the people are those who seek to exterminate public liberty, either by force or by cunning.

6. Those deemed enemies of the people are those who have instigated the re-establishment of monarchy, or have sought to disparage or dissolve the National Convention and the revolutionary and republican government of which it is the center;

Those who have betrayed the Republic in the command of places and

From *Bulletin des Lois de la République Française*, vol. 1, no. 1 (Paris, 1794). Trans. Thomas G. Barnes.

armies, or in any other military function; carried on correspondence with the enemies of the Republic, labored to cause the failure of the provisioning or the service of the armies;

Those who have sought to impede the provisioning of Paris, or to create scarcity within the Republic;

Those who have supported the designs of the enemies of France, either by countenancing the withdrawal and the impunity of conspirators and the aristocracy, by persecuting and calumniating patriotism, by corrupting the mandataries of the people, by abusing the principles of the Revolution, the laws or measures of the government, by false and perfidious applications;

Those who have deceived the people or the representatives of the people, in order to lead them into undertakings contrary to the interests of liberty;

Those who have sought to inspire discouragement, in order to favor the enterprises of the tyrants leagued against the Republic;

Those who have disseminated false news in order to divide or trouble the people;

Those who have sought to mislead opinion and to impede the instruction of the people, to deprave morals and to corrupt the public conscience, to pervert the energy and the purity of revolutionary and republican principles, or to arrest the progress thereof, either by counter-revolutionary or insidious writings, or by any other machination;

Contractors of bad faith who compromise the safety of the Republic, and squanderers of the public fortune, other than those included in the provisions of the law of 7 Frimaire; [1]

Those who, charged with public office, abuse it in order to serve the enemies of the Revolution, to harass patriots, or to oppress the people;

Finally, all who are designated in previous laws relative to the punishment of conspirators and counter-revolutionaries, and who, by whatever means or by whatever appearances they assume, have made an attempt against the liberty, unity, and security of the Republic, or labored to impede the strengthening thereof.

7. The penalty provided for all offences pertaining to the jurisdiction of the Revolutionary Tribunal is death.

8. The proof necessary to convict enemies of the people comprises every kind of evidence, whether material or moral,[2] oral or written, which can naturally secure the approval of every just and reasonable mind; the rule of judgments is the conscience of the jurors, enlightened by love of the *Patrie;* their aim, the triumph of the Republic and the ruin

---

[1] Law of November 27, 1793, against embezzlers of provisions. — T. G. B.

[2] Moral evidence is founded on analogy or induction, experience, or the testimony of witnesses, as distinct from physical evidence. Without developing an absolute certainty, it does develop a high degree of probability. — T. G. B.

of its enemies; the procedure, the simple means which good sense dictates in order to arrive at knowledge of the truth, in the forms determined by law.

It is confined to the following points.

9. Every citizen has the right to seize conspirators and counter-revolutionaries, and to cite them before the magistrates. He is bound to denounce them as soon as he knows of them.

10. Nobody may cite anyone before the Revolutionary Tribunal except the National Convention, the Committee of Public Safety, the Committee of General Security, the representatives of the people who are commissioners of the Convention, and the public prosecutor at the Revolutionary Tribunal.

11. The constituted authorities in general may not exercise such right without having notified the Committee of Public Safety and the Committee of General Security and obtained their authorization.

12. The accused shall be interrogated publicly at the hearing; the formality of preceding secret examination is suppressed as superfluous; it shall take place only in particular circumstances in which it is deemed useful for knowledge of the truth.

13. If either material or moral proofs exist, independently of the testified proof, there shall be no further hearing of witnesses, unless this formality appears necessary, either to discover accomplices or for other important considerations of public interest.

14. In case there is occasion for this proof, the public prosecutor shall cause to be called witnesses who are able to enlighten justice, without distinction as to witnesses for or against the accusation.

15. All testimony shall be given in public, and no written deposition shall be received, unless witnesses cannot come before the Tribunal; and in this case an express authorization of the Committees of Public Safety and General Security shall be necessary.

16. The law provides sworn patriots as counsel for calumniated patriots; it does not grant them to conspirators.

17. The trial completed, the jurors shall formulate their verdicts, and the judges shall pronounce the penalty in the manner determined by law.

The president shall propound the question with clarity, precision, and simplicity. If it is presented in an equivocal or inexact manner the jury may ask that it be propounded in another manner.

18. The public prosecutor may not, on his own authority, discharge an accused person sent to the Tribunal, or one whom he himself has caused to be cited before it; in case there is no ground for accusation before the Tribunal, he shall make a written report of his reasons to the chamber of the council, which shall decree therein. But no accused person may be discharged from trial before the decision of the chamber has been communi-

Establishment of the Revolutionary Tribunal 197

cated to the Committees of Public Safety and General Security, which shall examine it.

19. A duplicate register shall be kept of the persons cited before the Revolutionary Tribunal, one for the public prosecutor and the other for the Tribunal, and all accused persons shall be enrolled thereon as they are cited.

20. The Convention repeals all those provisions of previous laws which are at variance with the present law, and it does not intend that laws concerning the organization of the ordinary courts should apply to the crimes of counter-revolution and to the functioning of the Revolutionary Tribunal.

21. The report of the Committee shall be appended to the present act as an instruction.

THE NAPOLEONIC ERA
Chapter 10

On December 15, 1799, Roger Ducos, Abbé Emmanuel-Joseph Siéyès, and First Consul General Napoleon Bonaparte declared that the French Revolution was ended. They were the three consuls established by the coup d'état a month earlier, during which Bonaparte had almost lost everything by a failure of nerve and was rescued only by the intervention of his brother Lucien. The coup had succeeded in overthrowing the Directory, and Ducos and Siéyès, both former Directors, were the window dressing of continuity for the new regime. They were men of the past. Siéyès was the golden pen of the first days of revolution whose rhetorical question, "What is the Third Estate?" and whose rhetorical answer, "Everything!" had electrified the Estates-General and the Parisian masses alike. Bonaparte was the man of the future, and for fifteen years that future, from the Atlantic to the Urals, bore his mark — indelibly, as events would prove.

Napoleon still looms too large in the historiography of the European world to be encapsulated in a few documents. In his day, contemporaries compared him to Alexander the Great and Julius Caesar (to his gratification), and a quarter-century ago Hitler's contemporaries compared *him* to Napoleon (to his gratification). All comparisons, forward and backward, are worthless. Napoleon was unique, an inimitable combination of statesman, politician, general, soldier, patriot, internationalist, visionary, propagandist, builder, destroyer, law-giver, despot, man, machine. He ended the Revolution in France, broadcast it throughout Europe, and was destroyed by it on the battlefields of Europe. Though he was a dictator with tools too imperfect to implement the essentials of dictatorship, he recast French institutions into the form that they bear today. He lost all, and yet his specter haunted Europe for a century, only to be dispelled finally in the cataclysmic years between 1914 and 1918.

He is best left to speak for himself: in that terse proclamation declaring the end of the Revolution in words that were both real and prophetic; in his code of laws, which is still his most lasting monument (from Paris to Tokyo, including the Moscow that was a burning shambles when he reached it in 1812); in his own words over his whole career, words of exhortation, of assertion, of self-adulation and self-justification, of vision, and of despair.

Napoleon Ends the Revolution, December 15, 1799

The proclamation of the consuls of the Republic of 24 Frimaire, Year VIII of the French Republic, ended the revolution. It was prophetic because Napoleon had no assurance that he would succeed in halting the revolutionary dialectic or that his regime would not be just another stage through which the Revolution would move.

Proclamation of 24 Frimaire, VIII

The Consuls of the Republic to the French:
A Constitution is presented to you.

It puts an end to the uncertainties which the provisional government introduced into external relations, into the internal and military situation of the Republic.

It replaces in the institutions which it establishes governors whose devotion has appeared necessary for its operation.

The Constitution is founded on the true principles of representative government, on the sacred rights of property, equality, liberty.

The powers which it institutes will be strong and stable, as they must be in order to guarantee the rights of citizens and the interests of the State.

Citizens, the Revolution is settled upon the principles which began it: It is ended.

Ducos
Siéyès
Bonaparte
Consuls of the Republic

From *Bulletin des Lois de la République Française*, 10th series, part 9, no. 335 (Paris, 1799). Trans. Thomas G. Barnes.

Laws of "the New Justinian"

As First Consul, Napoleon instructed a commission of eminent jurists to survey all existing French law and to rationalize it with reference to accepted standards of jurisprudence, using the great Roman law code of Justinian as the model for the form of the code and the source of much of its substance. Roman law had been living law in France since the sixteenth century at least (and, through its influence on the Church's canon law and the old customary laws at their origins, since much earlier), tending to displace the older customary laws of the French jurisdictions in the arena of litigation and becoming the preponderant law in the royal courts. Between March, 1803, and March, 1804, 2,281 articles comprising the Code Civil were promulgated. This code dealt with the substantive law of civil matters, including civil rights, persons, family law, property, succession and wills, contracts, sales, company, and mortgage. In subsequent years codes of civil procedure, commercial law, criminal procedure, and penal (criminal) law were promulgated. The whole comprised the Code Napoléon, the foundation of the law codes of most European countries, Egypt, several Latin American states, Japan, former French colonies, and a major influence on the law of Louisiana and of Russia and other now Communist countries in Eastern Europe. Its merits are clarity, comprehensiveness, equitableness, and applicability to a bourgeois and secular social order. It has readily accommodated change exacted by modernization and new developments internal and external to the law.

The Civil Code

PRELIMINARY TITLE. OF THE PUBLICATION, EFFECT,
AND APPLICATION OF THE LAWS IN GENERAL

1. The laws are executory throughout the whole French territory, by virtue of the promulgation thereof made by the First Consul.

They shall be executed in every part of the republic, from the moment their promulgation can be known.

The promulgation made by the First Consul shall be deemed to be known in the department which shall be the seat of government, one day after the promulgation; and in each of the other departments, after the expiration of the same interval augmented by one day for every ten myriameters (about twenty ancient leagues) [1] between the town where the

From *Conférence du Code Civil*, vols. 1–2 (Paris, 1805). Trans. Thomas G. Barnes.

[1] That is, 55¼ miles, the distance that could be covered in a day by horse-post relays. — T. G. B.

The Civil Code

promulgation shall have been made, and the chief place of each department.

2. The law ordains for the future only; it has no retrospective effect.

3. The laws of police and public security bind all the inhabitants of the territory.

Immoveable property, even that possessed by foreigners, is governed by the French law.

The laws concerning the legal status and rights of persons govern Frenchmen even if residing in a foreign country.

4. The judge who shall refuse to determine under pretext of the silence, obscurity, or insufficiency of the law may be prosecuted as guilty of a denial of justice.

5. Judges are forbidden to pronounce, by way of general and legislative determination, on the causes submitted to them.

6. None can derogate by private agreements from the laws concerning public order and good morals.

BOOK I. OF PERSONS

TITLE I. OF THE ENJOYMENT AND DEPRIVATION OF CIVIL RIGHTS

Chapter I. Of the Enjoyment of Civil Rights

7. The exercise of civil rights is independent of the quality of citizen, which is only acquired and preserved conformably to the constitutional law.

8. Every Frenchman shall enjoy civil rights.

9. Every individual born in France of a foreigner, may, during the year following the time of his majority, claim the quality of Frenchman; provided, that if he shall reside in France he declares his intention to fix his domicile there, and in case he shall reside in a foreign country, he makes his declaration to fix his domicile in France and establish himself there within a year, to be computed from the date of that declaration.

10. Every child born of a Frenchman in a foreign country is French. Every child born in a foreign country of a Frenchman who shall have lost the quality of a Frenchman, may at any time recover this quality by complying with the formalities prescribed in Article 9.

11. A foreigner shall enjoy in France the same civil rights as are or shall be accorded to Frenchmen by the treaties of that nation to which such foreigner shall belong.

12. The foreign woman who shall have married a Frenchman, shall follow the condition of her husband.

13. The foreigner who shall have been permitted by authorization of the government to establish his domicile in France, shall enjoy all civil rights so long as he shall continue to reside there.

14. A foreigner, although not resident in France, may be cited before the French courts, for execution of obligations contracted by him in France with a Frenchman; he may be brought before the courts of France, with respect to obligations contracted by him in a foreign country with Frenchmen.

15. A Frenchman may be summoned before a French court, for obligagions contracted by him in a foreign country, though with a foreigner.

. . . . .

Chapter II. Of the Deprivation of Civil Rights

SECTION I. OF THE DEPRIVATION OF CIVIL RIGHTS
BY THE LOSS OF THE QUALITY OF FRENCHMAN

17. The quality of Frenchman shall be lost (1) by naturalization acquired in a foreign country, (2) by acceptance, not authorized by the government, of public functions conferred by a foreign power, (3) by affiliation with any foreign association which shall require distinctions of birth, (4) in short, by any settlement made in a foreign country without intention of returning [to France].

Settlements for business [purposes] shall never be considered as having been made without intention of returning.

. . . . .

SECTION II. OF THE DEPRIVATION OF CIVIL RIGHTS
IN CONSEQUENCE OF JUDICIAL PROCEEDINGS

22. Sentences to punishments, the effect of which is to deprive the party condemned of all participation in the civil rights hereafter expressed, shall imply civil death.

23. Sentence to natural death shall imply civil death.

24. Other perpetual afflictive punishments shall not imply civil death, except so far as the law shall have attached that effect to them.

25. By civil death, the party condemned loses the property in all the estate which he possessed; his succession is open for the benefit of his heirs, on whom his estate devolves, in the same manner as if he were naturally dead and intestate.

He can no longer inherit any estate, nor transmit, by this title, the property which he has acquired in consequence.

He can neither dispose of his property in whole or in part, either by gift or by will, nor can he take by such title, except for the purpose of sustenance of life.

He cannot be named guardian, nor interfere in affairs relative to guardianship.

He cannot be a witness to any solemn or authentic act, nor be admitted to bear testimony in law.

He cannot proceed in law, either as defendant or plaintiff, but in the name and by the ministry of a special curator, appointed for him by the court in which the action is brought.

He is incapable of contracting a marriage which can produce any civil effect.

Marriage that has been contracted previously by him, is dissolved, as to all its civil effects.

His spouse and his heirs may respectively exercise the rights and actions to which his natural death would have given rise.

. . . . .

TITLE V. OF MARRIAGE

Chapter VI. Of the Respective Rights and Duties of Married Persons

212. The married persons owe mutually to each other fidelity, succor, assistance.

213. The husband owes protection to his wife, the wife obedience to her husband.

214. The wife is obliged to live with the husband, and to follow him everywhere he judges it proper to reside; the husband is obliged to receive her, and to furnish everything necessary for the needs of life, according to his means and his station.

. . . .

Chapter VII. Of the Dissolution of Marriage

227. Marriage is dissolved, first, by the death of one of the partners; second, by divorce lawfully pronounced;[2] third, by condemnation, become final, of one of the partners to a punishment implying civil death.

. . . .

TITLE VI. OF DIVORCE

Chapter I. Of the Causes for Divorce

229. The husband can ask for divorce on the ground of his wife's adultery.

230. The wife can ask for divorce on the ground of her husband's adultery, when he shall have brought his concubine into the married home.

231. The married persons can reciprocally ask for divorce on the

---

[2] Divorce was abolished by a decree of March 8, 1816, following the restoration of the Bourbon monarchy by Louis XVIII. The canon law did not allow divorce (that is, dissolution of a valid marriage), and the repeal was to bring French civil law into line with the canon law, as might be expected of the monarchy. Napoleon himself did not favor divorce, though he was divorced from his first Empress, Josephine, in order to remarry and secure a male heir. The Civil Code was far in advance of virtually all other European legal systems in the matter of divorce. — T. G. B.

ground of outrageous conduct, mistreatment, or grievous injury of one by the other.

232. Condemnation of one of the partners to an infamous punishment shall be to the other a ground for divorce.

233. The mutual and unwavering consensus of the married persons, expressed in the manner prescribed by law, under the conditions and after the proofs which it determines, shall prove sufficiently that their common life is insupportable to them, and that there exists, in respect to them, a conclusive ground for divorce.

Napoleon Speaks for Himself

The following selection is taken from a collection of Napoleon's speeches, communiqués, memoirs, and quotations. The compiler is an American historian, Robert Matteson Johnston, who was fascinated by "the Corsican." It is not a work of critical scholarship. Undoubtedly it contains some apocryphal matter, and the translations leave something to be desired. Yet the collation does provide an opportunity to assess Napoleon on the basis of his own testimony. The brief excerpts here reward patient analysis with incredible insight into the man every European of his day at some time or another thought must be a superman.

Exhortation, Assertion, Self-Adulation, and Despair

[*On October 30, 1784, Cadet Napoleon Bonaparte left the military school at Brienne for the military college at Paris.*]

March 28th, 1785, Paris: We have lost our father, the sole support of our youth. Our country has lost a keen, enlightened, and honest citizen. It was so decreed by the Supreme Being!

(To Madame Buonaparte.) My dear mother: It is for you to console us, the event demands it. Our affection, our devotion, will be doubled, to make you forget, so far as it is possible, the incalculable loss of a beloved husband.

April 26th, 1786, Valence: To-day Paoli [1] enters his sixty-first year. The

---

From *The Corsican: A Diary of Napoleon's Life in His Own Words*, ed. R. M. Johnston (Boston, 1910). Reprinted by permission of Houghton Mifflin Company.

[1] Napoleon's father, an early supporter of Pasquale Paoli, the Corsican patriot, had later allied himself to the French government's administration of Corsica. — T. G. B.

Corsicans have already, in a just cause, shaken off the yoke of the Genoese; they can do as much with that of the French. Amen!

May 3d. Always solitary among men, I am here, within doors, dreaming, and giving full vent to all my melancholy. To what will it drive me to-day? To thoughts of death. Still at the dawn of life, I may hope for many days to come. It is now six or seven years since I last saw my country. What madness, then, drives me to self-destruction? Doubtless it is the hollowness of life. If one is to die, why not kill one's self? What spectacle awaits me when I return to my own people? My compatriots laden with chains, and kissing in fear the hand that strikes them!

9th. Virtue and the love of truth are not enough to enable a man to argue against Rousseau. He was human; and so, one may easily believe, liable to error.

July 29th. (To M. Borde, bookseller, Geneva.) Sir: This is to request you to forward me the *Memoirs of Mme. de Valens* (sic), sequel to the *Confessions* of J. J. Rousseau. Pray send me also the *History of the Revolutions of Corsica,* and a list of books you may have relating to the island of Corsica, or that you could get for me quickly. I will remit the correct amount on hearing from you. Address your letter: Monsieur Buonaparte, Officer of artillery, regiment of La Fère, Valence, Dauphiné.

September 20th, Lyons: I leave Lyons with even more reluctance than I did Valence. I like the place so much, I would be content to spend the rest of my days here; but a man must follow his fate, and must accept the conditions of his profession. A soldier can be constant to nothing but his flag.

[*Bonaparte was an early enthusiast for the Revolution, not least because he saw it as a means to attain Corsican independence. Yet, during the popular insurgency in Paris, Bonaparte came to detest the mob. He served with distinction in the War of the First Coalition, beginning in 1792, his artillery breaking the British hold on Toulon in December, 1793. He was promoted to general of brigade a few days later. He was less successful in 1794, and upon the Thermidorean Reaction he was relieved of his command, largely through the distrust of a fellow Corsican, a legislator, Antoine-Christophe Saliceti.*]

April 1st. [1795]. Saliceti has done me a grievous injury. He broke my career just as it was opening out. He withered my ideas of glory on their stem. That man is my evil genius. No, I can forgive; but forget — that is another matter.

[*The outburst in Paris of a moderate and royalist faction against the continuation of the Revolution on 13 Vendémiaire — October 5, 1795 — was repressed in large part by Bonaparte and led to his rehabilitation and promotion in the revolutionary army.*]

5th [October, 1795] (13 Vendémiaire), morning: The news was very bad. They then put the matter in my hands, and set to discussing whether they had the right to repel force by force. Do you intend to wait — said I — until the people give you permission to fire at them? You have appointed me, and I am compromised; it is only fair that I should do the business my own way. On that I left the lawyers to drown themselves in their own flood of words, and got the troops on the move.

[November 7, 1796. Rivoli in Italy]. Soldiers! I am no longer proud of you! You have shown no discipline, no steadiness, no courage; you have abandoned every position. Men of the 39th and of the 85th, you are no longer French soldiers. Chief of staff — put on their flags: *They are no longer of the army of Italy!*

[*Bonaparte's reputation was made in the Italian campaign. Following the treaty with Austria signed at Campo Formio in October, 1797, Bonaparte returned to Paris.*]

January 1st [1798] Paris: Paris has a short memory. If I remain longer doing nothing, I am lost. In this great Babylon one reputation quickly succeeds another. After I have been seen three times at the theatre, I shall not be looked at again; I shall therefore not go very frequently.

[*Bonaparte's campaign in Egypt, from July, 1798, to August, 1799, ended not only in defeat but threatened him with political oblivion.*]

[Around August, 1799]. If ever I have the luck to set foot in France again, the reign of chatter is over.

[*He set foot in France again, and the "reign of chatter" ended with the overthrow of the Directory in November, 1799.*]

[February 25, 1800]. When a Frenchman has to choose between a policeman and the devil, he is for the devil, but when it is between the devil and fashion, he follows fashion, and providing the government does well, all that it does will be in the fashion.

[June 4]. (To Talleyrand.) Please have a pamphlet printed with the following title: *Letter of a patriotic member of the Germanic body on the policy of the House of Austria.* The object is to show that Austria has always striven to enlarge herself at the expense and to the detriment of the Empire. It would be a good thing to have this letter printed in German and to have it distributed broadcast in Germany.

[July 4]. I! a royal maggot! I am a soldier, I come from the people, I have made myself! Am I to be compared with Louis XVI? I listen to everybody, but my own mind is my only counsellor. There are some men who have done France more harm than the wildest revolutionaries, — the talkers, and the rationalists. Vague and false thinkers, a few lessons of geometry would do them good!

My policy is to govern men as the great number wish to be governed. That, I think, is the way to recognize the sovereignty of the people.

14th. To the 14th of July! To the French people, the sovereign of us all!

[August 13]. Wealth cannot confer a privilege. I have no intention of preaching collectivism; I am speaking between ourselves; I even want to have rich men, for that is the only way of supporting the poor; but I cannot admit that wealth is entitled to social or political distinction.

How can a state be well governed without the aid of religion? Society cannot exist save with inequality of fortune, and inequality of fortune cannot be supported without religion. When a man dies of hunger by the side of another who is gorged, he cannot accept that disparity without some authority that shall say to him: "God has decreed it thus: there must be rich and poor in the world; but in the hereafter, and for all eternity, it will be the other way about."

It was by becoming a Catholic that I pacified the Vendée and a Mussulman that I established myself in Egypt; it was by becoming ultramontane [2] that I won over public opinion in Italy. If I ruled a people of Jews, I would rebuild the temple of Solomon! Paradise is a central spot whither the souls of men proceed along different roads; every sect has a road of its own.

December 1st. You don't want a general in that position;[3] you want a civilian. The army will obey a civilian better than it will a soldier. If three or four years from now I were dying in my bed, of a fever, and if to crown my romance I were to make my will, I would warn the nation against a military government; I would tell it to choose a civilian for its first magistrate.

March 1st. [1801]. Lafayette is an obstinate political monomaniac; he cannot understand me; I regret it, because he is an honest man. I wanted to make him Senator; he refused. Let him go his own way then, I can get on without him.

4th. There shall be held in Paris, each year, an exhibition of the products of French industry.

20th. Do you know why I allow such free discussion in the Council of State? It's because I'm the best of them all in an argument. I let them attack me because I know how to defend myself.

I am a doctor of laws!

[*On March 27, 1802, Bonaparte concluded an uneasy peace with Britain, which with earlier settlements with the other powers brought France's*

---

[2] A pro-Papal Catholic. — T. G. B.
[3] First Consul. — T. G. B.

first respite from war in a decade. He turned to domestic reform, albeit within the repressive confines of Joseph Fouché, his minister of police, who had made his name — and nickname, "the slaughterer of Lyon" — by the massacres he had organized in Lyon in 1794 as the agent of the Jacobin Terror.]

[February 19, 1802]. (To Fouché.) As the reestablishment of peace with the Powers gives me time to pay special attention to the police, I want to be posted in the smallest details, and to work with you at least once, sometimes twice a day, when necessary. The most convenient hours for me are in the morning at eleven and at night at eleven.

[In 1801, Bonaparte had reached an agreement with Pope Pius VII, the Concordat, by which the most radical features of the Revolution's Civil Constitution of the Clergy were removed, though it left the appointment of bishops in the hands of the government, with confirmation by the Pope, and also retained payment of the clergy by the government.]

April 9th. (To Portalis.) The intention of the First Consul is to present each archbishop and bishop, at his consecration, with a cross, a crozier, and a mitre. You will therefore arrange to have these articles ready in time, and bought as cheaply as possible.

12th. Note the insolence of the priests who, in the division of authority with what they call the temporal power, reserve for themselves the dominion of the mind, of the noble part of man, and have the pretension of leaving me dominion over the body. They keep the soul and throw me the carcase!

There will be no stable political conditions until we have a teaching body acting on fixed principles. So long as men are not taught from childhood whether to be republican or monarchist, Catholic or freethinking, the state will not be a nation.

May 4th. In every country force bows to the civilian virtues. The bayonets fall before the priest who speaks in the name of religion, and before the man of science. I foretold that a military government would never take in France unless the nation were degraded by fifty years of ignorance. Every attempt would fail, and their authors would be the first victims. It is not as a general that I govern, but because the nation believes that I have civilian qualities that make me fit for governing, otherwise the government could not maintain itself. I knew what I was about when, as a general, I assumed the title of Member of the Institute; my meaning was clear even to the last drummer of the army.

We cannot argue on the analogy of the dark ages. We are thirty millions of men held together by enlightenment, property, and commerce; three or four hundred thousand soldiers are nothing in such a mass. The soldiers themselves are the children of the citizens. The army is the nation.

The distinctive mark of the soldier is that all his desires are despotic; that of the civilian is that he submits everything to discussion, to truth, to reason.

14th, Paris: By virtue of clause 87 of the Constitution concerning military rewards, and to recompense distinction and service among civilians, a Legion of Honour shall be instituted.

Where is the republic, ancient or modern, that has not granted honours? Call them trifles if you like, but it is by trifles that men are influenced. I would not utter such a sentiment as this in public, but here, among statesmen and thinkers, things should be spoken of as they are. In my opinion the French do not care for liberty and equality; they have but one sentiment, that of honour. Therefore that sentiment must be gratified; they must be given distinctions. Do you suppose you can persuade men to fight by a process of analysis? Never; that process is valid only for the man of science in his study. The soldier demands glory, distinction, rewards.

[November] 10th, Dieppe: I passed through Fécamp and St. Valéry. As the road from Havre to Dieppe is only a crossroad, our carriages were often brought to a walk, which enabled the inhabitants of the neighbouring villages to follow me all the way; so we held frequent conversations.

[December] 30th. My power proceeds from my reputation, and my reputation from the victories I have won. My power would fall if I were not to support it with more glory and more victories. Conquest has made me what I am; only conquest can maintain me.

Friendship is only a word; I love nobody; no, not even my brothers. Perhaps Joseph a little; even then it's a matter of habit, it's because he is my elder. — Duroc? Ah, yes, I love him; but why? His character attracts me: he is cool, dry, severe; and Duroc never sheds tears. As for me, you don't suppose I care; I know perfectly well I have no real friends. As long as I remain what I am, I shall have as many as I need so far as the appearance goes. Let the women whimper, that's their business, but for me, give me no sentiment. A man must be firm, have a stout heart, or else leave on one side war and government.

January 12th [1803], Paris: Until I was sixteen I would have fought for Rousseau against all the supporters of Voltaire. Now it's the other way about.

September 6th. The winter will be a severe one; meat very high. There must be plenty of employment in Paris.

Push on the construction of the Ourcq canal.

Start work on the quais Desaix and d'Orsay.

Have the new streets paved.

Get other work for the masses.

October 1, Paris: There shall be erected in Paris, in the centre of the *place Vendôme,* a column on the same lines as that erected at Rome in honour of Trajan. The column shall be surmounted by a pedestal adorned with an olive wreath on which there shall be a statue of Charlemagne.

[*Upon the proclamation of the Empire, May 18, 1804.*]

Everything that can increase the happiness of the country is completely bound up with my own. I accept a title that you believe will be of service to the nation. I will submit to the people the law concerning the hereditary power. I hope that France will never regret the honours she has showered on my family.

[*A plebiscite overwhelmingly confirmed "the hereditary power"!*]

November 4th [1804]. It is from a sense of justice that I will not divorce her![4] It may be that my personal interests, or even the interests of my system call for my marrying again. But I said to myself: How can I put away this excellent woman, just because I am becoming great? No, that is beyond me. I have the heart of a man; it was not a tigress gave me birth. When she dies I will marry again, and perhaps I shall have children. But I will not make her unhappy.[5]

Joseph is not marked out for my succession; he is older than I am; I shall probably outlive him, my health is good; and then he was not born in a high enough rank to maintain the illusion. I was born in poverty; he also was born in the most mediocre of surroundings; I have risen by my deeds; he has remained where his birth placed him. To reign in France, one must be born great, have been seen in childhood in a palace, surrounded with guards, or else be a man capable of raising himself above all others.

My mistress is power; I have done too much to conquer her to let her be snatched away from me. Although it may be said that power came to me of its own accord, yet I know what labour, what sleepless nights, what scheming, it has involved.

[April 24, 1805]. (To Fouché.) Have some well written articles published deriding the military movements of the Russians, the interview of the Emperor of Russia with the Emperor of Austria, and the absurd reports, phantoms born of the fogs and the spleen of England. Get active, and keep public opinion up. Tell the editors that although I am far away, I still read the papers, and that if they continue on the present tack I shall close their accounts.

[4] His childless wife, Josephine. — T. G. B.
[5] Bonaparte did divorce Josephine in 1809. — T. G. B.

Napoleon

(To Marshal Soult.) Let me know whether the horses, the supplies, the men, will all be ready for embarkation in two weeks. Don't reply in terms of metaphysics, but inspect your magazines and depots.

[*Napoleon's invasion of England was not launched; his attention turned elsewhere.*]

[August 13]. I have made up my mind: I will either attack Austria and reach Vienna before November — to face the Russians, should they put in an appearance; or else my will, and that is the word, is that there should be but one Austrian regiment in the Tyrol. I want to be left to conduct my war against England in quiet.

[January 7, 1806]. (To Cardinal Fesch.) On the 13th of November the Pope wrote me a letter of the most ridiculous, most insane, character: those people think I am dead! I am a religious man, but I am not a bigoted idiot.

For the Pope I am Charlemagne, because like Charlemagne I unite the Crowns of France and of the Lombards, and my Empire touches the East. I will reduce the Pope to be the mere bishop of Rome.

March 1st. I want to create in France a lay state. Up till now the world has only known two forms of government, the ecclesiastic and the military. Constantine was the first to establish, by means of the priests, a sort of civilian state; Clovis succeeded in founding the French monarchy only with this same support. Monks are the natural enemies of soldiers, and have more than once served to check them. The lay order will be strengthened by the creation of a teaching body, and even more strengthened by the creation of a great corporation of magistrates.

I think it is unnecessary to take into consideration a system of education for girls, they can get no better teaching than that of their mothers. A public education does not suit them, for the reason that they are not called on to live in public; for them habit is everything, and marriage is the goal.

If we are to establish the nation, we must hasten to regulate by means of codes the principal fields of legislation. The Civil Code, though imperfect, has done much good. Every one is familiar now with the first principles of conduct, and governs his property and business accordingly.

[March 4]. As for me, it is not the mystery of the Incarnation that I see in religion, but the mystery of social order. Heaven suggests an idea of equality which saves the rich from being massacred by the poor. To look at it another way, religion is a sort of inoculation or vaccine which, while satisfying our sense of the supernatural, guarantees us from the charlatans and the magicians: the priests are better than the Cagliostros, the Kants, and all the dreamers of Germany.

I need a special Tribunal to judge public functionaries for certain infractions of the laws. There must be some arbitrary exercise of power in such a matter, and this should not be left in the hands of the Sovereign, because he will either abuse it or neglect to use it. I complain every day of the number of arbitrary acts I am made to commit; they would come with more propriety from such a tribunal. I want the State to be governed according to law, and that the things that have to be done despite the law should be legalized by the operation of a duly constituted body.

[*Bonaparte placed his older brother Joseph on the throne of Naples in 1806.*]

[August 17]. (To the King of Naples.) It would be a good thing if the Neapolitan rabble attempted a revolt. So long as you have not made an example you will not be their master. Every conquered nation should revolt at least once, and I would view an insurrection at Naples as the father of a family views measles in his children, providing the patient is not too much weakened. It marks a healthy crisis.

19th. (To Fouché.) If you know where General Dumoulin is, send for him and question him about a lady named Keilenfels, whom he married two months before abducting Mlle. d'Eckhardt. I have no power over the judges, and there must be an exemplary punishment for so detestable an offence. Does this general realize that the Criminal Court will condemn him to the galleys? How can he have been so unmindful of the laws of honour? The whole business is very humiliating for the French army.

[*On October 14, 1806, Bonaparte crushed and routed the Prussian army at Jena and Auerstädt; two weeks later, he occupied the Prussian capital, Berlin.*]

[October 27]. The Emperor has visited the tomb of Frederick the Great [of Prussia]. He has presented to the [Military Hospital of the] Invalides at Paris, Frederick's sword, his ribbon of the Black Eagle, his General's sash, and the standards carried by his Guard in the Seven Years' War.

[*In 1806, Bonaparte transformed the Batavian Republic, set up in the Netherlands under the aegis of the Revolution by the Dutch Patriots in 1795, into the Kingdom of Holland. Predictably, he put another brother, Louis, on that throne.*]

[April 4, 1807]. (To the King of Holland.) A prince who in the first year of his reign gets so great a reputation for benevolence is a prince who in the second year is despised. The affection inspired by kings must be a virile one, a blend of respectful fear and of high esteem. When it is said of a king that he is a good man, the reign is a failure.

19th. (Notes.) There have been historiographers of France, but it is true to say that they have accomplished nothing. And yet an institution of this sort might serve a purpose; but it would be best to avoid the word historiographer. It is accepted that the historian is a judge who is to be the organ of posterity, and so many qualities, so many perfections, are expected of him that it is difficult to believe that a good history can be made to order. What can be obtained to order from men of well-regulated talent are historical monographs, the results of laborious research, setting out authentic documents, with critical observations that tend to clear up our view of events. If these researches and these documents are framed in a good narrative, a piece of work of this sort will bear some sort of resemblance to history, and yet its author would not be a historian in the sense in which we use the word.

[*Napoleon detested Madame de Staël, an outspoken critic of him, with unusual passion. Wife of a Swedish ambassador to France and daughter of Necker, Louis XVI's last principal minister of his own choosing, she was an early, gushing, admirer of Rousseau and his proto-romanticism. She exercised a formative influence on romanticism, less by reason of her profundity than by virtue of her volubility and capacity for self-advertisement. She detested Napoleon.*]

[April 19]. (To Fouché.) Among the thousand and one products of Mme. de Staël's pen that fall into my hands, you may judge from the enclosed letter how excellent a French patriot she is. One day an aristocratic toady and the next a nationalizing democrat, in truth one can hardly restrain one's indignation in seeing all the shapes that this . . . takes. I shall not tell you the plans this ridiculous clique have made in the happy event of my death, as a Minister of Police may be supposed to know all about that.

[*On June 14, 1807, Bonaparte decisively defeated the Russian army at Friedland. Tsar Alexander I concluded a truce on June 22 and, with the King of Prussia, entered into the Treaties of Tilsit in early July.*]

[June 22, to the Grand Army of France]. Frenchmen, you have been worthy of yourselves and of me. You will return to France covered with laurels, and after having secured a glorious peace containing guarantees for its permanence. The end must come, and our country must be able to live quietly, freed from the malign influence of England. The rewards I will grant will prove all my gratitude and my affection for you.

[October 22]. The Civil and Commercial Codes, and the Code of Procedure, have met with success. The Criminal Code will come before the Legislative Body this session. The Civil Code is the code of the century;

its provisions not only preach toleration, but organize it — toleration the greatest privilege of man.

Liberty is the need of only a small class, endowed by nature with higher faculties than common men. Equality, on the contrary, is what appeals to the mass.

[May 31, 1809, after the battle of Aspern, against the Austrians]. (To the Empress Josephine.) I am in great grief for the loss of the Duke of Montebello,[6] who died this morning. And so all things come to their end! Good-bye, dear friend; do anything you can to console the Marshal's poor wife.

[Retrospectively, Bonaparte wrote] there are some wounds to which death itself is preferable. It is at the moment of leaving life that a man clings to it with all his might. Lannes, the bravest of men, Lannes, deprived of his two legs, did not want to die, and said to me that the two surgeons who had treated a Marshal so brutally and with such scant respect ought to be hanged. With his remnant of life he clung to me; he wanted only me, thought only of me. A sort of instinct! For surely he loved his young wife and his children more than he did me; yet he never spoke of them, which was because he expected no help from them. But I was his protector; for him I was some vague and superior power; I was his Providence, and he was imploring. . . .

[October 12]. At parade to-day a young man of seventeen, the son of a Lutheran pastor of Erfurt, tried to get near me. Some officers stopped him, and as the boy showed confusion, suspicion was aroused, he was searched, and a dagger was found on him. I have ordered him to be brought before me.

What did you want of me?

(Staps: To kill you.)

What have I done to you? Who made you my judge?

(I wanted to bring the war to an end.)

Why didn't you go to the Emperor Francis [of Austria]?

(He? What for? He doesn't count. And if he died another would succeed him; but after you the French would disappear from Germany.)

Do you repent?

(No!)

Would you do it again?

(Yes!)

What, even if I spared you?

(To Fouché.) The wretched boy, who seems to be pretty well educated, told me that he wanted to assassinate me to rid Austria of the presence of the French. I could find in him no traces of religious or of political fanaticism. He seemed to have no clear idea of who Brutus was. His excitement

---

[6] Marshal Lannes. — T. G. B.

Napoleon

prevented my finding out more. He will be questioned after he has cooled down and fasted. Possibly it all amounts to nothing.

I have sent you the news of this incident to prevent its importance being exaggerated. I hope nothing will be said about it; if there should be talk, make out that the fellow is insane. If there is none, keep the matter a close secret. There was no scene at the parade; I myself had no notion that anything had happened.

[*Between his defeat of Austria in 1809 and his attack on Russia in 1812, Bonaparte remade the map of Europe.*]

[June 6, 1812]. Imperial headquarters, Wilkowyski: (Proclamation to the Grand Army.) Soldiers! The second Polish war has begun; the first ended at Friedland and Tilsit. At Tilsit Russia pledged an eternal alliance with France, and war on England! To-day her oath is broken. She refuses all explanations of her strange conduct unless the French eagles recross the Rhine. Fate draws Russia on; her destiny must be accomplished! Does she then think us degenerate? Are we no longer the soldiers of Austerlitz? She places us between dishonour and war; can our choice be in doubt? Forward, then, across the Niemen, and let us carry the war on to her own soil!

[*Thus Bonaparte and the Grand Army began the drive into Russia that would physically destroy the latter and politically destroy the former: the disastrous battle of Borodino, September 7, the French occupation of Moscow a week later, the fire that raged throughout the city, September 15 to 19, and the retreat begun a month later.*]

[September 20] Moscow: Despite the poet's art, all the imaginary details of the burning of Troy can never equal the reality of that of Moscow. The city was built of wood, the wind was very strong, all the fire engines had been removed. It was literally an ocean of fire!

23d. I have just levied a conscription of 140,000 men in France, and of 30,000 in Italy. The result of the battle of Borodino and our entry into Moscow must not reduce our energy.

[November 18]. Doubrovna: (To Maret.) Since my last letter to you our situation has become worse. Ice and frost of near zero (Fahr.) have killed off nearly all our horses, say 30,000. We have been compelled to burn nearly 300 pieces of artillery, and an immense quantity of transport wagons. The cold has greatly increased the number of stragglers. The Cossacks have turned to account our absolute want of cavalry and of artillery to harass us and cut our communications, so that I am most anxious about Marshal Ney, who stayed behind with 3000 men to blow up Smolensk.

29th, Zanivki: (To Maret.) The army is numerous but in a frightful state of disbandment. We need two weeks to reform the men into regiments, and where can we get two weeks? Cold and privation have broken up the army. We shall soon reach Vilna; can we stay there? Yes, if we can hold on for eight days; but if we are attacked during the first eight days, it is doubtful whether we can stay there. Food! food! food! Otherwise there are no horrors which this undisciplined mob is not capable of wreaking on the city. Possibly the army cannot be rallied short of the Niemen [River]. . . .

[December 3]. Molodetchna: (Bulletin.) [After detailing considerable loss of horses and equipment on the retreat from Moscow]. The enemy, marching in the footsteps of the frightful calamity that had overtaken the French army, tried to profit by it. All our columns were surrounded by Cossacks who, like the Arabs in the desert, picked up every cart or wagon that lagged behind. This contemptible cavalry, which only knows how to shout and couldn't ride down so much as a company of light infantry, became formidable from the force of circumstances! . . .

It may be concluded from what has been said that the [French] army needs to reestablish its discipline, to be reequipped, to remount its cavalry, its artillery, and its transport.

[*The Grand Army left behind in Russia nearly a half-million soldiers. In March, 1813, the German states east of the Elbe rose against France, in alliance with Russia. In August, Austria declared war on France. On October 18, a nine-hour battle near Leipzig, with an allied army of Prussia and other German states, Russia, and Austria, cost Bonaparte 30,000 men and forced his retreat.*]

[October 28, 1813]. On the road near Schluchterne: (To the Polish officers.) Is it true that the Poles want to leave me?

I went too far. I have made mistakes. Fortune has turned her back on me these last two years; but she's a woman, and will change. Who can tell? Perhaps it is your evil star has drawn mine on? In any case have you lost confidence in me? Is there no . . . left in my . . . ? Do I look thinner?

I only hope the Allies will burn down two or three of my good cities of France; it would give me a million of soldiers. I would offer them battle, I would beat them, and I would drive them at tap of drum all the way back to the Vistula.

I have been informed as to what you want. As Emperor, as general, I have nothing but gratitude for all you have done; I have nothing to reproach you with, you have acted loyally towards me; you have not been willing to abandon me without notice, and you have even undertaken to reconduct me to the Rhine. To-day, I want to give you good advice. If

Napoleon

you abandon me I shall no longer have the right of speaking for you; and I imagine that in spite of our disasters I am still the most powerful monarch of Europe.

[*Bonaparte would write later: "I could see clearly enough the fatal hour coming! My star was growing paler; I felt the reins slipping from my fingers; and I could do nothing." Three weeks after Leipzig, the British General Wellington crossed the Spanish-French frontier, defeated Marshal Soult on French soil, and drove toward the French city of Bayonne.*]

[November 15]. St. Cloud: Order, in the event of the English reaching the château of Marracq [near Bayonne], that the château and all the buildings belonging to me there be burnt down, so that they may not sleep in my bed. All the furniture may be removed and stored at Bayonne.

[*The allies, driving toward Paris, took it while Bonaparte was attempting a final strike eastward. The Senate on April 1, 1814, pronounced his abdication causing Bonaparte's hold on the army to break, and on April 4 he was virtually deserted by the only remaining source of power, his troops.*]

[April 11, 1814]. The Emperor Napoleon renounces for himself, his heirs and successors, all right of sovereignty over the French Empire, the Kingdom of Italy, and all other countries.

The island of Elba, chosen as his abode by the Emperor Napoleon, shall, during his lifetime, be an independent principality.

The French Imperial Guard shall furnish a detachment of 1200 to 1500 men to serve as an escort. H. M. the Emperor Napoleon may keep for his own guard 400 men who shall volunteer for this service.

13th. Providence has decreed it, — I shall live! Who can fathom the future? In any case, my wife and my son will be enough for me.

[*Louis XVIII, younger brother of Louis XVI, returned to France and the throne, with the émigrés — those who had learned nothing and forgotten nothing — in his train. Bonaparte, on Elba, watched closely the failure of the new ancien régime to establish itself. February 26, 1815, he slipped away to the mainland with 1,000 men.*]

[February 28, 1815] at sea: I shall reach Paris without firing a shot.

March 1st, Golfe Jouan: (To the army.) Soldiers! we were not defeated! Soldiers! In my exile I have heard your voice. I have come to you through every obstacle, every danger. Your general, called to the throne by the voice of the people and raised on your bucklers, is back among you; come to him! Pluck off the colours that the nation has proscribed, and that, for twenty-five years, were the rallying point of all the enemies of France. Put on the tricolour cockade; you wore it in our great days. Here are the eagles you had at Ulm, at Austerlitz, at Jena, at Eylau, at Friedland, at Tudela, at Eckmühl, at Essling, at Wagram, at Smolensk, at the Moskowa, at Lützen, at Wurschen, at Montmirail! Do you believe that the little handful of Frenchmen who are so arrogant to-day can support their sight? They will return whence they came; there let them reign as they pretend that they did reign these last nineteen years.

Soldiers, rally around the standard of your chief! Victory will advance at the double! The Eagle, with the national colours, will fly from steeple to steeple to the towers of Notre Dame. Then will you be able to display your honourable scars. Then will you be able to claim the credit of your deeds, as the liberators of your country. In your old age, surrounded and honoured by your fellow-citizens, all will respectfully listen while you narrate your great deeds; you will be able to say with pride: "And I also was one of that Grand Army that twice entered the walls of Vienna, of Rome, of Berlin, of Madrid, of Moscow, and that cleansed Paris from the stain left on it by treason and the presence of the enemy!"

[*On March 19, Bonaparte reached Paris; Louis XVIII had already departed. The throne that Louis XVIII was not prepared to fight for, the powers of Europe were prepared to deny Bonaparte. He accepted the challenge, crossed into Belgium on June 14, and on June 18 fell upon Wellington's army near Waterloo. But the French general charged with preventing the arrival of the Prussian army failed, and late in the afternoon General Blücher's fresh troops routed the last of Bonaparte's grand armies.*]

[June 22], morning: If they mean to use force with me, I shall not abdicate. I must be left to come to my decision in peace. Tell them to wait.

4 P.M.: Lucien, write: When I began the war to maintain the national independence, I counted on the unanimous support of every individual, of every official. I had good reason to anticipate success. Circumstances appeared to be changed. I offer myself as a sacrifice to the hatred of the enemies of France. I only hope that their declaration may prove sincere, and that their hostility is solely to my person. Let all unite for the public safety and to remain an independent nation. I proclaim my son, under the style of Napoleon II, Emperor of the French.

[*A British warship carried Bonaparte to the bleak island of St. Helena in the south Atlantic. There for almost six years he dreamed, reminisced, and fashioned his justification to history, increasingly pained by the cancer that would kill him.*]

[November 29]. My Code alone, because of its simplicity, has done more good in France than the sum total of all the laws that preceded it. My schools are preparing unknown generations. And so during my reign crime diminished rapidly, whilst on the contrary among our neighbors in England it increased with frightful rapidity. And that is enough, I think, to give a clear judgment on the two governments.

People take England on trust, and repeat that Shakespeare is the greatest of all authors. I have read him: there is nothing that compares with Racine or Corneille: his plays are unreadable, pitiful.

[May 1, 1816]. They may change, and chop, and suppress, but after all they will find it pretty difficult to make me disappear altogether. A French historian cannot very easily avoid dealing with the Empire; and, if he has a heart, he will have to give me back something of my own. I sealed the gulf of anarchy, and I unravelled chaos. I purified the revolution, raised the people, and strengthened monarchy. I stimulated every ambition, rewarded every merit, and pushed back the bounds of glory! All that amounts to something!

[June 1, 1816]. When any one of my ministers, or other high personages, had blundered badly, and it was necessary to get annoyed, really angry, furious, I always took care to have a third party present at the scene; my rule was that when I had decided to strike, the blow should fall on a good many; the one on whom it fell was neither more nor less resentful; while the witness, whose face and embarrassment were worth seeing, would go off and discreetly spread far and wide what he had seen and heard: a healthy terror circulated through the veins of the social body. Things went better; I had to punish less frequently; I profited much and without doing much harm.

[January 29, 1818]. To be a good general a man must know mathematics; it is of daily help in straightening one's ideas. Perhaps I owe my success to my mathematical conceptions; a general must never imagine things, that is the most fatal of all. My great talent, the thing that marks me most, is that I see things clearly; it is the same with my eloquence, for I can distinguish what is essential in a question from every angle. The great art in battle is to change the line of operations during the course of the engagement; that is an idea of my own, and quite new.

The art of war does not require complicated manoeuvres; the simplest are the best, and common sense is fundamental. From which one might wonder how it is generals make blunders; it is because they try to be clever. The most difficult thing is to guess the enemy's plan, to sift the truth from all the reports that come in. The rest merely requires common sense; it's like a boxing-match, the more you punch the better it is. It is also necessary to read the map well.

[October 22, 1820]. My power lasted only a flash of time, but never mind, it was full, it was gorged with useful institutions; I consecrated the revolution; I infused it into our laws.

[April 28, 1821]. After my death, which cannot be far off, I want my body to be opened; I also want, I exact, that no English doctor shall touch me. I further wish you to take my heart, place it in spirits of wine, and take it to my dear Marie Louise at Parma. You will tell her that I loved her tenderly, you will relate to her all you have seen, all that concerns my situation here, and my death.

[Napoleon began to lose coherence.]

May 2d, 2 A.M.: Steingel! Desaix! Masséna! Ah, victory is ours; go, haste, press home the charge; they are ours!

[General Steingel, Bonaparte's artillery commander, had been killed in the Italian campaign of 1796; General Desaix died leading the victorious charge at Marengo in 1800; Marshal Masséna, Bonaparte's "darling boy of the victory in Italy" 1796, had died in 1817.]

3d, 3 P.M.: You have shared my exile, you will be faithful to my memory, you will do nothing to injure it.

5th, 5:30 P.M.: . . . head . . . army . . .

[Napoleon Bonaparte died of cancer of the stomach at 5:50 P.M., May 5, 1821, at the age of 51.]